CONTENTS

Contributors	vii
Introduction	ix
ENGLAND AND WALES: D. M. Loades	1
Journals and Society publications consulted	3
Section 1: Books and parts of books	10
2: Dictionaries and bibliographies	53
3: Academic journals	57
4: Society publications	108
5: Reviews	121
6: Completed theses	167
SCOTLAND: J. K. Cameron	181
Journals and Society publications consulted	183
Section 1: Books and parts of books	184
2: Academic journals, society and occasional publications	190
3: Reviews	212
4: Completed theses	215
IRELAND: Derek Baker	219
Journals and Society publications consulted	221
Section 1: Books and parts of books	223
2: Dictionaries and bibliographies	228
3: Academic journals and society publications	230
4: Reviews	241
5: Completed theses	242

THE BIBLIOGRAPHY OF THE REFORM 1450–1648

relating to the United Kingdom and Ireland for the years 1955–70

edited by
DEREK BAKER

compiled by
D. M. Loades (England and Wales)
J. K. Cameron (Scotland)
Derek Baker (Ireland)

for
the British Sub-Commission
Commission Internationale
d'histoire Ecclésiastique Comparée

BASIL BLACKWELL · OXFORD

©Basil Blackwell 1975

All rights reserved. No part of this publication may be reproduced, stored in a retrieval system, or transmitted in any form or by any means, electronic, mechanical, photocopying, recording or otherwise, without the prior permission of the publisher

ISBN 0 631 15960 6

Reformation – Great Britain – bibliography
" – Ireland – "

Typeset by Preface Limited, Salisbury, Wilts and printed in Great Britain by Compton Printing Limited, Aylesbury

CONTRIBUTORS

D. M. Loades, lecturer in history, University of Durham
J. K. Cameron, professor of ecclesiastical history, University of St Andrews
Derek Baker, lecturer in history, University of Edinburgh

INTRODUCTION

The project for an international bibliography of the Reform (1450—1648) was initiated by the Commission Internationale d'Histoire Ecclésiastique Comparée, and the preparation of the first lists, to cover the years 1940—55, was entrusted to the national sub-commissions. These national lists, which conformed to no common conventions of presentation or content, were printed as they were completed, combined into a series of fascicles, and published at Leyden over more than a decade. In 1972 the Bureau of the International Commission proposed to the national sub-commissions the continuation of the bibliography for the years 1955—70. In response to this the British Sub-Commission nominated compilers, submitted a scheme, and suggested that the lists for England and Wales, Scotland and Ireland should be combined in one volume. These proposals the Bureau of the C.I.H.E.C. approved, and the present volume of three inter-related sections is the result.

Each compiler has been responsible for the selection of the titles printed in his list, and minor differences in the presentation of the material will be evident between the lists, occasioned by the abundance or lack of material under particular sectional headings. In general, however, each list conforms to a common pattern and order, and is numbered consecutively throughout. Titles discovered or notified at a late stage of preparation have not been placed in a supplementary section, but have been inserted into the lists at the appropriate place and bear suffixed numbers — for example, 256A. Items which bear the name of more than one author or editor are listed in full under the first name in the ascription, the other names appearing in the lists with cross-references to the main entry. It has not been thought necessary, or desirable, to supply an index of names or of subjects. Where the name of the author is known the alphabetical nature of the lists makes consultation easy. Where information on a particular topic or field is required it is felt that a subject index, inevitably the result of personal categorisation, would inhibit rather than aid the full employment of these lists.

'Reform', as in the first fascicles of these bibliographies, has been interpreted in a wide sense, and the limits of the period dealt with have not been over-rigidly observed. The aim of the compilers has been to make the lists as inclusive as possible, and works whose main theme, or period, lie outside the scope of the bibliography have been listed if they touch on, or illuminate, some aspect of 'Reform', or overlap the chronological limits of the period. At the individual discretion of the compiler reviews of importance have been included, and completed theses are listed for the first time.

Few bibliographies are ever finally complete, or comprehensive. While we have done our best to achieve accuracy and completeness we know that there will be errors in, and omissions from, our lists, and we shall be grateful for information from those who use this bibliography which will enable us to repair these deficiencies. In the future it is hoped to bring out two-yearly supplements to this volume, and corrections and additions will be included in these.

We are grateful to the British Academy and the Twenty-Seven Foundation for generous help with the production of this Bibliography.

Derek Baker
Edinburgh

ENGLAND AND WALES

compiled by

D. M. LOADES

JOURNALS AND SOCIETY PUBLICATIONS CONSULTED

1. JOURNALS

American Historical Review	Washington
American Journal of Legal History	Philadelphia
American Literature	Durham, North Carolina
Ampleforth Journal	Market Weighton, Yorkshire
Analecta Augustiniana	Rome
Analecta sacri ordinis Cisterciensis	Rome
Anglia	Tübingen
Annales	Paris
Annali della fondazione italiana per la storia amministrativa	Milan
Antiquaries Journal	London
Anthologia Annua	Rome
Arbor	Madrid
Archaeological Journal	London
Archiv für das Studium der neueren Sprachen (und Literaturen)	Brunswick
Archiv für katholisches Kirchenrecht	Mainz
Archiv für Reformationsgeschichte	Gütersloh
Archives de sociologie des religions	Paris
Archives internationales d'histoire des sciences	Paris
Archivum. Revue internationale des archives	Paris
Archivum Franciscanum historicum	Florence
Archivum Fratrum Praedicatorum	Rome
Archivum Hibernicum	Maynooth
Archivum historiae pontificiae	Rome
Archivum historicum Societatis Jesu	Rome
Augustiniana	Louvain
Bibliotheca Sacra	Dallas (Texas)
Bibliothèque d'humanisme et renaissance	Geneva
Bodleian Library Record	Oxford
Biographical Studies	Bognor Regis, Sussex
Bulletin de la Commission royale d'histoire	Brussels
Bulletin de l'Association Guillaume Budé	Strasbourg and Paris
Bulletin de la Societé de l'histoire du protestantisme Français	Paris
Bulletin de théologie ancienne et médiévale	Louvain

Bulletin of the Institute of Historical Research	London
Bulletin of the John Rylands Library	Manchester
Bulletin of the New York Public Library	New York
Burlington Magazine	London
Cahiers d'histoire mondiale	Neuchâtel
(Cambridge) Historical Journal	Cambridge
Canadian Historical Review	Toronto
Catholic Historical Review	Washington
Church History	Chicago
Church Quarterly Review	London
Civiltà cattolica	Rome
Cîteaux. Commentarii Cistercienses	Achel, Belgium
Clergy Review	London
Collectanea Franciscana	Rome
Collectanea Ordinis Cisterciensium Reformatorum	Westmalle (Belgium)
Comparative Literature	Eugene (Oregon)
Concilium. Revue internationale de théologie	Tours
De Gulden Passer	Antwerp
Deutsche Vierteljahrsschrift für Literaturwissenschaft und Geistesgeschichte	Stuttgart
Downside Review	Downside Abbey, Bath
Dublin Review	London
Durham University Journal	Durham
Economic History Review	Welwyn Garden City, Herts
English Studies	Amsterdam
Ephemerides theologicae Lovanienses	Louvain
Erasmus	Wiesbaden
Folklore	London
Franciscan Studies	St. Bonaventure, New York
Giornale storico della letteratura italiana	Turin
Greek Orthodox Theological Review	Brookline, Mass.
Gregorianum	Rome
Harvard Theological Review	Cambridge, Mass.
Heythrop Journal	Oxford
Hispania	Madrid
Historische Zeitschrift	Munich
Historisches Jahrbuch	Munich
Historisk tidskrift	Stockholm

History	London
History and Theory	Middletown, Conn.
History Today	London
Huntington Library Quarterly	San Marino, California
International Review of Social History	Assen
Irénikon	Amay-Chevetogne, Belgium
Irish Ecclesiastical Record	Dublin
Irish Historical Studies	Dublin
Irish Theological Quarterly	Maynooth
Istina	Paris
Jahrbuch des Kölnischen Geschichtsvereins	Cologne
Journal of the American Academy of Religion	Philadelphia
Journal of the Bible and Religion	Brattleboro, Vermont
Journal of the British Archaeological Association	London
Journal of Ecclesiastical History	London
Journal of Economic History	New York
Journal of English and German Philology	Urbana
Journal of the Historical Society of the Church in Wales	Cardiff
Journal of the History of Ideas	Ephrata, Penn. and New York
Journal of the History of Philosophy	Berkeley and Los Angeles
Journal of Religion	Chicago
Journal of Religious History	Sydney
Journal of Theological Studies	London
Journal of the Warburg and Courtauld Institutes	London
Les Études philosophiques	Paris
Library	Oxford
L'Information historique	Paris
Lumière et vie	Lyons
Manuscripta	St. Louis (Missouri)
Medieval Studies	Toronto
Medium Aevum	Oxford
Mennonite Quarterly Review	Goshen, Indiana
Mid America	Chicago
Miscelánea Comillas	Santander
Modern Language Quarterly	Seattle

Modern Languages Review	London
Modern Philology	Chicago
Month	London
Moreana	Angers
Moyen âge	Brussels
Musica disciplina	Rome
Nederlands archief voor Kerkgeschiedenis	Leyden
Neophilologus	Groningen
Neuphilologische Mitteilungen	Helsinki
New Testament Studies	London and New York
Nouvelle Revue théologique	Louvain
Numen	Leyden
Oxoniensia	Oxford
Paedagogica Historica	Ghent
Past and Present	London
Philological Quarterly	Iowa City
Reality	Dubuque, Iowa
Recherches de science religieuse	Paris
Recusant History	Bognor Regis, Sussex
Renaissance and Modern Studies	Nottingham
Renaissance News	New York
Renaissance Quarterly	New York
Review of English Studies	Oxford
Review of Politics	Notre Dame
Review of Religion	New York
Revista Española de derecho canónico	Madrid
Revue Belge de philologie et d'histoire	Brussels
Revue d'histoire de l'église de France	Paris
Revue d'histoire des sciences et leurs applications	Paris
Revue d'histoire ecclésiastique	Louvain
Revue d'histoire et de philosophie religieuses	Strasburg and Paris
Revue d'histoire moderne et contemporaine	Paris
Revue de littérature comparée	Paris
Revue de théologie et de philosophie	Lausanne
Revue des sciences humaines	Lille
Revue historique	Paris
Revue philosophique de la France et de l'étranger	Paris
Rivista critica di storia della filosofia	Florence
Rivista di storia e letteratura religiosa	Florence
Sacris erudiri	Steenbrugge, Bruges

Schweizer Beiträge zur allgemeinen Geschichte	Berne
Sciences ecclésiastiques	Montreal
Scottish Historical Review	Edinburgh
Scuola cattolica, La	Varese
Shakespeare Quarterly	New York
Soviet Studies in History	White Plains, New York
Speculum	Cambridge, Mass.
Studi medievali	Spoleto
Studi Romani	Rome
Studi Urbinati	Urbino
Studia monastica	Montserrat, Barcelona
Studia neophilologica	Uppsala
Studia theologica	Arrhus
Studies in Bibliography	Charlottesville, Virginia
Studies in English Literature, 1500–1900	Houston, Texas
Studies in Philology	Chapel Hill
Studies in the Renaissance	New York
The Thomist	Washington
Theological Studies	Woodstock
Theologie und Glaube	Paderborn
Theologie und Philosophie	Fribourg
Theologische Literaturzeitung	Leipzig and Berlin
Theologische-praktische Quartalschrift	Linz
Theologische Revue	Münster-en-W
Theology Today	Princeton, New Jersey
Thought	New York
Tijdschrift voor filosofie	Louvain
Tijdschrift voor geschiedenis	Groningen
Traditio	New York
Trierer Theologische Zeitschrift	Triers
University of Birmingham Historical Journal	Birmingham
Zeitschrift der Savigny-Stiftung für Rechsgeschichte: Kanonistische Abteilung	Weimar
Zeitschrift für Kirchengeschichte	Stuttgart
Zentralblatt für Bibliothekswesen	Leipzig

2. SOCIETY PUBLICATIONS

American Philosophical Society	Philadelphia
Archaeologia Cantiana	London

Bedfordshire Historical Society	Luton
Bibliographical Society	London
Bristol and Gloucester Archaeological Society	Bristol
British Academy	London
British Records Association	Cambridge
British Record Society	London
British Society of Franciscan Studies	London
Cambridge Bibliographical Society	Cambridge
Canterbury and York Society	London and Torquay
Catholic Record Society	London
Catholic Truth Society	London
Chetham Society	Manchester
Church Historical Society	London
Cumberland and Westmorland Antiquarian and Archaeological Society	Kendal
Devon and Cornwall Record Society	Exeter
Dugdale Society	London and Stratford-on-Avon
Early English Text Society	London
East Yorkshire Local History Society	York
Ecclesiastical History Society	London, Leyden and Cambridge
Edmonton Hundred Historical Society	London
Essex Archaeological Society	Chelmsford
Faversham Society	Faversham, Kent
Folio Society	London
Henry Bradshaw Society	Chichester
Historical Association	London
Huguenot Society of London	London
Leeds Philosophical and Literary Society	Leeds
Lincoln Record Society	Lincoln
London Record Society	London
Malone Society	London
Modern Language Association of America	Menasha, Wisconsin
Northampton Record Society	Northampton
Oxford Historical Society	Oxford
Oxfordshire Record Society	Oxford and London
Royal Historical Society (Transactions and Camden Series)	London
Sitzungsberichte der bayerischen Akademie der Wissenschaften	Munich
Somerset Archaeological and Natural History Society	Yeovil

England and Wales

Somerset Record Society	Yeovil
Staffordshire Parish Register Society	Willenhall, Staffs.
Suffolk Record Society	Ipswich
Surtees Society	Durham
Sussex Archaeological Society	Lewes
Sussex Record Society	Lewes
Yorkshire Archaeological Society	Leeds

SECTION 1. BOOKS AND PARTS OF BOOKS

1 Abbundo, V. — *Tommaso Moro, Saggio.* In appendice: La prima traduzione italiana dell' *Utopia* ald 1548 (Naples 1962).

2 Adams, R. P. — *The Better Part of Valor. More, Erasmus, Colet and Vives on humanism, war and peace 1496–1535* (Seattle 1962)

3 Addy, J. — *The Archdeacon and Ecclesiastical Discipline in Yorkshire, 1598–1714. Clergy and the Churchwardens* (London 1963).

3a Aitken, W. A. — See 97.

4 Albert, M. H. — *The Divorce. A re-examination by an American writer of the great Tudor controversy* (London 1966).

5 Alexander, H. G. — *Religion in England, 1558–1662* (London 1968).

6 Allen, J. W. — *A History of Political Thought in the 16th Century* (3 ed London 1960).

7 Allison, C. F. — *The Rise of Moralism. The proclamation of the Gospel from Hooker to Baxter* (London 1966).

8 Andreasen, N. J. C. — *John Donne, Conservative Revolutionary* (London 1967).

9 Anglo, S. — *Spectacle, pageantry and early Tudor Policy* (Oxford 1969).

10 Anstruther, G. — *A Hundred Homeless Years. The English Dominicans 1558–1658* (London 1958).

11 Anthony, E. — *Anne Boleyn* Translated from English by G. Rives (Paris 1958).

12 Ashley, M. — *The Greatness of Oliver Cromwell* (London 1957).

13 ——— *Oliver Cromwell and the Puritan Revolution* (London 1958, 2 ed 1970).

14 ——— *Oliver Cromwell and the Puritan revolt* (London 1967).

15 Aveling, H. — *Northern Catholics. The Catholic Recusants of the North Riding of Yorkshire, 1558–1790* (London 1966).

England and Wales

16	Axelrod, A. J.	*Un Malcontent Elizabéthain; John Marston, 1576–1634* (Paris 1955).
17	Bagley, J. J.	*Henry VIII* (London 1962).
17a	Baker, D. (ed)	*Miscellane Historiae Ecclesiasticae III* (Louvain 1970).
18	Bald, R. C.	*Donne and the Drurys* (London 1959).
19	———	*John Donne. A Life* (London 1970).
20	Barker, A. E.	*Milton and the Puritan Dilemma 1641–60* (2 ed London 1956).
21	Baskerville, G.	*English Monks and the Suppression of the Monasteries* (new ed London 1965).
22	Bassett, B.	*Born for Friendship. The Spirit of Sir Thomas More* (London 1965).
23	———	*The English Jesuits. From Campion to Martindale* (London 1968).
24	Baumer, F. Le Van	*The Early Tudor Theory of Kingship* (repr New York 1966).
25	Bayne, C. G.	*Anglo Roman Relations, 1558–1565* (repr London 1968).
26	Beales, A. C. F.	*Education under penalty. English Catholic education from the Reformation to the fall of James II 1547–1689* (London 1963).
26a	Beardwood, A.	See 605
27	Beckinsale, B. W.	*Elizabeth I* (London, 1963).
28	Bennett, H. S.	*English books and readers, 1558–1603. Being a study in the history of the book trade in the reign of Elizabeth I* (London 1965).
29	———	*English books and readers, 1603–1640. Being a study in the history of the book trade in the reigns of James I and Charles I* (London 1970).
30	Bennett, J.	*Sir Thomas Browne* (New York 1962).
31	Benson, L. F.	*The English hymn. Its development and use in worship* (Richmond, Virginia, 1962).
32	Berry, L. E.	*The Geneva bible. A facsimile of the 1560 edition* (Madison 1969).
32a	Bindoff, S. T.	See 140.

33 Binns, L. E. E.	*The reformation in England* (new ed London 1966).
34 Bishop, J. G.	*Lancelot Andrewes, bishop of Chichester 1605–1609* (Chichester 1963).
35 Black, J. B.	*The reign of Elizabeth 1558–1603* (2 ed London 1959)
36 Blatt, T. B.	*The Plays of John Bale. A study of ideas, techniques and style* (Copenhagen 1968).
37 Blench, J. W.	*Preaching in England in the late XVth and XVIth Centuries. A study of English sermons 1450 to ca. 1600* (Oxford 1964).
38 Blitzen, C.	*The commonwealth of England, 1641–1660* (London 1963).
39 Bolam, C. G.; Goring J.; Short, H. L.; & Thomas, R.	*The English Presbyterians from Elizabethan puritanism to modern Unitarianism* (London 1968).
40 Booty, J. E.	*John Jewel as an apologist of the Church of England* (London 1963).
41 Bond, S.	*The chapter acts of the dean and canons of Windsor; 1430, 1523–1672* (London 1967).
42 Bowker, M.	*The secular clergy in the diocese of Lincoln 1495–1520* (London 1968).
43 Bowle, J.	*Henry VIII* (London 1965).
44 Boyce, P.	*The polemic character, 1640–1661. A chapter in English literary history.* (Lincoln, Nebraska 1955).
45 Boyd, M. C.	*Elizabethan music and musical criticism* (2 ed London 1963).
46 Boyton, P. A. & Lamb, G. R.	*Francis Tregian, Cornish Recusant* (London 1955).
47 Brailsford, H. N.	*The Levellers and the English revolution,* ed C. Hill (London 1961).
48 ———	*I livellatori e la rivoluzione inglese,* I–II (Milan 1962).
49 Braithwaite, W. C.	*The beginnings of Quakerism* (2 ed London 1955).
50 Brandreth, H. R. T.	*Episcopi vagantes and the Anglican church* (London 1961).
51 Breslow, M. A.	*A mirror of England. English puritan views on foreign nations 1618–1640, Harvard historical*

England and Wales

		studies, fasc 84 (Cambridge, Mass. 1970).
52	Brett, S. R.	*The Tudor Century* (London 1962).
53	Breword, I.	*The work of William Perkins. Introduced and edited.* The Courtenay Library of Reformation Classics, III (Appleford, Abingdon, Berks 1970).
54	Brindenbough, C.	*Vexed and troubled Englishmen, 1590–1642* (New York 1968).
55	Brinkworth, E. R. C.	*South Newington churchwardens' accounts 1553–1684* (Banbury, Oxon 1964).
56	Broadbent, J. B.	*Some graver object. An essay on Paradise Lost* (New York 1960).
57	Bromiley, G. W.	*Thomas Cranmer, theologian* (London 1956).
58	Brook, V. J. K.	*Whitgift and the English Church* (London 1957).
59	———	*A life of Archbishop Parker* (London 1962).
60	Brooks, P.	*Thomas Cranmer's doctrine of the Eucharist. An essay on historical development* (London 1965).
60a	Brown, N. P.	See 345.
61	Brown, W. J.	*The life of Rowland Taylor, Ll.D., rector of Hadleigh in the Deanery of Bocking* (London 1959).
62	Bryant, J. A. Jnr.	*Hippolyta's view. Some christian aspects of Shakespeare's plays* (Lexington 1961).
63	Bullock, F. W. B.	*Voluntary religious societies. 1520–1799* (St Leonards on Sea, Sussex 1964).
64	———	*Evangelical conversion in Great Britain 1516–1695* (St Leonards on Sea, Sussex 1966).
65	Burne, R. V. H.	*Chester Cathedral, from its founding by Henry VIII to the accession of Queen Victoria* (London 1958).
66	———	*The monks of Chester* (London 1962).
67	Bush, D.	*The renaissance and English humanism* (London 1957).
68	Butterwoth, C. C. & Chester, A. G.	*George Joye, 1495–1553. A chapter in the history of the*

	English bible and the English reformation. (London 1962).
69 Calder, I.	*Activities of the puritan faction in the church of England 1625–1633* (London 1957).
70 Campbell, L. B.	*Divine poetry and drama in XVIth century England* (London 1959).
71 Caraman, P.	*William Weston. The autobiography of an Elizabethan* (London 1956).
72 ———	*The other face. Catholic life under Elizabeth I.* (London 1960).
73 ———	*Vogelvrij, 1588–1606. Herinneringen van John Gerard.* translated from English by C. Benkens. (Bilthoven, 1961).
74 ———	*Henry Garnet and the gunpowder plot* (London 1964).
75 ———	*The years of siege. Catholic life from James I to Cromwell* (London 1966).
76 Cardwell, E.	*The reformation of the ecclesiastical laws as attempted in the reigns of King Henry VIII, King Edward VI and Queen Elizabeth* (repr London 1968).
77 Carlson, L. H.	*The Writings of Henry Barrow, 1587–1590,* Sir Halley Stewart Trust publications, *Elizabethan Nonconformist texts* 3 (London 1962).
78 ———	*The writings of John Greenwood, 1587–1590 together with the joint writings of Henry Barrow and John Greenwood, 1587–1590,* Sir Halley Stewart Trust publications, *Elizabethan Nonconformist texts,* 4 (London 1962).
78a Carr, D.	See 126.
79 Carter, H.	'Archbishop Laud and scandalous books from Holland' *Studia bibliographica in honorem Herman de la Fontaine Verwey* (Amsterdam 1968) pp 43–55.
80 Castelli, A.	*Tommaso Moro: Il Dialogo del conforto nelle triboluzione. Traduzione e note* (Rome 1970).

80a	Chambers, D. S.	*Cardinal Bainbridge at the Court of Rome, 1509–1514* (London 1965).
81	———	*Faculty office registers, 1534–1549. A Calendar of the first two registers of the Archbishop of Canterbury's Faculty Office* (Oxford 1966).
82	Chapman, H. W.	*The last Tudor King. A study of Edward VI. Oct. 12. 1537– July 5 1553.* (London 1958).
83	Chauviré, R.	*Le temps d' Elisabeth.* (Paris 1960).
84	Chester, A. G.	*Selected sermons of Hugh Latimer,* Folger documents of Tudor and Stuart civilization (Charlottesville 1968).
85	Chidsey, D. B.	*Elizabeth I* (New York 1955).
86	Clancy, T. H.	*Papist pamphleteers. The Allen-Parsons party and the political thought of the Counter-Reformation in England, 1572–1615* (Chicago 1964).
87	Claridge, M.	*Margaret Clitherow (1556?–1586)* (London 1966).
88	Clark, F.	*Anglican orders and defect of intention* (London 1957).
89	Clebsch, W. A.	*England's earliest protestants, 1520–1535* (New Haven 1964).
90	Cobban, A. B.	*The King's Hall within the University of Cambridge in the late Middle Ages* (London 1969).
91	Cocks, H. F. L.	*The religious life of Oliver Cromwell* (London 1961).
92	Cohn, N.	*The pursuit of the millenium* (London 1957)
93	Collinson, P.	*A mirror of Elizabethan Puritanism. The Life and letters of 'Godly Master Dering',* Friends of Dr Williams Library, 17th Lecture, 1963 (London 1964).
94	———	*The Elizabethan puritan movement* (London 1967).
95		*F. J. Colgan O. F. M. 1592–1658. Essays in commemoration of the third centenary of his death,* ed T. O'Donnell (Dublin 1959).
96	Coltman, I.	*Private men and public causes.*

97		*Philosophy and politics in the English Civil war* (London 1962). *Conflict in Stuart England. Essays in honour of Wallace Notestein*, ed W. A. Aitken and B. D. Henning (London 1960).
98	Cook, G. H.	*Letters to Cromwell and others on the suppression of the Monasteries* (London 1965).
99	Coolidge, J. S.	*The Pauline renaissance in England. Puritanism and the Bible.* (London 1970).
99a	Cooper, J. P.	See 422.
100	Costello, W. T.	*The scholastic curriculum at early XVIIth century Cambridge* (Cambridge, Mass., 1958).
101	Coulton, G. C.	*Fate of medieval art in the Renaissance and Reformation* (New York 1958).
101a	Cross, M. C.	*The Puritan Earl: The Life of Henry Hastings, Third Earl of Huntingdon* (London, 1966).
102	———	*The royal supremacy in the Elizabethan church* (London 1969).
103	Cuming, G. J.	*A history of Anglican Liturgy* (London, New York 1969).
104	Curry, W. C.	*Milton's ontology, cosmogany and physics* (Lexington 1957).
105	Curtis, M. H.	*Oxford and Cambridge in transition, 1558–1642* (Oxford 1959).
106	Daiches, D.	*Milton* (London 1957).
107	Danielsson, B.	*Sir Thomas Smith. Literary and Linguistic works I: Certaigne Psalmes or Songues of David, 1549* (Stockholm 1963).
108	Dankbaar, W. F.	*Marten Micron. De Christliche Ordinancien der Nederlantscher Ghemeinten te London (1554)* Kerkhistorische Studien behorende bij het *Nederlands Archief voor Kerkgischiedenis*, 7 (The Hague 1956).
109	Darbishire, H.	*The poetical works of John Milton, I: Paradise Lost. II: Paradise regain'd;*

110 Davies, H.	*Sampson Agonistes; Poems upon Several occasions, both English and Latin* (Oxford 1955). *Worship and theology in England, Vol. I From Cranmer to Hooker, 1534–1603* (Princeton 1970).
110a Davis, H.	See 141.
111 Davis, W. R.	*The works of Thomas Campion* (New York 1967).
111a De Cugis, C.	See 506.
112 Dedegen, C.	*Dante en Angleterre. Fasc. 1. Moyen âge, Renaissance* (Paris 1961).
113 Dempsey, W. S.	*The Story of the catholic church in the Isle of Man* (London 1958).
114 Denonain, J. J.	*La personnalité de Sir Thomas Browne*, Publication de la Fac. des lettres d'Alger, 33 (Paris 1959).
115 D'Entrèves, A. P.	*The medieval contribution to political thought. Thomas Aquinas, Marsilius of Padua and Richard Hooker* (2 ed London 1960).
116 Devlin, C.	*The Life of Robert Southwell, Poet and Martyr* (London 1956, 2 ed 1967).
117 Dewar, M.	*Sir Thomas Smith. A Tudor intellectual in Politics* (London 1964).
118 Dickens, A. G.	*Robert Holgate, Archbishop of York, President of the King's Council in the North* (London 1955).
119 ———	*The Marian reaction in the diocese of York: I – the clergy* (London 1957).
120 ———	*The Marian reaction in the diocese of York: II – the laity* (London 1957).
121 ———	*Thomas Cromwell and the English Reformation* (London 1959).
122 ———	*Lollards and Protestants in the diocese of York 1509-1558* (London 1959).
123 ———	*The English reformation* (London 1964).

124	———	'The English reformation and religious tolerance', in *XII congrès international des sciences historiques.* Rapports. I, Grands thèmes pp 177-89 (Vienna 1965).
125	———	*Thomas Cromwell and the English Reformation* (re-issue London 1970).
126	——— & Carr, D.	*The Reformation in England to the accession of Elizabeth I* (London 1967).
126a	Dodwell, C. R.	See 152.
127	Doernberg, E.	*Henry VIII and Luther* (London 1961).
128	Donnelly, G. J.	*A translation of St. Thomas More's Responsio ad Lutherum, with an introduction and notes.* The Catholic University of America, *Medieval and Renaissance Latin Language and Literature*, fasc 23 (Washington, 1962).
128a	Doyle, A. I.	See 182.
129	Du Boulay, F. R. H.	*Registrum Thome Bourchier* (London 1957).
130	Duffield, G. E.	*The Work of William Tyndale*, Courtenay Library of Reformation Classics, I (Appleford, 1964).
131	Dugmore, C. W.	*The Mass and the English Reformers* (London 1958).
132	Dunlop, C. and Smyth C. H.	*Thomas Cranmer. Two Studies* (London 1956).
133	Dunn, C. M.	*Peter Ramus. The Logicke of the most excellent philosopher P. Ramus Martyre. Tr. Roland MacIlwaine (1574)* (Northridge, California 1969).
134	Dwyer, J. D.	*Reginald Pole. Pole's Defence of the unity of the church.* Translated and with introduction. (Westminster, Maryland, 1965).
135	Echlin, E. P.	*The Anglican eucharist in ecumenical perspective. Doctrine and rite from Cranmer to Seabury.* (New York 1968).
136	Edden, G.	*The Description of England by William Harrison* (London 1968).

137 Edwards, F.   *Guy Fawkes. The real story of the Gunpowder Plot?* (London 1970).

138 Edwards, R. D.   'The Irish Catholics and the Puritan Revolution', *Father Luke Wadding. Commemorative volume* (Dublin 1957) pp 93-118.

139 Egretier, N. M.   *Reginald Pole; Defense de l'unité de l'Église. En quatre livres.* Texte trad. presenté et annoté (Paris 1967).

140   *Elizabethan government and society: Essays presented to Sir John Neale*, edited by S. T. Bindoff, J. Hurstfield, and C. H. Williams (London 1961).

141   *Elizabethan and Jacobean studies. Presented to Frank Percy Wilson in honour of his 70th birthday*, ed H. Davis and H. Gardner (New York 1959).

142 Ellrodt, R.   *L'Inspiration personnelle et l'esprit du temps chez les poètes métaphysiques anglais. 1er partie: T. I. John Donne et les poètes de la tradition chretienne T. II Poètes de transition, poètes mystiques.* (Paris 1960).

143 ———   *L'Inspiration personnelle et l'esprit du temps chez les poètes métaphysiques anglais. 2me partie: Les origines sociales, psychologiques et litteraires de la poèsie métaphysique au tournant du siècle.* [Thése de lettres. Paris] (Paris 1960).

144 Elton, G. R.   *England under the Tudors* (London 1955).

145 ———   *The Tudor Revolution in Government* (repr London 1959).

146 ———   *The Tudor constitution. Documents and Commentary* (Cambridge 1960).

147 ———   *England, 1200-1640* (London 1969).

147a ———   See 420.

148 Emden, A. B.   'Northerners and Southerners in the organisation of the University

		to 1509'. *Oxford Studies presented to Daniel Callus* (Oxford 1964) pp 1–30.
149	——	*A survey of Dominicans in England based on the ordination lists in episcopal registers, 1268-1538*, Dissertationes historicae 18 (Rome 1967).
150	Emerson, E. H.	*English puritanism from John Hooper to John Milton* (Durham, North Carolina, 1968).
151	Empson, W.	*Milton's God* (London 1961, 2 ed 1965).
152		*The English Church and the continent*, ed C. R. Dodwell (London 1959).
153	Eusden, J. D.	*Puritans, lawyers and politics in early XVIIth century England*, Yale studies in religious education, 23 (New Haven 1958).
154		*Essex Recusant*, I, ed D. Shanahan (London 1959).
155	Evans, I.	See 372.
156	Evans, J. M.	*Paradise Lost and the Genesis tradition* (London 1968).
157	Evans, M.	*English poetry in the XVIth century* (London 1955).
158	Farrington, B.	*The philosophy of Francis Bacon* (Liverpool 1964).
159	Farrow, J.	*The story of Thomas More* (London 1956).
160	Ferguson, A. B.	'Circumstances and the sense of history in Tudor England: The coming of the historical revolution', *Medieval and Renaissance Studies* (Chapel Hill 1968) pp 170-205.
161	Ferguson, C. W.	*Naked to mine enemies. The life of Cardinal Wolsey* (Boston 1958).
162	Ferris, P.	*The Church of England* (London 1962).
163	Ferry, A. D.	*Milton's epic voice. The narrator in Paradise Lost.* (Cambridge, Mass. 1963).
164	Feuerlicht, R. S.	*The life and world of Henry VIII* (New York 1970).

165 Finch, J. S.	*Sir Thomas Browne* (New York 1962).
166 Firpo, L.	'La Chiesa italiana di Londra vel Cinquecento e i suoi rapporti con Ginevra'. *Ginevra e l'Italia*, (Florence 1959) pp 307-412
167 Fisch, H.	*Jerusalem and Albion. The Hebraic factor in XVIIth century literature* (London 1964).
168 Fixler, M.	*Milton and the Kingdoms of God* (London 1964).
169 Fletcher, H. F.	*The intellectual development of John Milton, I: The institution to 1625. From the beginnings through grammar school* (Urbana 1956).
170 ———	*The intellectual development of John Milton, II: The Cambridge University period: 1625-1632* (Urbana 1962).
171 Ford, B.	*A guide to English literature, II: The age of Shakespeare* (London 1955).
172 Fox, L.	*English historical scholarship in the XVIth and XVIIth centuries* (London 1956).
173 Frede, C. de	*La restaurazione cattolica in Inghilterra sotto Maria Tudor nel carteggio di Girolamo Seripando* (Naples 1971).
174 French, A.	*Charles I and the Puritan upheaval* (London 1955).
175 Frye, N.	*The return of Eden. Five essays on Milton's epics* (Toronto 1965).
176 Frye, R. M.	*God, man and Satan. Patterns of Christian thought and life in Paradise lost, Pilgrims' Progress and the great theologians* (London 1961).
177 ———	*Shakespeare and Christian doctrine* (Princeton 1963).
177a Furniss, W. T.	See 650.
178 Fussner, F. S.	*The historical revolution. English historical writing and thought, 1580-1640* (London 1962).
179 Gardner, H.	*The Elegies and Songs and Sonnets*

		of John Donne. Edited with introduction and commentary (Oxford 1965).
179a	———	See 141.
180	Garrett, C. H.	The Marian exiles (repr London 1966).
181	George, C. H. and George, K.	The protestant mind of the English reformation 1570-1640 (Princeton 1961).
182	Gibby, G. W. and Doyle, A. I.	Durham bishops: John Cosin 1594-1672 (Washington, County Durham, 1970).
183	Goldschmidt, E. P.	The first Cambridge Press in its European setting (Cambridge 1955).
184	Goring, J.	See 39.
185	Gray, B. K.	A history of English philanthropy. From the dissolution of the monasteries to the taking of the first census. (new ed London 1967).
186	Grayeff, F.	Heinrich der Achte. Das Lebel eines Königs. Schicksal eines Reiches (Hamburg 1961).
187	———	Henri VIII, prince de la Renaissance. Trad. de l'all. par J. Lancrey – Javal et L. Waintraub (Paris 1963).
188	Greaves, R. L.	The puritan revolution and educational thought. Background for reform (New Brunswick 1970).
189	Green, V. H. H.	The Later Plantagenets. A survey of English history between 1307 and 1485 (London 1955).
190	Greg, W. W.	Some aspects and problems of London publishing between 1550 and 1650 (London 1956).
191	Gros, L. G.	John Donne. Un tableau synoptique de la vie et les oeuvres de John Donne et des événements artistique, litteraires et historiques de son époque. Une étude sur l'écrivain. Choix de textes, Écrivains d'hier et d'aujourd'hui 15 (Paris 1964).
192	Grün, R. H.	Das Menschenbild John Miltons in Paradise Lost. Eine interpretation seines Epos im Lichte d.

		Bergriffes 'Disobedience', Frankfurter Arbeiten aus d. Gebiet d. Anglistik und Amerika Studien, Fasc 2 (Heidelberg 1956).
193	Guilday, P.	*The English catholic refugees on the continent 1558-1795* (London 1969).
194	Gumbley, Walter	*Obituary notices of the English Dominicans, 1555-1952* (London 1956).
195	Hackett, F.	*Henry VIII, 1491-1547*. Translated from English by S. Champaux, *Historia* (Paris 1960).
196	Halewood, W. H.	*The poetry of grace. Reformation themes and structures in English XVIIth century poetry* (New Haven 1970).
197	Halkett, J. G.	*Milton and the idea of matrimony. A study of the divorce tracts and Paradise Lost* (London 1970).
198	Hall, D. D.	*The Antinomian controversy 1636-8. A documentary history.* Ed with introduction and notes (Middletown, Conn. 1968).
199	Haller, W.	*Liberty and Reformation in the Puritan revolution* (New York 1955).
200	———	*The rise of puritanism, or the way to the New Jerusalem as set forth in pulpit and press from Thomas Cartwright to John Lilburn and John Milton* (New York 1957).
201	———	*Foxe's Book of Martyrs and the elect nation* (London 1963).
202	———	*Elizabeth I and the puritans.* (Ithaca 1964).
203	———	*Tracts on liberty in the Puritan revolution, 1638-47. Records of Civilisation* 1-3 (London 1968).
204	Hamilton, K. G.	*The Protestant Way* (London 1956).
205	Handover, P. M.	*The second Cecil. The rise to power 1563-1604, of Sir Robert Cecil, later 1st Earl of Salisbury* (London 1959).

206	Harbison, E. H.	*The Christian scholar in the age of the reformation* (New York 1956).
207	Hardacre, P. H.	*The royalists during the Puritan revolution* (London 1956).
208	Harrison, F. L.	*The Eton Choirbook I, Musica Britannica* 10 (London 1956).
209	Harrison, G. B.	*Elizabethan Journals, being a record of those things most talked of during the years 1591-1603* 4 vols (new ed London 1955).
210	———	*A second Jacobean Journal 1607-1610* (Ann Arbor 1958).
211	Hart, A. T.	*The country clergy in Elizabethan and Stuart times, 1558-1660* (London 1958).
212	———	*The country priest in English history* (London 1959).
213	———	*Clergy and Society: 1600-1800* (London 1968).
214	Haugaard, W. P.	*Elizabeth and the English reformation. The struggle for a stable settlement of religion* (London 1968).
215	Havran, M. J.	*The Catholics in Caroline England* (Stanford 1962).
216	Haward, I.	*The secret rooms of Yorkshire* (Clapham, via Lancaster, 1956).
217	Hays, R. W.	*A history of the Abbey of Aberconway 1186-1537* (Cardiff 1963).
218	Head, R. E.	*Royal supremacy and the trials of bishops. 1558-1725* (London 1962).
219	Headley, J. M.	*St. Thomas More, Responsio ad Lutherum*, edited by J. M. Headley, English translation by S. Mandeville, vol 2, The Yale edition of the complete works of St. Thomas More, (New Haven 1969).
220	Healy, T. S.	*John Donne, Ignatius his conclave.* An edition of the Latin and English texts, with introduction and commentary (Oxford 1969).
221	Heath, P.	*The English parish clergy on the eve of the Reformation* (London 1969).

222	Hembry, P. M.	*The bishops of Bath and Wells, 1540-1640. Social and economic problems* (London 1967).
222a	Henning, B. D.	See 97.
223	Herbrüggen, H. Schulte	*Sir Thomas More, Neue Briefe. Mit einer Einführung in die epistolographische Tradition*, Neue Beiträge zur englischen Philologie 5 (Münster-en-W 1966).
223a	Hexter, J. H.	See 561.
224	Hicks, L.	*An Elizabethan problem. Some aspects of the careers of two exile-adventurers.* (Thomas Morgan and Charles Paget) (New York 1965).
225	Higham, F.	*Catholic and Reformed. A study of the Anglican Church 1559-1662* (London 1962).
226	Hill, C.	*Economic problems of the church. From archbishop Whitgift to the Long Parliament* (Oxford 1956).
227	———	*Puritanism and revolution* (London 1958).
228	———	*The century of revolution 1603-1714* (London 1961).
229	———	*Society and Puritanism* (London 1964).
230	———	*Intellectual origins of the English revolution* (London 1965).
231	———	*God's Englishman. Oliver Cromwell and the English revolution* (London 1970).
232	Hill, J. W. F.	*Tudor and Stuart Lincoln* (London 1956).
233	Hillerdal, G.	*Reason and revelation in Richard Hooker* (Lund 1962).
234	Hills, E. F.	*The King James version defended. A Christian view of the New Testament* (Des Moines, Iowa, 1956).
235	Hinnebusch, W. A.	'Foreign Dominican students and professors at the Oxford Blackfriars'. *Oxford studies presented to Daniel Callus* (Oxford 1964) pp 101-34.

236 Hoare, C. — *Anglican ordinations in the reign of Queen Mary* (St Leonards on Sea, 1957).

237 ——— *The Edwardine Ordinal* (Bristol 1958).

238 Hockey, S. F. — *Quarr Abbey and its lands 1132-1631* (Leicester 1970).

239 Hogrefe, P. — *The Sir Thomas More circle. A program of ideas and their impact on secular drama* (Urbana 1959).

240 ——— *The life and times of Sir Thomas Elyot Englishman* (Iowa State University Press 1967).

241 Holden, W. P. — *Anti-puritan satire 1572-1642*, Yale studies in English 126 (New Haven 1954).

242 Hollaender, A. E. J. — 'Articles of Almayne. An English version of German peasants' *Gravamina* 1525' *Studies presented to Sir Hilary Jenkinson*, ed J. C. Davies (Oxford 1957) pp 164-77.

243 Holmes, G. — *The later middle ages, 1272-1485* (London 1962).

244 Hoopes, R. — *Right reason in the English Renaissance* (London 1962).

245 Horden, J. — *Francis Quarles; Hosanna or Divine poems in the Passion of Christ, and Threnodes* (Liverpool 1960).

246 Horn, J. M. — *John Le Neve. Fasti Ecclesiae Anglicanae, 1300-1541. III. Salisbury diocese* (London 1962).

247 ——— *John Le Neve, Fasti Ecclesiae Anglicanae 1300-1541. II. Hereford diocese* (London 1962).

248 ——— *John Le Neve. Fasti Ecclesiae Anglicanae, 1300-1541. V. St. Pauls, London* (London 1963).

249 ——— *John Le Neve. Fasti, Ecclesiae Anglicanae, 1300-1541. VII. Chichester diocese* (London 1964).

250 ——— *John Le Neve, Fasti Ecclesiae Anglicanae 1300-1541. IX. Exeter diocese* (London 1964).

251 ——— John Le Neve, Fasti Ecclesiae Anglicanae 1300-1541. XIII. Introduction, errata and index (London 1967).
251a Horsman, A. E. Dobson's Drie Bobbes (Oxford 1955).
252 Horton, D. The answer to the whole set of questions of the celebrated Mr. William Apollonius, pastor of the church of Middleburg, looking towards the resolution of certain controveries concerning church government now being agitated in England; By John Norton. Translated from Latin (London 1958).
253 Howell, R. Newcastle upon Tyne and the Puritan revolution. (London 1967).
254 Howell, W. S. Logic and rhetoric in England 1500-1700 (Princeton 1956).
255 Hughes, J. J. Stewards of the Lord. A reappraisal of Anglican Orders (London 1970).
256 Hughes, M. T. The piety of Jeremy Taylor (London 1960).
257 Hughes, M. Y. The complete prose works of John Milton, III: 1648-9 (New Haven 1963).
258 Hughes, P. The Reformation in England (new ed London 1963).
259 Hughes, P. E. The theology of the English Reformers (London 1965).
260 Hughes, P. L. and Larkin, J. F. Tudor royal proclamations, I. The early Tudors 1485-1553. (New Haven and London 1964).
261 ——— Tudor royal proclamations, II, 1553-1587. III, 1588-1603 (London 1969).
262 Hunt, E. W. Dean Colet and his theology (London 1956).
263 Hunt, J. E. English and Welsh crucifixes 670-1550 (London 1956).
264 Hunt, P. Fifteenth century England (London 1962).

265	Huntly, F. L.	*Sir Thomas Browne. A biographical and critical study* (Ann Arbor 1962).
266	Hurstfield, J.	*Elizabeth I and the unity of England* (London 1960).
266a	———	See 140.
267	Ives, E. W. (ed)	*The English Revolution, 1600-1660* (London 1968).
268	Jackson, R. S.	*John Donne's christian vocation* (Evanston 1970).
269	Jacob, E. F.	*The fifteenth century, 1399-1485* (London 1961).
270	Jayne, S.	*John Colet and Marsilio Ficino* (London 1963).
271	Jenkins, E.	*Elizabeth the Great* (London 1958).
272	———	*Elizabeth and Leicester* (London 1961).
273	Jessup, F. W.	*Background to the English civil war* (London 1966).
274	Johnson, J. T.	*A society ordained by God. English puritan marriage doctrine in the first half of the XVIIth Century* (Nashville 1970).
275	Johnson, R. S.	*More's Utopia. Idealism and illusion* (London 1969).
276	Jones, B.	*John Le Neve, Fasti Ecclesiae Anglicanae 1300-1541. IV. Monastic cathedrals (Southern province)* (London 1963).
277	———	*John Le Neve, Fasti Ecclesiae Anglicanae, 1300-1541. VI. Northern Province (York, Carlisle, Durham)* (London 1963).
278	———	*John Le Neve, Fasti Ecclesiae Anglicanae, 1300-1541. VIII. Bath and Wells diocese* (London 1964).
279	———	*John Le Neve, Fasti Ecclesiae Anglicanae, 1300-1541. X. Coventry and Lichfield diocese* (London 1964).
280	———	*John Le Neve, Fasti Ecclesiae Anglicanae, 1300-1541. XI. The Welsh dioceses* (London 1965).
281	Jones, D.	*The Church in Chester 1300-1540* (Manchester 1957).

282 Jones, G. — *History of the law of charity, 1532-1827* (London 1969).
283 Jones, W. R. D. — *The Tudor Commonwealth, 1529-1559* (London 1970).
284 Jordan, W. K. — *Philanthropy in England 1480-1660. A study of the changing pattern of English social aspirations* (London 1959).
285 ——— *The charities of London 1480-1660.* (London 1961).
286 ——— *Charities of rural England. 1480-1660* (London 1961).
287 ——— *The chronicle and political papers of King Edward VI* (London 1966).
288 ——— *Edward VI: the young King. The Protectorship of the Duke of Somerset* (London 1968).
289 ——— *Edward VI: the threshold of power. The dominance of the Duke of Northumberland, 1549-1553* (London 1970).
290 Judd, A. — *The life of Thomas Bekynton, secretary to King Henry VI and bishop of Bath and Wells. 1443-1465* (Chichester 1961).
291 Kearney, H. — *Scholars and gentlemen. Universities and Society in pre-Industrial Britain, 1500-1700* (London 1970).
292 Kelley, M. W. — *This great argument. A study of Milton's De doctrina christiana as a gloss upon Paradise Lost.* (Gloucester, Mass. 1962).
293 Kelly, H. A. — *Divine providence in the England of Shakespeare's histories* (Cambridge, Mass. 1970).
294 Kelly, K. T. — *Conscience, dictator, or guide? A study in XVIIth century English protestant moral theology* (London 1967).
295 Kemp, E. W. — *An introduction to canon law in the church of England* (London 1957).
296 Kendall, P. M. — *Richard the Third* (New York 1956).

297	———	*Richard III*. Translated from English by A. Seiffhart and H. Rinn (Munich 1957).
297a	Kenyon, J. P.	*The Stuart Constitution* (London 1966).
298	Ketton-Cremer, R. W.	*Norfolk in the Civil War. A portrait of a society in conflict* (London 1969).
299	King, H. P. F.	*John Le Neve, Fasti Ecclesiae Anglicanae 1300–1541. I. Lincoln diocese* (London 1962).
300	Kingdon, R. M.	*The execution of justice in England; by William Cecil: and A true, sincere and modest defence of English catholics; by William Allen* (New York 1965).
301	Klein, A. J.	*Intolerance in the reign of Elizabeth* (new ed London 1968).
302	Knachel, P. A.	*The case of the Commonwealth of England stated; by Marchamont Nedham* (Charlottesville, Virg., 1969).
303	Knight, G. W.	*Shakespeare and religion* (London 1967).
304	Knowles, D.	*The Religious Orders in England, II. The end of the middle ages* (Cambridge 1955).
305	———	*The Religious Orders in England, III. The Tudor Age* (Cambridge 1959).
306	———	'The English bishops. 1070-1532' *Medieval studies presented Aubrey Gwynn S.J* (Dublin 1961) pp 283-96.
307	Knox, D. B.	*The doctrine of faith in the reign of Henry VIII* (London 1961).
308	———	*James Ussher, Archbishop of Armagh* (Cardiff 1967).
309	Knox, S. J.	*Walter Travers, paragon of Elizabethan puritanism* (London 1962).
310	Kranidas, T.	*New essays on Paradise lost* (Berkeley/Los Angeles 1969).
311	Kurth, B. O.	*Milton and Christian heroism. Biblical epic themes and forms in*

312 Laisney, M-Cl.   S. Thomas More. *Dialogue du réconfort dans les tribulations*. Translated from English (Namur 1959).
312a Lamb, G. R.   See 46.
313 Lamont, W. M.   *Marginal Prynne, 1600–1669* (Toronto 1963).
314 ———   *Godly rule. Politics and Religion, 1603–1660* (London 1969).
315 Lander, J. R.   *Conflict and stability in 15th century England* (London 1969).
315a Larkin, J. F.   See 260, 261.
316 Laslett, T. P. R.   *The world we have lost* (London 1965).
317 ———   *Un monde que nous avons perdu. Famille, communauté et structure sociale dans l'Angleterre pré-industrielle*. Trad. de l'anglais par C. Campas (Paris 1969).
318 Lavater Sloman, M.   *Herrin der Meere. Elisabeth I, Königin von England* (Zurich 1956).
319 Law, A.   *Augustine Baker* (New York 1970).
320 Le Compte, E.   *Grace to a witty sinner. A life of Donne* (New York 1965).
321 Lehmberg, S. E.   *Sir Thomas Elyot, Tudor humanist* (Austin 1960).
322 ———   *The Reformation Parliament, 1529–1536* (London 1970).
323 Le Huray, P.   *Music and Reformation in England, 1549–1660* (London 1967).
324 Leonard, E. M.   *The early history of English poor relief* (new ed London 1965).
325 Leroy, A.   *Le grand schisme d'Angleterre. 1533–1660* (Paris 1967).
326 Levy, F. J.   *Tudor historical thought* (San Marino, California 1967).
327 Lewalski, B. K.   *Milton's brief epic. The genre, meaning and art of Paradise Regained* (Providence 1966).
328 Leys, M. D. R.   *Catholics in England* (London 1961).
329 Linsday, J.   *Civil war in England* (London 1967).

[preceding entry, top of page:] XVIIth century England (Berkeley 1959).

330 Linnell, C. — *Some East Anglian clergy* (London 1961).
331 Loades, D. M. — *The Oxford Martyrs* (London 1970).
332 ——— *Two Tudor Conspiracies* (Cambridge 1965).
333 Loane, M. L. — *Makers of religious freedom in the 17th century* (Grand Rapids 1961).
334 ——— *Pioneers of the reformation in England* (London 1964).
335 Lockyer, R. — *Tudor and Stuart Britain, 1471–1714* (London 1965).
336 Logan, F. D. — *Excommunication and the secular arm in Medieval England. A study in legal procedure from the XIIIth to the XVIth century* (Toronto 1968).
337 Loomie, A. J. — *The Spanish Elizabethans* (New York 1963).
338 Lunt, W. E. — *Financial relations of the papacy with England 1327–1534* (Cambridge, Mass. 1962).
339 Lupton, J. H. — *A life of John Colet D. D., Dean of St. Paul's and founder of St. Paul's School.* With an appendix of some of his English writings (Hamden, Conn. 1961).
340 Lutard, O. — *Les Niveleurs, Cromwell et la république* [Archives] (Paris 1967).
341 McAdoo, H. R. — *The spirit of Anglicanism* (London 1965).
342 MacCaffrey, I. G. — *Paradise Lost as myth* (London 1959).
343 MacCaffrey, W. — *The shaping of the Elizabethan regime. Elizabethan politics, 1558–1572* (London 1969).
344 McConica, J. K. — *English humanists and Reformation politics* (London 1965).
345 McDonald, J. H. and Brown, N. P. — *The poems of Richard Southwell, S. J.* (Oxford 1967).
346 McElwee, W. — *The wisest fool in Christendom. The reign of King James I and VI* (London 1958).
347 MacFarlane, A. — *Witchcraft in Tudor and Stuart*

348 McGinn, D. J.   *England. A regional and comparative study* (London 1970).
John Penry and the Marprelate controversy (New Brunswick 1966).
349 McGrath, P.   *Papists and puritans under Elizabeth I* (London 1967).
350 MacGregor, G.   *The thundering Scot. John Knox* (London 1958).
351 Macklem, M.   *The anatomy of the world. Relations between natural and moral law from Donne to Pope* (Minneapolis 1958).
352 McLelland, J. C.   *The visible words of God. An exposition of the sacramental theology of Peter Martyr Vermigli 1500—1562* (Edinburgh/London 1957).
353 Maclure, M.   *The Paul's Cross sermons 1534—1642* (Toronto 1958).
353a Madsen, W. G.   See 650.
354 Major, J. M.   *Sir Thomas Elyot and Renaissance humanism* (Lincoln, Nebraska 1964).
355 Malfatti, C. V.   *Accession, coronation and marriage of Mary Tudor as related in four MSS of the Escorial* (Oxford 1967).
356 Manley, F.   *John Donne. The Anniversaries.* Ed with introduction and commentary (Baltimore 1963).
357 Manning, R. B.   *Religion and society in Elizabethan Sussex* (Leicester 1969).
358 ———   'The spread of the popular Reformation in England' *Sixteenth Century essays and studies, I* (Saint Louis 1970) pp 35-52.
359 Marc'hadour, G.   *S. Thomas More. Lettre à Dorp. La supplication des âmes* En. introd: Thomas More vu par Erasme (Namur 1962).
360 ———   *Thomas More et la Bible. La place des livres saints dans son apologetique et sa spiritualité.* (Paris 1969).
361 ———   *The Bible in the works of Thomas*

362	———	More. 1: Old Testament (Nieuwkoop 1969). The Bible in the works of Thomas More. 2. The four Gospels. 3. The Acts, epistles and Apocalypse (Nieuwkoop 1969-70).
363	Marchant, R. A.	The puritans and the church courts 1560–1642 (London 1960).
364	———	The church under the law. Justice, administration and discipline in the diocese of York, 1560–1640 (London 1969).
365	Marklem, M.	God have mercy. The life of John Fisher of Rochester (Ottowa 1967).
366	Marshall, J. S.	Hooker and the Anglican Tradition (London 1964).
367	Martin, F. X.	Friar Nugent. A study of Francis Levalin Nugent (1569–1635) agent of the Counter Reformation (Rome/London 1962).
368	———	'A thwarted project: The Capuchin mission to England and Scotland in the XVIIth century, 1608–1660' Miscellanea Melchor de Pobladura II (Rome 1964) pp 211-41.
369	Martin, H.	The private prayers of Lancelot Andrewes (London 1957).
370	Martz, L. L.	The paradise within. Studies in Vaughn, Traherne and Milton (New Haven 1964).
371	Masan, H. A.	Humanism and poetry in the early Tudor period (London 1959).
372	Mathew, D and Evans, I. (et al)	Catholicisme anglais (Paris 1958).
373	Mathias, R.	Whitsun riot. An account of a commotion amongst Catholics in Herefordshire and Monmouthshire in 1605 (London 1963).
374	Matrat, J.	Oliver Cromwell (Paris 1970).
375	Mattingly, G.	'William Allen and Catholic propaganda in England' Aspects de la propagande religieux (Geneva 1957) pp 325-39.
376	Maxwell, W. D.	The liturgical portions of the

		Genevan service book: John Knox's Genevan service book, 1556. Text in Latin and English (London 1965).
377	Mayfield, G.	*The Church of England, its members and its business* (London 1958).
378	Maynard, T.	*The life of Thomas Cranmer* (London 1956).
379	Maynard Smith, H.	*Pre-reformation England* (repr London 1963).
380	Mercer, E.	*English Art, 1553–1625* (London 1963).
381	Merle d'Aubigné, J. H.	*The Reformation in England.* Translated from the French by H. White and edited by S. M. Houghton. 2 vols (London 1962).
382	Meyer, A. O.	*England and the catholic church under Queen Elizabeth.* Translated from German by J. R. McKee (new ed London 1967).
383	Meyer, C. S.	*Elizabeth I and the religious settlement of 1559* (St Louis 1960).
384	———	'Melanchthon's influence on English thought in the XVIth century' *Miscellanea historiae ecclesiasticae II* (Louvain 1967) pp 163-85.
385	Miles, L.	*St. Thomas More. A dialogue of comfort against tribulation.* Edited with a critical introduction and notes (Bloomington 1965).
386	———	*John Colet and the Platonic tradition* (London 1962).
387	Mitchell, R. J.	*John Free. From Bristol to Rome in the XVth century* (London 1955).
388	Mitchell, W. M.	*The rise of the revolutionary party in the English House of Commons 1603–1629* (London 1958).
389	Möbus, G.	*Politik und Menschlichkeit in Leben des Thomas Morus* (2 ed Mainz 1966).
390	Moir, T. L.	*The addled parliament of 1614* (London 1958).
391	Moore, E. G.	*An introduction to English canon law* (London 1967).

392	Morgan, E. S.	*Roger Williams, The Church and the State* (New York 1967).
393	———	*The Puritan family. Religion and domestic relations in XVIIth century New England* (2 ed New York 1966).
394	Morgan, I.	*Prince Charles's puritan chaplain* [John Preston] (London 1957).
395	———	*The Godly preachers of the Elizabethan church* (London 1965).
395a	Mori, G.	See 506.
396	Morison, S.	*The likeness of Thomas More. An iconographical survey over the centuries.* Ed and supplemented by N. Barker (London 1963).
397	Morris, C.	*The Tudors* (London 1955).
398	Morris, H.	*Elizabethan literature* (London 1958).
399	Morton, A. L.	*The world of the Ranters. Religious radicalism in the English revolution* (London 1970).
400	Mosse, G. L.	*The holy pretence. A study of Christianity and reason of state from William Perkins to John Winthrop* (Oxford 1957).
401	Mueller, W. R.	*John Donne, preacher* (London 1963).
402	Muir, K.	*John Milton* (London 1955).
403	———	*The life and letters of Sir Thomas Wyatt* (Liverpool 1963).
404	Muldrow, G. M.	*Milton and the drama of the soul. A study of the theme of the restoration of man in Milton's later poetry* (La Haye 1970).
405	Muller, J. A.	*Stephen Gardiner and the Tudor reaction* (repr New York 1970).
406	Murray, R. H.	*The political consequences of the reformation. Studies in 16th century political thought* (New York 1961).
407	Mutschmann, H and Wentersdorf, K.	*Shakespeare and catholicism* (2 ed New York 1969).
408	Myers, A. R.	*English historical documents. IV. 1327–1485* (London 1969).

409 Myerscough, J. A. *The martyrs of Durham and the North East* (Glasgow 1956).
410 ——— *A procession of Lancashire martyrs and confessors* (Glasgow 1958).
411 Nathanson, L. *The strategy of truth. A study of Sir Thomas Browne* (London 1968).
412 Neale, J. E. *Elizabeth and her parliaments, 1584–1601* (new ed London 1957).
413 ——— *Essays in Elizabethan history* (London 1958).
414 ——— *Queen Elizabeth I* (new ed New York 1959, London 1967).
415 ——— *Königin Elisabeth*. Translated from English by G. Goyert (Munich 1967).
416 Nédoncelle, M. 'L'Humour d'Érasme et l'humour de Thomas More' *Scrinium Erasmianum II* (Leyden 1969) pp 569-93.
417 Neill, S. *L'Anglicanisme et la communion anglicane*. Trad. de l'anglais par J. Marrou (Paris 1961).
418 New, J. F. H. *Anglican and Puritan. The basis of their opposition, 1558–1640* (Stanford 1964).
419 *The New Cambridge Modern History I. The Renaissance 1493–1520*, ed G. R. Potter (Cambridge 1957).
420 *The New Cambridge Modern History II. The Reformation 1520–1559*, ed G. R. Elton (Cambridge 1958).
421 *New Cambridge Modern History. III. The Counter Reformation and Price Revolution 1559–1610*, ed R. B. Wernham (Cambridge 1968).
422 *New Cambridge Modern History IV. The Decline of Spain and the Thirty Years War. 1609–1648/59*, ed J. P. Cooper (Cambridge 1970).
423 Nugent, E. M. *The thought and culture of the Renaissance. An Anthology of Tudor prose 1480–1555* (New York 1956).

424 Nuttall, G. F.	*Visible saints. The Congregational way, 1640–1660* (Oxford 1957).
425 ———	*The Welsh saints 1640–1660. Walter Cradock, Vavasor Powell, Morgan Lloyd* (Cardiff 1957).
426 ———	*Richard Baxter* (London 1966).
427 O'Connell, M. R.	*Thomas Stapleton and the Counter Reformation* (New Haven 1964).
427a O'Connor, D.	See 543.
427b O'Donnell, T.	See 95.
428 Oliver, M.	*Mary Ward 1585–1645* (London 1960).
429 Osborn, J. M.	*The Quenes Maiesties passage through the Citie of London* (New Haven 1960).
430 ———	*The Autobiography of Thomas Whythorne* (Oxford 1961).
431 Owen, D. M.	'The enforcement of the reformation in the diocese of Ely' *Miscellanea historiae ecclesiasticae III* (Louvain 1970) pp 167-74.
432 Owen, G. D.	*Elizabethan Wales* (Cardiff 1962).
433 Owen, H. W.	'Another Augustine Baker Manuscript', *Dr. L. Reypensalbum* (Antwerp 1964) pp 269-80.
434 Owst, G. R.	*Literature and pulpit in medieval England. A neglected chapter in the history of English letters and of the English people* (Oxford 1961).
435 Oxley, J. E.	*The reformation in Essex to the death of Mary* (Manchester 1965).
436 Packer, J. W.	*Transformation of Anglicanism, 1643–1660. With Special reference to Henry Hammond* (Manchester 1970).
437 Pallett, H.	*Come-to-good and the early Quakers in Cornwall* (London 1968).
438 Parker, W. R.	*Milton. A biography, I. The life: II, Commentary, notes, index and finding list* (Oxford 1968).
439 Parmiter, G. de C.	*The King's great matter. A study of Anglo-Papal relations. 1527–1554* (New York 1967).

440	Parry, R. H. (ed)	*The English Civil War and after. 1642–58* (Berkeley 1970).
441	Patrick, J. M.	*Milton's conception of sin as developed in Paradise Lost* (Logan, Utah 1960).
442	Patrides, C. A. (ed)	*Approaches to Paradise Lost* (Toronto 1968).
443	———	*Milton and the Christian tradition* (London 1966).
444	Paul, J. E.	*Catherine of Aragon and her friends* (London 1966).
445	Paul, L. A.	*Sir Thomas More* (New York 1960).
446	Paul, R. S.	*The Lord Protector. Religion and politics in the life of Oliver Cromwell* (London 1955).
447	Pearl, V.	*London and the outbreak of the puritan revolution. City government and national politics 1625–1643* (Oxford 1961).
448	Peck, A. L.	*Anglicanism and episcopacy* (London 1958).
449	Percy, L. E.	*John Knox* (Richmond 1964).
450	Peter, J.	*A critique of Paradise Lost* (London 1960).
451	Peters, R.	*Oculus episcopi. Administration in the archdeaconry of St. Albans, 1580–1625* (Manchester 1963).
452	———	'The training of the 'unlearned' clergy in England during the 1580s: a regional study' *Miscellanea historiae ecclesiasticae, III* (Louvain 1970) pp 184-97.
453	Pettet, E. C.	*Of paradise and light. A study of Vaughn's Silex scintillans* (London 1960
454	Pfaff, R. W.	*New liturgical feasts in later medieval England* (London 1970).
455	Pineas, R.	*Thomas More and Tudor polemics* (Bloomington, Indiana 1968).
456	Pollard, A. F.	*Thomas Cranmer and the English Reformation* (new ed London 1966).
456a	———	*Wolsey*, intro G. R. Elton (new ed London 1965).

457 ———	*England under Protector Somerset* (repr New York 1966).
458 Porter, H. C.	*Reformation and reaction in Tudor Cambridge* (London 1958).
458a ———	See 573.
458b Potter, G. R.	See 419.
459 ———	'The initial impact of the Swiss reformers on England', *Discordia concors. Festgabe für Edgar Bonjour, II* (Basle 1968) pp 391-400.
460 ——— and Simpson, E. M.	*The sermons of John Donne, IX and IV* (Berkeley/Los Angeles 1958—59).
461 ——— ———	*The Sermons of John Donne, X* (Berkeley 1962).
462 Prall, S. E.	*The agitation for law reform during the puritan revolution 1640—1660* (La Haye 1966).
463 Prévost, A.	*Thomas More et la crise de la pensée européenne* (Paris 1969).
464 Primus, J. H.	*The vestments controversy. An historical study of the earliest tensions within the church of England in the reigns of Edward VI and Elizabeth I* (Kampen 1960).
465 Procter, F. and Frere, W. H.	*A new history of the Book of Common Prayer* (3 impr, repr, London 1965).
466 Purvis, J. S.	*The York cycle of Mystery plays* (London 1957).
467 ———	*The condition of Yorkshire church fabrics 1300—1800* (York 1958).
468 Raab, F.	*The English face of Machiavelli. A changing interpretation, 1500—1700* (London 1964).
469 Read, C.	*Mr. Secretary Cecil and Queen Elizabeth* (London 1955).
470 ———	*Lord Burghley and Queen Elizabeth* (London 1960).
471 ———	'The government of England under Elizabeth' *Life and letters in Tudor and Stuart England* (Ithaca 1962) pp 481-510.

472 Redpath, T. — *John Donne. Songs and Sonnets* (London 1956).
473 Reidy, M. F. — *Bishop Lancelot Andrewes. Jacobean court preacher. A study in early XVIIth century religious thought* (Chicago 1955).
474 Reilly, C. — *Francis Line, S. J. An exiled English scientist. 1595–1675* (Rome 1969).
475 Reynolds, E. E. — *Saint John Fisher* (London 1955).
476 ——— *Margaret Roper, eldest daughter of Sir Thomas More* (London 1960).
477 ——— *John Southworth, priest and martyr* (London 1962).
478 ——— *The lives of St. Thomas More by William Roper and Nicholas Harpesfield* (London 1963).
479 ——— *The trial of St. Thomas More* (London 1964).
480 ——— *The field is won. The life and death of St. Thomas More* (London 1968).
481 Ribner, I. — *Jacobean tragedy. The quest for moral order* (New York 1962).
482 Richards, M. — *The liturgy in England* (London 1966).
483 Richardson, W. C. — *History of the Court of Augmentations, 1536–1554* (London 1962).
484 Ridley, J. — *Nicholas Ridley. A biography* (London 1957).
485 ——— *Thomas Cranmer* (London 1962).
486 ——— *John Knox* (London 1968).
487 Robins, H. F. — *If this be heresy. A study of Milton and Origen* (Urbana 1963).
488 Roberts, J. R. — *A critical anthology of English recusant devotional prose 1558–1603* (Pittsburgh 1966).
489 Rogers, E. F. — *St. Thomas More. Selected letters* (New Haven 1961).
490 Rogers, P. G. — *The fifth Monarchy men* (London 1966).
491 Roog, S. H. — *The theology of missions in the puritan tradition. A study of*

representative puritans: Richard Sibbes, Richard Baxter, John Eliot, Cotton Mather, and Jonathan Edwards (Delft 1965).

492 Roots, I. *The great rebellion, 1642–1660* (London 1966).

493 Rosenberg, E. *Leicester, patron of letters* (New York 1955).

494 Rossiter, A. P. *English drama from early times to the Elizabethans* (London 1958).

495 Roth, F. *The English Austin friars, 1249–1538, II; Sources* (New York 1961).

496 ——— *The English Austin Friars. 1249–1538, I; History* (New York 1966).

497 Rouschausse, J. *Saint John Fisher. Discours. Traité de la prière. Ecrits de prison.* Textes traduits et presentés (Namur 1964).

498 Routh, E. M. G. *Sir Thomas More and his friends, 1477–1535* (New York 1963).

499 Routley, E. *The music of Christian hymnody. A study of the development of the hymn tune since the reformation, with special reference to English protestantism* (London 1957).

500 Rowse, A. L. *Tudor Cornwall* (repr London 1957).

501 ——— *Raleigh and the Throckmortons* (London 1962).

502 Runes, D. D. *The Gospel according to St. John, in the words of the King James version of the year 1611* (New York 1967).

503 Rupp, G. *Six makers of English religion* (New York 1957, 2 ed London 1969).

504 ——— *Studies in the making of the English Protestant tradition* (new ed London 1967).

505 Ryken, L. *The apocalyptic vision in Paradise Lost* (Ithaca 1970).

506 *Saggi sulla rivoluzione inglese del 1640*, Ed by C. Hill, translated from English by C. De Cugis and G. Mori, *I fatti e le ide, II* (Milan 1957).

507 Saillens, E. *John Milton, poète combattant* (Paris 1959).

508 Saltmarsh, J.	'The founder's statutes of King's College, Cambridge' *Studies presented to Sir Hilary Jenkinson* (London 1957) pp 337-60.
509 Samuel, I.	*Dante and Milton* (Ithaca 1966).
510 Sasek, L. A.	*The literary temper of the English puritans* (Baton Rouge 1961).
511 Sawada, P. A.	'Das Imperium Heinrichs VIII und die erste Phase seiner Konzilpolitik' *Reformata reformanda. Festgabe für Hubert Jedin, I* (Münster-en-W 1965) pp 476-507.
512 Scarisbrick, J. J.	*Henry VIII* (London 1968).
513 Schlatter, R.	*Richard Baxter and puritan politics* (New Brunswick 1957).
514 Schleiner, W.	*The imagery of John Donne's sermons* (Providence 1970).
515 Schmidt, A. M.	*Calvin. Lettres anglaises 1548–1561* (Paris 1959).
516 Schmidt, M.	'Die Rechtfertigungslehre bei Richard Hooker', *Geist und Geschichte der Reformation. Festgabe Hanns Rückert* (Berlin 1966) pp 377-96.
517 Schoeck, R. J.	'Thomas More and the Italian heritage of early Tudor humanism', *Arts libéraux et philosophie au moyen âge* (Montreal et Paris, 1969) pp 1191-7.
518 ———	'Common law and canon law in the writings of Thomas More. The affair of Richard Hunne'. *Proceedings of the third international congress of medieval canon law. Strassburg, 1968* (Vatican City 1971).
519 Scholes, P. A.	*The puritans and music in England and New England* (repr London 1970).
520 Schücking, L. L.	*Die puritanische Familie in Literar-soziologischer* (Berne 1964).
520a ———	*The Puritan Family*, trans Brian Buttershaw (London 1969).
521 Schultz, H.	*Milton and forbidden knowledge* (London 1956).

522	Seaver, P. S.	*The puritan lectureships. The politics of religious dissent, 1560–1662* (Stanford 1970).
522a	Shanahan, D.	See 155.
523	Shaw, D.	'John Willock' *Reformation and Revolution. Essays in honour of Dr. Hugh Watt* (Edinburgh 1967). pp 42-69.
524	Shirley, T. F.	*Thomas Thirlby, Tudor bishop* (London 1964).
524a	Short, H. L.	See 39.
525	Siegel, P. M.	*Shakespearean tragedy and the Elizabethan compromise* (New York 1957).
526	Simon, J.	*Education and society in Tudor England* (London 1966).
527	Simons, E.	*Henry VII* (London 1968).
528	Simons, J.	*Robert Parsons, S. J. Certamen Ecclesiae Anglicanae. A study of an unpublished MS.* [Diss. Nimègue] (Assen 1965).
529	Simpson, A.	*Puritanism in Old and New England* (Chicago 1955).
529a	Simpson, E. M.	See 460, 461.
530	Simpson, M. A.	'Of the troubles begun at Frankfurt, A.D. 1554' *Reformation and revolution. Essays in honour of Dr. Hugh Watt* (Edinburgh 1967) pp 17-33.
531	Sims, J. H.	*The bible in Milton's Epic* (Gainsville 1962).
532	Sirluck, E.	*John Milton. Complete prose works, II; 1643-1648* (New Haven 1959).
533	Sitwell, G.	*Holy wisdom, or Directions for the prayer of contemplation: by Fr. Augustine Baker OSB* (London 1964).
534	Slavin, A. J.	*Humanism, Reform and Reformation in England* (London/New York 1969).
534a	Smyth, C. H.	See 132.
535	Snape, R. H.	*English monastic finances in the late Middle Ages* (new ed New York 1968).

536	Snell, L. S.	Documents towards a history of the reformation in Cornwall: II The Edwardian Inventories of Church goods for Cornwall (London 1956).
537	———	Documents towards a history of the Reformation in Devon: The Chantry certificates for Devon and the city of Exeter (Exeter 1961).
536	———	The suppression of the religious foundations of Devon and Cornwall (Marazion, Cornwall 1967).
539	Solt, L. F.	Saints in arms. Puritanism and democracy in Cromwell's army (Stanford 1959).
540	Southgate, W. M.	John Jewel and the problem of doctrinal authority (Cambridge, Mass. 1962).
541	Speaight, R.	Nature et grâce dans les tragedies de Shakespeare. Trad de l'angl. par H. Lemaitre (Paris 1957).
542	Stampher, J.	John Donne and the metaphysical gesture (New York 1970).
543	Stanwood, P. G. and O'Connor, D.	John Cosin. A collection of private devotions (1627) (Oxford 1967).
544	Stavig, M.	John Ford and the Traditional Moral Order (Madison 1968).
545	Steadman, J. M.	Milton and the Renaissance Hero (London 1967).
546	Stearns, M.	Elizabeth I of England (New York 1970).
547	Stevens, D.	Thomas Tomkins 1572–1656 (New York 1957).
548	Stevens, J.	Music and poetry in the early Tudor court (London 1961).
549	Stevenson, R.	Shakespeare's religious frontier (La Haye 1958).
550	Storey, R. L.	Diocesan administration in the XVth Century (London 1959).
551	———	The reign of Henry VII (London 1968).
552	Story, G. M.	Lancelot Andrewes: Sermons (Oxford 1967).
553	Stranks, C. J.	Anglican devotion (London 1961).
554	Strong, R.	Holbein and Henry VIII (London 1967).

555	———	*The English icon: Elizabethan and Jacobean portraiture* (New Haven, Conn. 1970).
556	Stroup, T. B.	*Religious rite and ceremony in Milton's poetry* (Lexington 1968).
557	Summers, J.	*The Muse's method. An introduction to Paradise Lost* (Cambridge, Mass. 1962).
558	Surman, C. E.	*Supplementary Index of 'Intruders' and others* [Supplementary to A. G. Matthews' *Walker revised* (Oxford 1948)] (London 1956).
559	Surtz, E. L.	*The praise of wisdom* [the treatment of morality and religion by More in the *Utopia*] (Chicago 1957).
560	———	*The works and days of John Fisher. An introduction to the position of St. John Fisher (1469–1535), bishop of Rochester, in the English renaissance and reformation* (Cambridge, Mass. 1967).
561	——— and Hexter, J. H.	*The Yale edition of the complete works of St. Thomas More: IV Utopia* (New Haven/London 1965).
562	Svendson, K.	*Milton and science* (Cambridge, Mass. 1956).
563	Sykes, N.	*Old priest and new presbyter* (London 1956).
564	———	*The English religious tradition. Sketches of its influence in church, state and society* (London 1961).
565	Tavard, G. H.	*Holy Writ or Holy Church. The crisis of the protestant reformation* (London 1960).
566	Thieme, H.	*Die Ehescheidung Heinrichs VIII als europäischer Rechtsfall*, Syntagma Friburgense. Historische Studien Herman Aubin dargebracht (Lindau/Constance 1956).
567	———	*Die Ehescheidung Heinrichs VIII und die europäischen Universitäten.* [Jursitiche Studiengesellschaft Karlsruhe. Schriftenreihe fasc. 31] (Karlsruhe 1957).

567a	Thomas, R.	See 39.
568	Thompson, A. H.	*The English Clergy and their organisation in the later Middle Ages* (new ed London 1966).
569	Thompson, C. R.	'The bible in English 1525–1611' *Life and letters in Tudor and Stuart England* (Ithaca 1962) pp 185-206.
570	———	'The English church in the XVIth century' *Life and letters in Tudor and Stuart England* (Ithaca 1962) pp 225-83.
571	———	'Schools in Tudor England' *Life and letters in Tudor and Stuart England* (Ithaca 1962) pp 285-322.
572	———	'Universities in Tudor England' *Life and letters in Tudor and Stuart England* (Ithaca 1962) pp 335-70.
573	Thomson, D. F. S. and Porter, H. C.	*Erasmus and Cambridge*. The Cambridge letters of Erasmus translated by D.F.S.T. Introduction, commentary and notes by H.C.P. (London 1964).
574	Thomson, J. A. F.	*The later Lollards, 1414–1520* (London 1965).
575	Thomson, P.	*Sir Thomas Wyatt and his background* (Stanford 1964).
576	Thornton, M.	*Margery Kempe, an example in the English pastoral tradition* (London 1960).
577	Tillyard, E. M. W.	*The metaphysicals and Milton* (London 1956).
578	———	*The Elizabethan World Picture* (repr London 1963).
579	Tjernagel, N.	*Henry VIII and the Lutherans* (London 1966).
580	Toledano, D.	*Histoire de l'Angleterre chrétienne* (Paris 1955).
581	———	*Une Église du silence en Angleterre sous Elisabeth Ire* (Paris 1957).
582	Torrance, T. F.	*Kingdom and church. A study in the theology of the Reformation.* (Edinburgh/London 1956).

583 Trevor Roper, H. R.	*Historical essays* (London 1957).
584 ———	*Archibishop Laud* (2 ed London 1962).
585 ———	*Religion, the Reformation and social change, and other essays* (London 1967).
586 Trimble, W. R.	*The catholic laity in Elizabethan England 1558–1603* (Cambridge, Mass. 1964).
587 Tucker, N.	*North Wales in the Civil War* (London 1958).
588 Tuve, R.	*Images and themes in five poems by Milton* (Cambridge, Mass. 1957).
589 Vaissier, J. J.	*A devout treatyse called The Tree and XII fruits of the holy ghost, edited from Ms McClean 132, Fitzwilliam Museum, Cambridge.* With a collation of the other MSS and the printed edition of 1534–5 (STC 13608) together with notes on the MSS language and contents (Groningen 1960).
590 Van der Essen, A.	'Les catholiques londoniens et l'ambassade d'Espagne (1633–1637)' *Scrinium Lovaniense. Mélanges historiques Etienne Van Cauwenbergh* (Gembloux/Louvain 1961) pp 475-85.
591 ———	'Hugh Owen, réfugié politique anglais aux Pays bas et le plan d'invasion de l'Angleterre de 1594' *Scrinium Lovaniense. Mélanges historiques Etienne Van Cauwenbergh* (Gembloux/Louvain 1961) pp 466-74.
592 Van Etten, H.	*George Fox and the Quakers*, trans from French by E. K. Osborn (London 1959).
593 Vassen, A. F.	*Two books of the histories of Ireland compiled by Edmund Campion feloe of St. John Baptistes College in Oxford.* Edited from MS Jones 6, Bodleian Library, Oxford (Assen 1963).

England and Wales

594	Vazques de Prada, A.	*Sir Thomas Moro Lord Canciller de Inglaterra* (Madrid 1962, 2 ed 1966).
595	Vyvyan, J.	*The Shakespearean ethic* (London 1959).
596	Wallace, K. R.	*Francis Bacon on the nature of man* (London 1968).
597	Walter, G.	*La révolution anglaise* (Paris 1963).
598	Walzer, M.	*The revolution of the saints. A study in the origins of radical politics* (Cambridge, Mass. 1965).
599	Wand, J. W. C.	*Anglicanism in history and today* (London 1961).
600	Ware, S. L.	*The Elizabethan parish in its ecclesiastical and financial aspects* (London 1962).
601	Watkin, E. I.	*Roman catholicism in England from the reformation to 1950* (London 1957).
602	Watson, F.	*The English grammar schools to 1660* (repr of 1908 ed London 1968).
603	Waugh, E.	*Edmund Campion* (London 1961).
604	———	*Edmund Campion.* Translated into Italian by M. R. Schisano (Rome 1966).
605	Weaver, J. R. H. and Beardwood, A.	*Some Oxfordshire wills proved in the prerogative court of Canterbury 1393–1510* (Oxford, Bodleian Library 1958).
606	Wedgewood, C. V.	*The Kings Peace, 1637–1641* (London 1955).
607	———	*The Kings War 1641–7* (London 1958).
608	Weiss, R.	*Humanism in England during the XVth century* (2 ed Oxford 1957).
609	Welsby, P. A.	*Lancelot Andrewes 1555–1626* (London 1958, 2 ed 1964).
610	———	*George Abbott, the unwanted Archbishop* (London 1962).
611	Wendel, F. (ed)	*M. Bucer Opera Latina, XV: De Regno Christi libri duo (1550)* (Gütersloh 1955).
611a	Wentersdorf, K.	See 407.

611b Wernham, R. B. — See 421.
612 Westfall, R. S. — *Science and religion in XVIIth century England* (New Haven 1958).
613 Whale, J. S. — *The protestant tradition. An essay in interpretation* (London 1955).
614 Whinney, M. — *Sculpture in Britain 1530–1830* (London 1964, 2 ed 1970).
615 White, H. C. — *Tudor books of saints and martyrs* (Madison 1963).
616 ——— *Social criticism in popular religious literature of the XVIth century* (new ed London 1966).
617 Whiting, G. W. — *Milton and this pendant world* (Austin 1958).
618 Wickham, G. — *Early English stages 1300–1600, I; 1300–1567* (New York 1959).
619 Wilding, M. — *Milton's Paradise Lost* (Sydney 1969).
620 Williams, C. H. — *English historical documents, V; 1485–1558* (London 1967).
620a ——— See 140.
621 Williams, D. — *John Penry. Three treatises concerning Wales* (Cardiff 1960).
622 Williams, Glanmor — *The Welsh church from the conquest to the Reformation* (Cardiff 1962).
623 ——— *Welsh reformation essays* (Cardiff 1968).
624 ——— *Reformation views of Church history* (London 1957).
625 Williams, G. H. — *Spiritual and Anabaptist writers. Documents illustrative of the radical reformation* (Philadelphia 1957).
626 ——— *The radical reformation* (Philadelphia 1962).
627 Williams, G. W. — *Image and symbol in the sacred poetry of Richard Crashaw* (Columbia 1963).
628 Williams, H. C. — *William Tyndale* (London 1969).
629 Williams, N. — *Elizabeth I. Queen of England* (New York 1968).
630 ——— *Elisabeth I von England.* Translated from English by L. Mickel (Stuttgart 1969).

England and Wales

631 Williams, W. O. — *Tudor Gwynedd. The Tudor age in the principality of North Wales* (London 1958).
632 Williamson, D. M. — *Lincoln muniments* (Lincoln 1956).
633 Williamson, H. R. — *The beginning of the English reformation* (London 1957).
634 Willis, A. J. — *Winchester consistory court depositions 1561–1602* (Folkestone 1960).
635 ——— *Hampshire marriage licences 1609–1640, 2nd part* (Folkestone 1960).
636 Willson, D. H. — *King James VI and I* (London 1956).
637 Wilson, J. F. — *Pulpit in Parliament, Puritanism during the English civil wars, 1640–48* (London 1970).
638 Winny, J. — *The preface to Donne* (Harlow 1970).
639 Wolfe, D. M. — *Milton in the puritan revolution* (London 1963).
640 ——— *Leveller manifestos of the Puritan revolution* (repr London 1967).
641 Wood-Legh, K. L. — *A small household of the XVth century, being the account book of Munden's chantry, Bridport* (Manchester 1956).
642 ——— *Perpetual chantries in Britain* (London 1965).
643 Woodward, G. W. O. — *Reformation and resurgence 1485–1603* (London 1963).
644 ——— *The dissolution of the monasteries* (London 1966).
645 Wormald, F. and Wright, C. E. — *The English Library before 1700. Studies in its history* (London 1958).
646 Wright, B. A. — *Milton's poems* (London 1956).
647 ——— *Milton's Paradise Lost* (London 1962).
647a Wright, C. E. — See 645.
648 Wright, L. B. — *Middle class culture in Elizabethan England* (Ithaca 1958).
649 Young, P. — *Oliver Cromwell* (London 1962).
650 Young, R. B., Furniss, W. T. and Madsen, W. G. — *Three studies in the renaissance: Sidney, Jonson, Milton* (Oxford 1958).

651 Yule, G.	*The independants in the English civil war* (London 1958).
652 Zagorin, P.	*The Court and the country. The beginning of the English Revolution* (New York 1970).
653 Zeeveld, W. G.	*Foundation of Tudor policy* (repr London 1969).
654 Ziff, L.	*John Cotton on the churches of New England* (Cambridge, Mass. 1968).

SECTION 2. DICTIONARIES AND BIBLIOGRAPHIES

The following seven works appeared annually throughout the period, or during the years indicated:

655 *Annual Bulletin of historical literature*, 40–54 (London, The Historical Association).
656 *Bibliographie Internationale de l'humanisme et de la Renaissance*, 1–6, Fédération internationales des sociétés et institutes pour l'étude de la Renaissance (Geneva 1966–1971).
657 *British National Bibliography*, ed A. J. Wells (London, British Museum, 1955–1967; Council of the British National Bibliography, 1968–70).
658 *Historical Research for University Degrees in the United Kingdom*; I, theses completed; II, theses in progress (London, University of London Institute of Historical Research).
659 *International Bibliography of the Historical Sciences*, International committee of Historical Sciences, Lausanne (Paris).
660 *International Bibliography of the History of Religions*, ed H. Boas, C. J. Bleeker et al (Leyden).
661 *Revue Historique; Bibliographie*, ed S. Hanssens 50–65 (Louvain).

662 Allison, A. F. and Rogers, D. M. — *Biographical studies 1534–1829. Materials towards a biographical dictionary of Catholic history in the British Isles from the break with Rome to Catholic emancipation.* III (1955).

663 ——— *A catalogue of Catholic Books in English printed abroad or secretly in England 1558-1640*, Biographical Studies, 3; pts 3 and 4 (Bognor Regis, Sussex 1956).

664 Anstruther, G. — *Seminary priests, Elizabethan, 1558–1603.* Vol I; A–L; Vol II; M–Z; (Woodchester, Stroud, Dominican Priory, 1966).

665 ——— *The Seminary Priests. A dictionary of the secular clergy of England and Wales, 1558–1850.* Vol I. Elizabethan, 1558–1603 (Durham 1968).

666 Beales, A. C. F. — 'A biographical catalogue of Catholic Schoolmasters in England

	from 1558–1700, with an index of places: I; 1558–1603.' *Recusant History*, 7, (1964) pp 268-89
667	*Bibliographie de la Réforme 1450–1648. Ouvrages parus de 1940 à 1955* Fasc 4, France, Angleterre, Suisse (Leyden 1963).
668	*Bibliography of British History. Tudor period 1485–1603*, ed C. Read (2 ed New York 1959).
669	*Bibliography of British history. Stuart period. 1603–1714*, ed G. Davies and M. F. Keeler, (Oxford 1970).
670 Bourde, A. J.	'Ouvrages récents sur l'époque élisabéthaine', *Revue Historique*, 229 (1963) pp 443-76.
671 Chambers, D. D. C.	'A catalogue of the library of Bishop Lancelot Andrewes (1555–1626)', *Transactions of the Cambridge Bibliographical Society*, 5, ii (1970) pp 99-121.
672 Christophers, R. A.	*George Abbot, archbishop of Canterbury, 1562–1633. A bibliography* (Charlottesville, Virginia 1966).
673 Clough, E. A.	*Short title catalogue arranged geographically of books printed and distributed by printers, publishers and booksellers in the English provincial towns, and in Scotland and Ireland up to and including 1700* (London 1970).
674 Curtis, M. H.	'Library catalogues in Tudor Oxford and Cambridge,' *Studies in the Renaissance* 5, (1958) pp 111-20.
674a	Davies, G. See 669.
675 Fitch, M.	*Index to parliamentary records in the Commissary court of London; (London division) now preserved in the Guildhall Library*, I, 1374–1488 (London 1969).
675a Fryde, E. B.	See 688.

England and Wales

676 Gibson, B. W. — *St. Thomas More. A preliminary bibliography of his works and Moreana to the year 1750.* With a bibliography of Utopiana compiled by R. W. Gibson and J. M. Patrick (New Haven 1961).

677 James, M. R. and Jenkins, C. — *A descriptive catalogue of the MSS in the Library of Lambeth Palace* (Cambridge 1955).

678 Jayne, S. and Johnson, F. R. — *The Lumley Library. The catalogue of 1609.* (London 1956).

679 Jayne, S. — *Library catalogues of the English Renaissance* (Berkeley 1956).

679a Keeler, M. F. — See 669.

680 Keynes, G. — *A bibliography of Dr. John Donne.* (3 ed London 1958).

681 Levine, M. — *Tudor England, 1485—1603.* A bibliographical handbook prepared for the Conference on British Studies (Cambridge 1968).

682 Lievsay, J. L. — *The Englishman's Italian Books, 1550—1700* (Philadelphia 1969).

683 Marc'hadour, G. — *L'Univers de Thomas More. Chronologie critique de More, Erasme, et leur époque (1477—1536)* (Paris 1963).

684 Miller, H. — 'L'Angleterre au XVI siècle' [bibliographie], *Revue Historique*, 241 (1969) pp 381-408.

685 Mortimer, J. E. — *The library catalogue of Anthony Higgin, dean of Ripon (1608—1624)*, Proceedings of the Leeds philosophical and literary society. Literary and historical section, X, 1 (Leeds 1962).

686 Petti, A. G. — 'A bibliography of the writings of Richard Verstegan c. 1550—1641,' *Recusant History*, 7 (1963) pp 82-103.

687 Pollard, A. W. and others — *Short title catalogue of books printed in England, Scotland and Ireland and of English books printed abroad, 1475—1640,*

		Bibliographical Society series (London 1970).
688	Powicke, F. M.	*Handbook of British chronology.* Second Edition by E. B. Fryde (London 1961).
689	Ramage, D.	*A finding list of English books to 1640 in libraries in the British Isles* (Durham 1958).
689a	Read, C.	See 668.
690		*Recusant books at St. Mary's Oscott, I; 1518-1687* (New Oscott, Warwickshire, n.d. but appearing 1963—5).
690a	Rogers, D. M.	See 662, 663.
691	Snell, L. S.	*Short guides to records, 6: Chantry certificates* (London 1962).
692	Twemlow, J. A.	*Calendar of entries in the papal registers relating to Great Britain and Ireland*, XIII. First and Second parts: Papal Letters 1471—1784 (London 1955).
693	———	*Calendar of entries in the papal registers relating to Great Britain and Ireland*, XIV. Papal Letters 1484—1492 (London 1960).
694	Williams, G. H.	'Studies in the radical reformation 1517—1618, a bibliographical survey of research since 1939', *Church History*, 27 (1958) pp 46-69, 124-60.
695	Zagorin, P.	'English history, 1558—1640. A bibliographical survey', *American Historical Review*, 68 (1962—3) pp 364-84.

SECTION 3. ARTICLES IN ACADEMIC JOURNALS

696 'A revolution in Tudor history?' — I. Dr. Elton's interpretation of the age; by P. Williams. II. Medieval government and statecraft; by G. L. Harris. III. The Tudor State: by P. Williams (*Past and Present*, 25, 1963, pp 3-58).

697 Abel, D. — 'The Elizabethan Archbishops' (*History Today*, 6, 1956, pp 686-94).

698 Adamson, J. H. — 'Milton's Arianism' (*Harvard Theological Review*, 53, 1960, pp 269-76).

699 ———— 'Milton and the creation' (*Journal of English and German Philology*, 61, 1962, pp 756-78).

700 Allen, D. C. — 'Milton and the descent to light' (*Journal of English and German Philology*, 60, 1961, pp 614-30).

701 Allen, P. R. — '*Utopia* and European humanism. The function of the prefatory verses and letters'. (*Studies in the Renaissance*, 10, 1963, pp 91-107).

702 Allen, W. — 'John Bois's notes' [concerning the translation of the King's bible] (*Renaissance News*, 19, 1966, pp 331-43).

703 Allison, A. F. — 'New light on the early history of the *Breve Compendio*. The background to the English translation of 1612'. (*Recusant History*, 4, 1957, pp 4-17).

704 ———— 'John Heigham of St. Omer (c. 1568–c. 1632)' (*Recusant History*, 4, 1958, pp 226-42).

705 ———— 'John Gerard and the Gunpowder plot'. (*Recusant History*, 5, 1959, pp 43-63).

706 ———— 'Sir Toby Matthew the author of *Charity mistaken*' (*Recusant History*, 5, 1959, pp 128-30).

707 Anderson, B. — 'Engelsk partihistoria, 1603–1660 Några aspekter' (*Historisk Tidskrift*, 3, 1968, pp 302-42).

708 Andreasen, N. J. C. — 'Donne's *Devotions* and the psychology of assent'. (*Modern Philology*, 62, 1964-5, pp 207-16).

709 Anglo, S. — 'An early Tudor programme of plays and other demonstrations against the Pope'. (*Journal of the Warburg and Courtauld Institutes*, 20, 1957, pp 176-9).

710 ———— 'The *British history* in early Tudor propaganda. With an appendix of manuscript pedigrees of the Kings of England, Henry VI to Henry VIII'. (*Bulletin of the John Rylands Library*, 44, 1961, pp 17-48).

711 ———— 'The Hampton court painting of the *Field of the cloth of Gold* considered as an historical document'. (*The Antiquaries Journal*, 46, 1966, pp 287-307).

712 Anstruther, G. — 'Lancashire clergy in 1639. A recently discovered list among the Towneley papers'. (*Recusant History*, 4, 1957, pp 38-46).

713 ———— 'The Ven. Robert Nutter O.P.' (d. 1600) (*Archivum Fratrum Praedicatorum*, 27, 1957, pp 359-402).

714 ———— 'The English Dominicans in Rome' (*Archivum Fratrum Praedicatorum*, 29, 1959, pp 168-99).

715 Antheunis, L. — 'La legislation persecutrice des catholiques sous le règne d'Elisabeth Ire d'Angleterre' (*Revue d'Histoire Ecclésiastique*, 50, 1955, pp 900-9).

716 ———— 'Quelques exiles anglais célèbres dont la sepulture se trouve en la collégiale St. Pierre a Louvain' (*Mededelingen v. de Geschied – en andheidk, Kring v. Leuven en amgeving*, I, 1961, pp 33-8).

717 Arthos, J. — 'Milton, Ficino and the *Charmides*' (*Studies in the Renaissance*, 6, 1969, pp 261-74).

718 Arundale, R. L. — 'Edmund Grindal and the northern

719 Ashton, R. 'Puritanism and progress'. (*Economic History Review*, second series 17, 1964-5, pp 579-87).

720 Aston, M. 'Lollardy and the reformation. Survival or revival?' (*History*, 49, 1964, pp 149-70).

721 ——— 'John Wycliffe's reformation reputation' (*Past and Present*, 30, 1965, pp 23-51).

722 Ault, W. O. 'Manor court and parish church in XVth century England. A study of village by-laws'. (*Speculum*, 42, 1967, pp 53-67).

723 Aveling, H. 'The catholic recusancy of the Yorkshire Fairfaxes', II (*Recusant History*, 4, 1957, pp 61-101).

724 ——— 'The catholic recusancy of the Yorkshire Fairfaxes', III-IV. (*Recusant History*, 6, 1961, pp 12-54, 95-111).

725 ——— Yorkshire notes: 1: 'St. Thomas More's family circle and Yorkshire'. 2: 'Predecessors of the Yorkshire Bretheren'. 3: 'A secret catholic printing press at Ripon in 1614'. (*Recusant History*, 6, 1961-2, pp 238-46).

726 ——— 'The marriages of catholic recusants, 1559-1642'. (*Journal of Ecclesiastical History*, 14, 1963, pp 68-83).

727 Avineri, S. 'War and slavery in More's *Utopia*'. (*International Review of Social History*, 7, 1962, pp 260-90).

728 Aylmer, G. E. '*Englands spirit unfoulded, or an incouragement to take the Engagement*. A newly discovered pamphlet by Gerrard Winstanley'. (*Past and Present*, 40, 1968, pp 3-15).

729 Bald, R. C. 'Dr. Donne and the booksellers' (*Bibliographical Studies*, 18, 1965, pp 69-81).

[Previous entry fragment:] province' (*Church Quarterly Review*, 160, 1959, pp 182-99).

730 Baldwin, R. G. 'Phineas Fletcher. His modern readers and his renaissance ideas'. (*Philological Quarterly*, 40, 1961, pp 462-75).

731 Bamber, J. E. 'The Ven. Christopher Robinson, martyred at Carlisle in 1597. The evidence concerning his place of birth, and place and date of execution'. (*Recusant History*, 4, 1957, pp 18-37).

732 Barry, J. C. 'The convocation of 1563' (*History Today*, 13, 1963, pp 490-501).

733 Beck, R. J. 'Milton and the spirit of his age' (*English Studies,* 42, 1961, pp 288-300).

734 Beesley, A. 'An unpublished source of the book of Common Prayer. Peter Martyr Vermigli's *Adhortatio ad coenam Domini mysticum*' (*Journal of Ecclesiastical History*, 19, 1968, pp 83-8).

735 Bekher, H. 'The religio-philosophical orientations of Vondel's *Lucifer*, Milton's *Paradise Lost* and Grotius' *Adamus exul.*' (*Neophilologus*, 44, 1960, pp 234-44).

736 Beier, A. L. 'Poor relief in Warwickshire, 1630-1660' (*Past and Present*, 35, 1966, pp 77-100).

737 Bell, P. I. 'The trial of Thomas More' (*The Month,* new series 23, 1960, pp 325-39).

738 Bennett, J. W. 'John Maren's Will: Thomas Linacre and prior Sellyng's Greek teaching' (*Studies in the Renaissance*, 15, 1968, pp 70-91).

739 Benson, D. R. 'Who 'bred' *Religio laici?*' (*Journal of English and German Philology*, 65, 1966, pp 238-51).

740 Bergeran, D. M. 'Venetian State Papers and English civic pageantry 1558-1642' (*Renaissance Quarterly*, 23, 1970, pp 37-47).

741 Bergsayel, J. D. 'An introduction to Ludford, c. 1485-c.1557' (*Musica disciplina*, 14, 1960, pp 105-30).

742 Berry, C. L. 'The coronation oath and the Church of England' (*Journal of Ecclesiastical History*, 11, 1960, pp 98-105).

743 Beumer, J. 'Die Opposition gegen das lutherische Schriftprinzip in der *Assertio Septem Sacramentorum* Heinrichs VIII von England' (*Gregorianum*, 42, 1961, pp 97-106).

744 ——— 'Lässt sich die *Utopia* des Thomas More 'ökumenisch' deuten?' (*Theologie und Philosophie*, 41, 1966, pp 75-83).

745 Bill, E. G. W. 'Two unprinted letters of Archbishop Laud.' (*The Bodleian Library Record*, 6, 1960, pp 617-20).

746 Bord, M. F. 'Chapter administration and archives at Windsor' (*Journal of Ecclesiastical History*, 8, 1957, pp 166-81).

747 Bossy, J. A. 'English catholics and the French marriage 1577-81' (*Recusant History*, 5, 1959, pp 2-16).

748 ——— 'A propos of Henry Constable' (*Recusant History*, 6, 1961-2, pp 228-37).

749 ——— 'The character of Elizabethan catholicism' (*Past and Present*, 21, 1962, pp 39-59).

750 ——— 'Rome and the Elizabethan catholics. A question of geography'. (*Historical Journal*, 7, 1964, pp 135-42).

751 ——— 'Henri IV, the Apellants and the Jesuits'. (*Recusant History*, 8, 1965, pp 80-122).

752 ——— 'More Northumbrian congregations' (*Recusant History*, 10, 1969, pp 11-29).

753 Boswell, J. C. 'Milton and prevenient grace'. (*Studies in English literature, 1500-1900*, 7, 1967, pp 83-94).

754 Bowker, M. — 'Non-residence in the Lincoln diocese in the early XVIth century'. (*Journal of Ecclesiastical History*, 15, 1964, pp 40-50).

755 Bradley, R. I. — 'Christopher Davenport and the 39 articles: A XVIIth century essay towards reunion'. (*Archiv für Reformationsgeschichte*, 52, 1961, pp 205-28).

755a Brass, M. F. — See 1205.

756 Braybrooke, N. — 'The Gunpowder plot. New facts to light' (*Clergy Review*, 40, 1955, pp 584-94).

757 Breen, T. H. — 'The non-existent controversy. Puritan and Anglican attitudes to work and wealth, 1600-1640'. (*Church History*, 35, 1966, pp 273-87).

758 Breward, I. — 'The significance of William Perkins' (*Journal of Religious History*, 4, 1966-7, pp 113-28).

759 Brewster, D. E. — 'Reconsidering the levellers. The evidence of the *Moderate*' (*Past and Present*, 46, 1970, pp 68-86).

760 Briggs, N. — 'The foundation of Wadham college, Oxford' (*Oxoniensia*, 21, 1956, pp 61-81).

761 Brinkworth, E. R. C. — 'The Laudian church in Buckinghamshire'. (*University of Birmingham Historical Journal*, 5, 1955, pp 31-59).

762 Brown, N. P. — 'The structure of Southwell's *Saint Peter's complaint*' (*Modern Languages Review*, 61, 1966, pp 3-11).

763 Brown, R. McA. — 'Tradition as a protestant problem'. (*Theology Today*, 17, 1960-1, pp 430-54).

764 Buchanan, C. — 'La réforme liturgique dans l'anglicanisme' (*Concilium*, 42, 1969, pp 95-104).

765 Burns, J. H. — 'John Knox and revolution, 1558' (*History Today*, 8, 1958, pp 565-73).

766 —— 'Catholicism in defeat. Ninian Winzet, 1579-1592' (*History Today*, 16, 1966, pp 788-95).

767 Burstein, S. R. 'Demonology and medicine in the XVIth and XVIIth centuries' (*Folk Lore*, 67, 1956, pp 16-33).

768 Bussy, F. 'George Morley, Caroline divine' (*Church Quarterly Review*, 165, 1964, pp 185-97).

769 Caldwell, J. 'Keyboard plainsong settings in England, 1500-1600'. (*Musica disciplina*, 19, 1965, pp 129-53).

770 Campion, L. 'The family of Edmund Campion'. (*The Month*, new series 16, 1956, pp 30-41).

771 Cargill-Thompson, W. D. J. 'A reconsideration of Richard Bancroft's Paul's Cross Sermon of 9 February 1588/9' (*Journal of Ecclesiastical History*, 20, 1969, pp 253-66).

772 —— 'Who wrote *The Supper of the Lord?*' (*Harvard Theological Review*, 53, 1960, pp 77-91).

773 Cashman, M. J. 'Two Newcastle martyrs' [Joseph Lambton and Edward Waterson] (*Recusant History*, 10, 1969-70, pp 231-40).

774 Catsonis, J. 'The validity of the Anglican orders' (*The Greek Orthodox Theological Review*, 1958).

775 Chambers, A. B. 'Chaos in *Paradise Lost*' (*Journal of the History of Ideas*, 24, 1963, pp 55-84).

776 Chambers, D. S. 'Cardinal Wolsey and the papal tiara' (*Bulletin of the Institute of Historical Research*, 38, 1965, pp 20-30).

777 Chaussy, Y. 'New evidence on the English Benedictines, 1: John Barnes (1581?–1661) 2: William Gifford, archbishop of Rheims'. (*Downside Review*, 88, 1970, pp 36-56).

778 —— 'William Gifford, archevêque de Reims. Documents nouveaux'

779 Chauviré, R. — (*MS Marne,* 85, 1970, pp 99-104).
'Elisabeth' (*Bulletin de l'Association Guillaume Budé,* 4 series, 4, 1956, pp 105-21).

780 Chitty, H. and Harvey, J. H. — 'Thurbern's chantry at Winchester college' (*The Antiquaries Journal,* 42, 1962, pp 208-25).

781 Clancy, T. H. — 'Notes on Persons's *Memorial for the Reformation of England* (1596)' (*Recusant History,* 5, 1959, pp 17-34).

782 ——— 'Pamphlets and politics under Elizabeth I. The Catholic contribution' (*The Month,* new series 23, 1960, pp 283-90).

783 ——— 'English catholics and the papal deposing power 1570-1640' (*Recusant History,* 6, 1961, pp 114-40).

784 ——— 'English catholics and the papal deposing power 1570-1640. II. The Stuarts' (*Recusant History,* 6, 1961-2, pp 205-27).

785 ——— 'English catholics and the papal deposing power. 1570-1640 III: The Stuarts' (*Recusant History,* 7, 1963, pp 2-10).

786 Claridge, M. — 'The blessed Margaret Clitherow and the York plays' (*The Month,* new series 31, 1964, pp 347-54).

787 Clark, E. M. — 'Milton and Wither' (*Studies in Philology,* 56, 1959, pp 626-46).

788 Clebsch, W. A. — 'The earliest translations of Luther into English' (*Harvard Theological Review,* 56, 1963, pp 75-86).

789 Clert-Rolland, L. — 'Jeremy Taylor et la tolérance religieux au XVII siècle' (*Revue d'Histoire et de Philosophie religieuses,* 49, 1969, pp 257-64).

790 Clive, H. P. — 'The Calvinists and the question of dancing in the XVIth century' (*Bibliothèque d'humanisme et renaissance,* 23, 1961, pp 296-323).

791 Clouse, R. G. — 'Johann Heinrich Alsted and English millenarianism'. (*Harvard Theological Review*, 62, 1969, pp 189-207).

792 Cohen, A. — 'Two roads to the puritan millenium. William Erbury and Vavasour Powell' (*Church History*, 32, 1963, pp 322-38).

793 Cole, A. — 'The Quakers and the English revolution' (*Past and Present*, 10, 1956, pp 39-54).

794 Coles, P. — 'The interpretation of More's *Utopia*' (*Hibbert Journal*, 56, 1957-8, pp 365-70).

795 Colie, R. L. — 'Time and eternity. Paradox and structure in *Paradise lost*'. (*Journal of the Warburg and Courtauld Institutes*, 23, 1960, pp 127-38).

796 Collinson, P. — 'The authorship of *A brief discours of the troubles begonne at Franckford*' (*Journal of Ecclesiastical History*, 9, 1958, pp 188-208).

797 ——— 'Letters of Thomas Wood, Puritan, 1566-77'. (*Bulletin of the Institute of Historical Research*, special supplement, 5, London, 1960).

798 ——— 'The 'nott conformytye' of the young John Whitgift' (*Journal of Ecclesiastical History*, 15, 1964, pp 192-200).

799 ——— 'The reformer and the archbishop. Martin Bucer and an English Bucerian'. (*Journal of Religious History*, 6, 1970-71, pp 305-30).

800 Cooper, J. P. — 'The Supplication against the ordinaries reconsidered'. (*English Historical Review*, 72, 1957, pp 616-41).

801 Couratin, A. H. — 'The service of Holy Communion, 1552-1662' (*Church Quarterly Review*, 163, 1962, pp 431-42).

802 ——— 'The Holy Communion, 1549' (*Church Quarterly Review*, 164, 1963, pp 148-59).

803 Courtney, F.   'English Jesuit colleges in the low countries, 1593-1794' (*Heythrop Journal*, 4, 1963, pp 254-63).

804 Courtenay, W. J.   'Cranmer as a nominalist. Sed contra' (*Harvard Theological Review*, 57, 1964, pp 367-80).

805 Crehan, J. P.   'The Return to obedience. New judgement on Cardinal Pole' (*The Month*, new series 14, 1955, pp 221-29).

806 ———— 'St. Ignatius and Cardinal Pole.' (*Archivum Historicum Societatis Jesu,* 25, 1956, pp 72-98).

807 ———— 'English spiritual writers. XV: Father Persons, S.J.' (*The Clergy Review,* 45, 1960, pp 145-57).

808 Cren, P. R.   'Approche de l'Anglicanisme' (*Lumière et vie,* 64, 1963, pp 5-29).

809 Croft-Murray, E.   'Lambert Barnard. An English early renaissance painter.' (*The Archaeological Journal*, 113, 1956, pp 108-25).

810 Cross, M. C.   'Noble patronage in the Elizabethan Church' (*Historical Journal*, 3, 1960, pp 1-16).

811 ———— 'The third Earl of Huntingdon and the trials of catholics in the north, 1581-1595.' (*Recusant History*, 8, 1965 pp 136-46).

812 Curtis, M. H.   'Hampton court conference and its aftermath.' (*History*, 46, 1961, pp 1-16).

813 ———— 'The alienated intellectuals of early Stuart England.' (*Past and Present,* 23, 1962, pp 25-43).

814 Daely, J. I.   'The episcopal administration of Matthew Parker, archbishop of Canterbury, 1559-1575.' (*Bulletin of the Institute of Historical Research*, 40, 1967, pp 228-231).

815 ———— 'Pluralism in the diocese of Canterbury during the administration of Matthew Parker, 1559-1575'. (*Journal of Ecclesiastical History*, 18, 1967, pp 33-49).

816 Dant, J. L. C.	'Thomas Becket and Thomas More. Were they both martyrs?' (*Church Quarterly Review*, 157, 1956, pp 35-46).
817 Datta, K. S.	'New light on Marvell's *A dialogue between the soul and body*'. (*Renaissance Quarterly*, 22, 1969, pp 242-55).
818 Davies, C. S. L.	'The Pilgrimage of Grace reconsidered' (*Past and Present*, 41, 1968, pp 54-76).
819 ———	'Les revoltes populaires en Angleterre, 1500-1700' (*Annales*, 24, 1969, pp 24-60).
820 Davies, H. N.	'The first English translation of Bellarmine's *De ascensione mentis*'. (*The Library*, 5 series 25, 1970, pp 49-52).
821 Davis, J. F.	'Lollards, reformers, and St. Thomas of Canterbury'. (*University of Birmingham Historical Journal*, 9, 1963, pp 1-15).
822 D'Elboux R. H.	'The Ven. Thomas Pylcher' (*Biographical Studies 1534-1829*, 3, 1956, pp 334-37).
823 Derrett, J. D. M.	'Henry Fitzroy and Henry VIII's 'scruple of conscience' '. (*Renaissance News*, 16, 1963, pp 1-9).
824 ———	'Neglected versions of the contemporary account of the trial of Sir Thomas More'. (*Bulletin of the Institute of Historical Research*, 33, 1960, pp 202-23).
825 ———	'The trial of Sir Thomas More' (*English Historical Review*, 79, 1964, pp 449-77).
826 Devereux, E. J.	'Elizabeth Barton and Tudor censorship' (*Bulletin of the John Rylands Library*, 49, 1966-67, pp 91-106).
827 ———	'The publication of the English *Paraphrases* of Erasmus'. (*Bulletin of the John Rylands Library*, 51, 1968-9, pp 348-67).
828 Devereux, J. A.	'The Collects of the first *Book of*

	Common Prayer as works of translation'. (*Studies in Philology*, 66, 1969, pp 719-38).
829 ———	'Reformed doctrine in the Collects of the first *Book of Common Prayer*'. (*Harvard Theological Review*, 58, 1965, pp 49-68).
830 De Vocht, H.	'Anecdota humanistica Lovaniensia II: John Ramridge exsul pro fide catholica d. 1568'. (*Sacris erudiri*, 7, 1955, pp 367-80).
831 Dickinson, J. C.	'The buildings of the English Austin canons after the dissolution of the monasteries' (*Journal of the British Archaeological Association*, 3 series, 31, 1968, pp 65-70).
832 Dobson, R. B.	'The last English monks on Scottish soil. The severance of Coldingham priory from the monastery of Durham, 1461-1478'. (*Scottish Historical Review*, 46, 1967, pp 1-25).
833 Dodd, A. H.	'Hugh Owen. A Welsh conspirator. 1538-1618' (*History Today*, 12, 1962, pp 329-35).
834 Dow, H. J.	'John Hudde and the English renaissance'. (*Renaissance News*, 18, 1965, pp 289-94).
835 Drake, G.	'The ideology of Oliver Cromwell' (*Church History*, 35, 1966, pp 259-72).
836 Driscoll, J. P.	'The supposed source of Persons' *Christian directory*' (*Recusant History*, 5, 1960, pp 236-45).
837 Du Boulay, F. R. H.	'The quarrel between the Carmelite Friars and the Secular clergy of London, 1464-1468' (*Journal of Ecclesiastical History*, 6, 1955, pp 156-74).
838 Dunning, R. W.	'The muniments of Syon Abbey. Their administration and migration in the XVth and XVIth centuries'. (*Bulletin of the Institute of Historical Research*, 37, 1964, pp 103-11).
839 ———	'Rural deans in England in the

	XVth Century'. (*Bulletin of the Institute of Historical Research*, 40, 1967, pp 207-13).
840 Duvall, R. F.	'Time, place, persons: The background for Milton's *Of Reformation*' (*Studies in English literature 1500-1900*, 7, 1967, pp 107-18).
841 Dwyer, J. J.	'Robert Southwell' (*The Month*, new series 16, 1956, pp 13-21).
842 Edelen, G.	'William Harrison, 1535-1593' (*Studies in the Renaissance*, 9, 1962, pp 256-72).
843 Edgerton, W. L.	'Nicholas Udall in the indexes of prohibited books' (*Journal of English and German Philology*, 55, 1956, pp 247-52).
844 Edwards, F.	'Most incomparable Lady. English catholics and the French marriage of 1625' (*The Month*, new series 24, 1960, pp 164-78).
845 Ellis, I. P.	'The Archbishop [Edwin Sandys, Archbishop of York 1577-88] and the usurers'. (*Journal of Ecclesiastical History*, 21, 1970, pp 33-42).
846 Elton, G. R.	'King or Minister? The man behind the Henrican Reformation'. (*History*, 39, 1955, pp 216-32).
847 ———	'The Quondam of Rievaulx' (*Journal of Ecclesiastical History*, 7, 1956, pp 45-60).
848 ———	'Thomas Cromwell' (*History Today*, 6, 1956, pp 528-35).
849 ———	'Sir Thomas More and the opposition to Henry VIII' (*Bulletin of the Institute of Historical Research*, 61, 1968, pp 19-34).
850 ———	See 696.
851 Emerson, E. H.	'Reginald Pecock, Christian rationalist' (*Speculum*, 31, 1956, pp 235-42).
852 Evans, J. X.	'The art of rhetoric and the art of dying in Tudor recusant prose' (*Recusant History*, 10, 1969-70, pp 247-72).

853	Evennett, H. O.	'The last stages of mediaeval monasticism in England' (*Studia monastica,* 2, 1960, pp 387-419).
854	Ferguson, A. B.	'Reginald Pecock and the Renaissance sense of history' (*Studies in the Renaissance,* 13, 1966, pp 147-65).
855	Fielding, E.	'John Donne and the new Christianity'. (*The Month,* new series, 42, 1969, pp 194-202).
856	Fines, J.	'Heresy trials in the diocese of Coventry and Lichfield 1511-1512' (*Journal of Ecclesiastical History,* 14, 1963, pp 160-74).
857	———	'The post-mortem condemnation for heresy of Richard Hunne'. (*English Historical Review,* 78, 1963, pp 528-31).
858	———	'A unnoticed tract of the Tyndale-More dispute?' (*Bulletin of the Institute of Historical Research,* 42, 1969, pp 220-30).
859	Finney, G. L.	'Music: a book of knowledge in Renaissance England'. (*Studies in the Renaissance,* 6, 1959, pp 36-63).
860	Fiore, A. P.	'The problem of XVIIth century soteriology in reference to Milton' (*Franciscan Studies,* 15, 1955-6, pp 48-59, 257-82).
861	Fisher, B.	'English spiritual writers XIII: St. Thomas More' (*The Clergy Review,* new series, 45, 1960, pp 1-10).
862	Fisher, P. F.	'Milton's theodicy' (*Journal of the History of Ideas,* 17, 1956, pp 28-53).
863	Flesseman-van Leer, E.	'The controversy about Scripture and Tradition between Thomas More and William Tyndale'. (*Nederlands archief voor Kerkgeschiedenis,* 43, 1959, pp 143-64).
864	Fletcher, J. M.	'The teaching of Arts at Oxford 1400-1520' (*Paedagogica historica,* 7, 1967, pp 417-54).
865	Forster, A. M. C.	'The Ven. George Errington' (*Biographical Studies, 1534-1829,* 3, 1956, pp 322-33).

865a	———	See 1262.
866	———	'Ven. William Southerne, another Tyneside martyr' (*Recusant History*, 4, 1958, pp 217-22).
867	———	'Who was John Norton, the martyr?' (*Recusant History*, 6, 1961, pp 56-67).
868	———	'Bishop Tunstall's priests' [Durham] (*Recusant History*, 9, 1967-8, pp 175-204).
869	Foster, S.	'The Presbyterian Independents exorcised. A ghost story for historians'. (*Past and Present*, 44, 1969, pp 52-75).
869a	———	See 1125.
870	Fry, E. J. B.	' 'Monsignor of England' Cardinal Pole before his final return to England' (*The Dublin Review*, 477, 1958, pp 236-45).
871	Frye, R. M.	'The teachings of classical Puritanism on conjugal love' (*Studies in the Renaissance*, 2, 1958, pp 148-59).
872	Fryer, W. R.	'The 'High Churchmen' of the earlier XVIIth century' (*Renaissance and Modern Studies*, 5, 1961, pp 106-48).
873	Garrett, J.	'Before and after Roger Williams'. (*Journal of Religious History*, 4, 1966-7, pp 1-13).
874	Garner, B. C.	'Francis Bacon, Natalis Comes and the mythological tradition'. (*Journal of the Warburg and Courtauld Institutes*, 33, 1970, pp 264-91).
875	George, C. H.	'English calvinist opinion on usury, 1600-1640' (*Journal of the History of Ideas*, 18, 1957, pp 455-74).
876	———	'Puritanism as history and historiography' (*Past and Present*, 41, 1968, pp 77-104).
877	George, C. H. and George, K.	'Protestantism and capitalism in pre-revolutionary England'. (*Church History*, 27, 1958, pp 351-70).
878	Gill, L. A.	'The anthems of Thomas Tomkins. An introduction'. [with transcriptions

878a Gibaud, H.   See 1034.

879 Glover, W. B.   'God and Thomas Hobbes'. (*Church History*, 1960, pp 275-97).

880 Gohn, E. S.   'The christian ethic of *Paradise lost* and *Samson Agonistes*'. (*Studia Neophilologica*, 34, 1962, pp 243-68).

881 Gottfried, R. B.   'The authorship of *A breviary of the history of England*'. (*Studies in Philology*, 53, 1956, pp 172-90).

882 Grace, W. J.   'Milton, Salmasius and the natural law' (*Journal of the History of Ideas*, 24, 1963, 323-36).

883 Grassmann, F.   'A religious allegory by Hans Holbein the Younger' (*Burlington Magazine*, 103, 1961, pp 491-4).

884 Greaves, R. L.   'The ordination controversy and the spirit of reform in Puritan England'. (*Journal of Ecclesiastical History*, 21, 1970, pp 225-41).

885 Greenleaf, W. H.   'Filmer's patriarchal history' (*Historical Journal*, 9, 1966, pp 157-71).

886 Griffiths, G. M.   'A St. Asaph 'register' of episcopal acts 1506-1571' (*Journal of the Historical Society of the Church in Wales*, 6, 1956, pp 25-49).

887 ———   'St Asaph episcopal acts 1536-1538' (*Journal of the Historical Society of the Church in Wales*, 9, 1959, pp 32-69).

888 Grun, R. E.   'A note on William Howard, author of *A Patterne of Christian loyaltie*' (*Catholic Historical Review*, 42, 1956, pp 330-40).

889 Habakkuk, H. J.   'The market for monastic property 1539-1603' (*Economic History Review*, 2 series 10, 1958, pp 362-80).

890 Habeggar, A.   'Preparing the soul for Christ. The contrasting sermon forms of John Cotton and Thomas Hooker'

890a Hadcock, R. M.   (*American Literature*, 41, 1969, pp 342-54). See 980.

891 Haines, R. M.   'Bishop Carpenter's injunctions to the diocese of Worcester in 1451' (*Bulletin of the Institute of Historical Research*, 40, 1967, pp 203-7).

892 ———   'Aspects of the episcopate of John Carpenter, bishop of Worcester 1444-1476' (*Journal of Ecclesiastical History*, 19, 1968, pp 11-40).

893 Hahlan, J. D.   'Richard Dering, Catholic musician of Stuart England' (*Catholic Historical Review*, 46, 1960, pp 428-52).

894 Hale, S.   'The background of divine action in *King Lear*' (*Studies in English literature 1500-1900*, 8, 1968, pp 217-33).

895 Hall, G. D. G.   'The Abbot of Abingdon and the tenants of Winkfield' (*Medium Aevum*, 28, 1959, 91-5).

896 Hamilton, C. L.   'The basis for Scottish efforts to create a reformed church in England, 1640-41' (*Church History*, 30, 1961, pp 171-8).

897 Hanley, T. O.   'A note on Cardinal Allen's political thought' (*Catholic Historical Review*, 45, 1959-60, pp 327-34).

898 Hardie, C.   'Dante and Milton' (*Deutches Dante-Jahrbuch*, 44-5, 1967, pp 42-99).

899 Hargrave, O. T.   'The Free willers in the English Reformation' (*Church History*, 37, 1968, pp 271-80).

899a Harris, G. L.   See 696.

900 Harris, P. R.   'William Fleetwood, Recorder of the City, and Catholicism in Elizabethan London' (*Recusant History*, 7, 1963, 166-72).

901 ———   'The reports of William Udall, informer, 1605-1612' (*Recusant*

902 Harris, W. O.   'Wolsey and Skelton's Magnyfycence. A re-evaluation' (*Studies in Philology*, 57, 1960, 99-122).

902a Harvey, J. H.   See 780.

903 Hattaway, M.   'Paradoxes of Solomon. Learning in the English Renaissance' (*Journal of the History of Ideas*, 29, 1968, pp 499-530).

904 Hauben, P. J.   'A Spanish calvinist church in Elizabethan London 1559-65' (*Church History*, 34, 1965, pp 50-6).

905 Haugaard, W. P.   'Katherine Parr. The religious convictions of a Renaissance Queen' (*Renaissance Quarterly*, 22, 1969, pp 346-59).

906 ———   'John Calvin and the Catechism of Alexander Nowell' (*Archiv für Reformationsgeschichte*, 61, 1970, pp 50-66).

907 Havran, M. J.   'Parliament and catholicism in England 1626-9' (*Catholic Historical Review*, 44, 1958, pp 273-89).

908 Hay, D.   'The Church of England in the later Middle Ages' (*History*, 53, 1968, pp 35-50).

909 Haynes, R.   'Augustine Baker' (*The Month*, new series 25, 1961, pp 160-72).

910 Head, C.   'Pope Pius II and the Wars of the Roses' (*Archivum Historiae Pontificiae*, 8, 1970, pp 139-78).

911 Headley, J. M.   'Thomas Murner, Thomas More, and the first expression of More's ecclesiology' (*Studies in the Renaissance*, 14, 1967, pp 73-92).

912 ———   'Thomas More and Luther's revolt' (*Archiv für Reformationsgeschichte*, 60, 1969, pp 145-60).

913 Heath, P.   'The treason of Geoffrey Blythe, bishop of Coventry and Lichfield 1503-31' (*Bulletin of the Institute of Historical Research*, 42, 1969, pp 101-9).

914	———	'The medieval archdeaconry and Tudor bishopric of Chester' (*Journal of Ecclesiastical History*, 20, 1969, pp 243-52).
915	Henderson, R. W.	'XVIth century community benevolences. An attempt to resacralise the secular' (*Church History*, 38, 1969, pp 421-8).
916	Henson, E. and Loomie, A. J.	'A register of the students of St. Gregory's College of Seville, 1501-1605' (*Recusant History*, 9, 1967, pp 163-70).
916a	Hexter, J. H.	See 1125.
917	Hicks, L.	'Sir Robert Cecil, Father Persons and the Succession' (*Archivum historicum Societatis Iesu*, 24, 1955, pp 95-139).
918	———	'Father Robert Persons, S. J. and the *Book of succession*' (*Recusant History*, 4, 1957, pp 104-37).
919	———	'The embassy of Sir Anthony Standen in 1603' I. (*Recusant History*, 5, 1959, pp 91-127).
920	———	'The embassy of Sir Anthony Standen in 1603' II. (*Recusant History*, 5, 1960, pp 184-222).
921	———	'The embassy of Sir Anthony Standen in 1603' III. (*Recusant History*, 6, 1961-2, pp 163-94).
922	———	'The embassy of Sir Anthony Standen in 1603', IV. (*Recusant History*, 7, 1963, pp 50-81).
923	Hill, C.	'Recent interpretations of the Civil War' (*History*, 41, 1956, pp 67-87).
924	———	'La révolution anglaise de XVIIe siècle. Essai d'interprétation' (*Revue Historique*, 221, 1959, pp 5-32).
925	———	'Puritanism, capitalism and the scientific revolution' (*Past and Present*, 29, 1964, pp 88-97).
926	———	'Science, religion and society in the XVIth and XVIIth centuries' (*Past and Present*, 32, 1965, pp 110-12).

926a ——— See 1181.

927 Hinton, R. W. K. 'The decline of parliamentary government under Elizabeth I and the early Stuarts' (*Cambridge Historical Journal*, 13, 1957, pp 116-32).

928 Hodgett, G. A. J. 'The unpensioned ex-religious in Tudor England' (*Journal of Ecclesiastical History*, 13, 1962, pp 195-202).

929 Hodgetts, M. 'In search of Nicholas Owen' (*The Month*, new series 26, 1961, pp 197-209).

930 ——— 'Nicholas Owen in East Anglia' (*The Month*, new series 28, 1962, pp 69-81).

931 Holaday, A. 'Giles Fletcher and the puritans' (*Journal of English and German Philology*, 54, 1955, pp 578-86).

932 Holmes, G. A. '*The libel of English policy*' (*English Historical Review*, 76, 1961, pp 193-216).

933 Hooykaas, R. 'Thomas Digges' Puritanism' (*Archives Internationales d'histoire des sciences*, 8, 1955, pp 145-59).

934 Hopf, C. 'An English version of parts of Bucer's reply to the Cologne *Antididagma* of 1544' (*Journal of Theological Studies*, new series 11, 1960, pp 94-110).

935——— 'Martin Bucer und England. Sein Beitrag zur englischen Reformationgeschichte' (*Zeitschrift für Kirchengeschichte*, 71, 1960, pp 82-109).

936 Howell, R. 'Henry Vane the younger and the politics of religion' (*History Today*, 13, 1963, pp 275-82).

937 Howse, W. H. 'Contest for a Radnorship rectory in the XVIIth century' (*Journal of the Historical Society of the Church in Wales*, 7, 1957, pp 69-79).

938 Huelin, G. ' 'The delight of the English nation'; William Juxon, 1582-1663' (*Church Quarterly Review*, 164, 1963, pp 311-21).

939 Hughes, J. J. — 'La validité des ordinations Anglicanes. Études récentes' (*Concilium*, 31, 1967, pp 113-22).

940 Hughes, M. Y. — 'Milton and the symbol of light' (*Studies in English literature, 1500-1900*, 4, 1964, pp 1-33).

941 Hume, A. — 'Spenser, puritanism and the 'Maye' ecologue'. (*Review of English Studies*, new series, 20, 1969, pp 155-67).

942 ——— 'William Roye's *Brefe dialogue* (1527). An English version of a Strassburg catechism'. (*Harvard Theological Review*, 60, 1967, pp 307-21).

943 Hunter, G. K. — 'The theology of Marlowe's *The Jew of Malta*' (*Journal of the Warburg and Courtauld Institutes*, 27, 1964, pp 211-40).

944 Hunter, W. B. — 'Milton's Arianism re-considered' (*Harvard Theological Review*, 52, 1959, pp 9-35).

945 ——— 'Milton on the incarnation; some more heresies' (*Journal of the History of Ideas*, 21, 1960, pp 349-69).

946 Hurstfield, J. — 'Burghley, minister to Elizabeth I' (*History Today*, 6, 1956, pp 791-9).

947 ——— 'Robert Cecil, Earl of Salisbury, minister of Elizabeth and James I' (*History Today*, 7, 1957, pp 279-89).

948 ——— 'Some Elizabethans' (*History*, 47, 1962, pp 18-31).

949 Hurwich, J. J. — 'The social origins of the early Quakers. Rejoinder by R. T. Vann' (*Past and Present*, 48, 1970, pp 156-64).

950 Huttar, C. A. — 'The christian basis of Shakespeare's Sonnet 146' (*Shakespeare Quarterly*, 19, 1968, pp 355-65).

951 Jack, R. I. — 'The ecclesiastical patronage exercised by a baronial family in the late Middle ages' [the Greys of Ruthin] (*Journal of Religious History*, 3, 1964-5, pp 275-95).

952 Jack, S. M.   'The last days of the smaller monasteries in England' (*Journal of Ecclesiastical History*, 21, 1970, pp 97-124).

953 ———   'Dissolution dates for the monasteries dissolved under the act of 1536' (*Bulletin of the Institute of Historical Research*, 43, 1970, pp 161-81).

954 Jackson, R. S.   'The 'inspired' style of the English bible' (*Journal of the Bible and Religion*, 29, 1961, 4-15).

955 James, M. E.   'Obedience and dissent in Henrician England. The Lincolnshire Rebellion of 1536' (*Past and Present*, 48, 1970, pp 3-78).

956 Jarvis, R. C.   'The administration of the anti-papist laws, with particular reference to the north of England'. (*Bulletin of the John Rylands Library*, 47, 1964-5, pp 79-100).

957 Jennings, B.   'The indictment of Fr. John Preston, Franciscan'. (*Archivum Hibernicum*, 26, 1963, pp 50-5).

958 Johnson, J. T.   'English Puritan thought on the ends of of marriage'. (*Church History*, 38, 1969, pp 429-36).

959 Jones, O. W.   'A Pembrokeshire sceptic'. [John Owen] (*Journal of the Historical Society of the Church in Wales*, 11, 1961, pp 57-64).

960 Jones, W. M.   'Uses of foreigners in the Church of Edward VI'. (*Numen*, 6, 1959, pp 142-53).

961 Josten, C. H.   'An unknown chapter in the life of John Dee'. (*Journal of the Warburg and Courtauld Institutes*, 28, 1965 pp 223-57).

962 Judd, A. F.   'The episcopate of Thomas Bekynton, bishop of Bath and Wells, 1443-1465'. (*Journal of Ecclesiastical History*, 8, 1957, pp 153-65).

963 Kamenetski, B. A.   'The shaping of the absolutist ideology in XVIth century England

964 Kapalan, L. 'Presbyterians and independants in 1643' (*English Historical Review*, 84, 1969, pp 244-56).

965 Karpman, D. M. 'William Tyndale's response to the Hebraic tradition'. (*Studies in the Renaissance*, 14, 1967, pp 110-30).

966 Kasteel, P. 'Reginald Pole 1500-1558' (*Streven*, 12, i, 1958, pp 260-68).

967 Kastor, F. S. 'Miltonic narration. Christs nativity' (*Anglia*, 86, 1968, pp 339-52).

967a Kearney, H. F. See 1181.

968 Kelley, M. 'Milton's Arianism again considered' (*Harvard Theological Review*, 54, 1961, pp 195-205).

969 Kelly, H. A. 'Canonical implications of Richard III's plan to marry his niece'. (*Traditio*, 23, 1967, pp 269-311).

970 Kennedy, D. E. 'The Jacobean episcopate' (*Historical Journal*, 5, 1962, pp 175-81).

971 Kenny, A. 'Anthony Munday in Rome' (*Recusant History*, 6, 1961-2, pp 158-62).

972 ——— 'A martyr manqué. The early life of Anthony Tyrell' (*Clergy Review*, 42, 1957, pp 651-68).

973 Kenrick, E. F. '*Paradise Lost* and the *Index* of prohibited books'. (*Studies in Philology*, 53, 1956, pp 485-500).

974 King, P. 'The episcopate during the civil wars, 1642-1649' (*English Historical Review*, 83, 1968, pp 523-37).

975 ——— 'Bishop Wren and the suppression of the Norwich lecturers' (*Historical Journal*, 11, 1968, pp 237-54).

976 ——— 'The reasons for the abolition of the Book of Common Prayer in 1645'. (*Journal of Ecclesiastical History*, 21, 1970, pp 327-39).

977 Kirby, J. L. 'Clerks in royal service'. (*History Today*, 6, 1956, pp 752-58).

[preceding entry continuation at top:] and its characteristics' (*Soviet Studies in History*, 9, 1970-71, pp 168-92).

978 Kissack, K. E. — 'Religious life in Monmouth 1066-1536' (*Journal of the Historical Society of the Church in Wales*, 14, 1964, pp 25-57).

979 Kliever, L. D. — 'General Baptist origins. The question of anabaptist influence'. (*The Mennonite Quarterly Review*, 36, 1962, pp 291-321).

980 Knowles, D. — 'English spiritual writers I: Father Augustine Baker' (*The Clergy Review*, 43, 1958, pp 641-57).

981 ——— 'The 'matter of Wilton' in 1528' (*Bulletin of the Institute of Historical Research*, 31, 1958, pp 92-6).

982 ——— and Hadcock, R. M. 'Additions and corrections to 'Medieval Religious Houses: England and Wales'. (*English Historical Review*, 72, 1957, pp 60-87).

983 Knox, R. B. — 'A Caroline trio: Ussher, Laud and Williams'. (*Church Quarterly Review*, 164, 1963, pp 442-547).

984 Kranidas, T. — ' 'Decorum' and the style of Milton's anti-prelatical tracts'. (*Studies in Philology*, 62, 1965, pp 176-87).

985 Krodel, G. G. — 'Luther, Erasmus and Henry VIII'. (*Archiv. für Reformationsgeschischte*, 53, 1963, pp 60-78).

986 Krueger, R. — 'The publication of John Donne's sermons'. (*Review of English Studies*, new series 15, 1964, pp 151-60).

987 Kuphal, E. — 'England und Köln. Zur Geschichte des englischen Königshauses aus dem J. 1498'. (*Jahrbuch des Kölnischen Geschichtsvereins*, 33, 1958, pp 200-11).

988 Lamont, W. M. — 'Episcopacy and a 'godly discipline' 1641-6' (*Journal of Ecclesiastical History*, 10, 1959, pp 74-89).

989 ——— 'William Prynne, 1600-1669. 'The mountainous ice' of Puritanism'

990 ——— (*History Today*, 11, 1961, pp 199-205).
'Puritanism as history and historiography. Some further thoughts'. (*Past and Present*, 44, 1969, pp 133-46).

991 Lampe, G. W. H. 'The concept of the mission of the church in the Anglican tradition'. (*Studia Theologica*, 16, 1962, pp 155-69).

992 Langley, K. M. 'The 'trial' of Margaret Clitherow'. (*The Ampleforth Journal*, 75, 1970, pp 335-64).

993 Laon, Th. F. van 'John Donne's *Devotions* and the Jesuit spiritual exercises' (*Studies in Philology*, 60, 1963, pp 191-202).

994 Lehmberg, S. E. 'Sir Thomas More's Life of Pico della Mirandola' (*Studies in the Renaissance*, 3, 1956, pp 61-74).

995 ——— 'Sir Thomas Elyot and the English reformation' (*Archiv für Reformationsgeschichte*, 48, 1957, pp 91-112).

996 ——— 'English humanists, the Reformation and the problem of counsel'. (*Archiv für Reformationsgeschichte*, 52, 1961, pp 74-91).

997 ——— 'Supremacy and vicegerency. A re-examination' (*English Historical Review*, 81, 1966, 225-35).

998 Le Huray, P. 'Towards a definitive study of pre-Restoration Anglican service music' (*Musica disciplina*, 14, 1960, pp 167-95).

999 Lennam, T. N. S. 'Francis Merbury 1555-1611' (*Studies in Philology*, 65, 1968, pp 207-22).

1000 Lerner, L. D. 'Puritanism and the spiritual autobiography'. (*Historical Journal*, 55, 1956-7, pp 371-86).

1001 Levany, D. 'George Herbert's *The Church militant* and the chances of history' (*Philological Quarterly*, 36, 1957, pp 265-8).

1002 Levine, M.   'Henry VIII's use of his spiritual and temporal jurisdictions in his great causes of matrimony, legitimacy and succession'. (*Historical Journal*, 10, 1967, pp 3-10).

1003 Lewalski, B. K.   'Theme and structure in *Paradise Regained*'. (*Studies in Philology*, 57, 1960, pp 186-220).

1004 Loades, D. M.   'The Essex Inquisitions of 1556'. (*Bulletin of the Institute of Historical Research*, 35, 1962, pp 87-97).

1005 ———   'The enforcement of reaction, 1553-1558'. (*Journal of Ecclesiastical History*, 16, 1965, pp 54-66).

1006 Lomax, D. W.   'Recusants in the Spanish Inquisition.' (*Recusant History*, 9, 1967-68, pp 53-9).

1007 Longhurst, J. E.   'The first English Lutherans in Spain'. (*Bibliothèque d'humanisme et renaissance*, 20, 1958, pp 143-57).

1008 Loomie, A. J.   'The authorship of *An advertisement written to a secretarie of M. L. treasurer of England*'. (*Renaissance News*, 15, 1962, pp 201-7).

1009 ———   'A catholic petition of the Earl of Essex'. (*Recusant History*, 7, 1963, pp 33-42).

1010 ———   'Religion and Elizabethan commerce with Spain'. (*Catholic Historical Review*, 50, 1964-5, pp 27-51).

1011 ———   'A Jacobean crypto-catholic, Lord Wotton'. (*Catholic Historical Review*, 53, 1967-8, pp 328-45).

1011a ———   See 916.

1012 Loomis, R.   'The Barrett version of Robert Southwell's *Short rule of good life*' (*Recusant History*, 7, 1964, pp 239-48).

1013 Lunn, M.   'William Rudesind Barlow, OSB, 1585-1656'. (*Downside Review*, 86, 1968, pp 139-54, 234-49).

1014 ——— 'English Benedictines and the oath of allegiance, 1606-1647' (*Recusant History*, 10, 1969, pp 146-63).

1015 Lutard, O. '*L'accord du peuple*, Londres, ler mai 1649. Texte presenté et traduit'. (*Annales*, 17, 1962, pp 501-16).

1016 Lyall, R. J. 'Alexander Barclay and the Edwardian Reformation 1548-1552'. (*Review of English Studies*, new series 20, 1969, pp 455-61).

1017 McAleer, J. 'More and his detractors'. (*The Month*, new series 26, 1961, pp 14-23).

1018 McCutchean, E. 'Lancelot Andrewes *Preces privatae*. A journey through time'. (*Studies in Philology*, 65, 1968, pp 223-41).

1019 ——— 'Thomas More, Raphael Hythlodeaus and the Angel Raphael'. (*Studies in English Literature 1500-1900*, 9, 1969, pp 21-38).

1020 McDonagh, E. 'The nature and membership of the church in the Anglican theology of the reformation 1530-1603'. (*Irish Theological Quarterly*, 25, 1958, pp 43-57, 209-26).

1021 McGee, F. K. 'Cranmer and Nominalism'. (*Harvard Theological Review*, 57, 1964, pp 189-216).

1022 McGrade, A. S. 'The coherence of Hooker's *Polity*. The books on power'. (*Journal of the History of Ideas*, 24, 1963, pp 163-82).

1023 ——— 'The public and the religious in Hooker's *Polity*'. (*Church History*, 37, 1968, pp 404-22).

1024 McKenna, J. W. 'The coronation oil of the Yorkist Kings'. (*English Historical Review*, 82, 1967, pp 102-4).

1025 Maclear, J. F. 'Popular anticlericalism in the puritan revolution'. (*Journal of the History of Ideas*, 17, 1956, pp 443-70).

1026 Macpherson, C. B. 'Harrington's 'opportunity State' ' (*Past and Present*, 17, 1960, pp 45-70).

1027 Magill, A. J.	'Spenser's Guyon and the mediocrity of the Elizabethan settlement'. (*Studies in Philology*, 67, 1970, pp 167-77).
1028 Main, C. F.	'New texts of John Donne'. (*Studies in Bibliography*, 9, 1957, pp 225-35).
1029 Malkiewiez, A. J. A.	'An eye witness's account of the coup d'état of October 1549'. (*English Historical Review*, 70, 1955, pp 600-9).
1030 Malloch, A. E.	'John Donne and the casuists'. (*Studies in English literature, 1500-1900*, 2, 1962, pp 57-76).
1031 Manning, R. B.	'Catholics and local office holding in Elizabethan Sussex'. (*Bulletin of the Institute of Historical Research*, 35, 1962, pp 47-61).
1032 ——	'Richard Shelley of Warminghurst and the English Catholic petition for toleration of 1585'. (*Recusant History*, 6, 1962, 265-74).
1033 Marc'hadour, G.	'Erasmus Englished by Margaret More' [Precatio dominica] (*The Clergy Review*, 43, 1958, pp 78-91).
1034 —— and Gibaud, H.	'Réponse de Thomas More à une moine anti-erasmien.' Presentation du document par GM. Trad française par HG et GM. (*Moreana*, 1970, pp 27-28, 31-82).
1035 Margolin, J. A.	'Thomas More et l'education des filles'. (*Revue Philosophique de la France et de l'étranger*, 146, 1956, pp 539-47).
1036 Marot, H.	'Aux origins de la théologie anglicane. Écriture et tradition chez Richard Hooker'. (*Irénikon*, 33, 1960, pp 321-93).
1037 ——	'Les ordinations anglicanes. Coup d'œil rétrospectif', (*Lumière et vie*, 64, 1963, pp 87-116).
1038 Marnish, P. S.	'Dr. Griffith Higgs, 1589-1659'. (*Oxoniensia*, 3, 1966, pp 117-38).

1039 Mavecty, S. R.	'Doctrine in Tyndale's New Testament. Translation as a tendentious art'. (*Studies in English literature, 1500-1900*, 6, 1966, pp 151-8).
1040 Mehl, D.	'Zur Interpretation des *Paradise regained*'. (*Deutsche Vierteljahrsschrift für Literaturewissenschaft und Geistesgeschichte*. 36, 1962, pp 340-55).
1041 Meijer, A. De,	'The attempts to re-establish the English Augustinian Province under Queen Mary Tudor'. (*Analecta Augustiniana*, 24, 1961, p 529).
1042 Mellano, M. Franca	'Rappresentanti italiani della corone inglese a Roma ai primi del Cinquecento'. (*Studi Romani*, 17, 1969, pp 438-59).
1043 Merchant, W. M.	'Bishop Francis Godwin, Historian and Novelist'. (*Journal of the Historical Society of the Church in Wales*, 5, 1955, pp 45-51).
1044 Merrill, T. F.	'John Donne and the word of God'. (*Neuphilologische Mitteilungen*, 69, 1968, pp 597-616).
1045 Mesnard, P.	'Un animateur de la renaissance anglaise: le Cardinal Wolsey, 1471-1530'. (*Revue des Sciences Humaines*, 101, 1961, pp 5-12).
1046 ———	'L'evangélisme politique de Martin Bucer 1491-1551'. (*Bulletin de la Societé de l'histoire du Protestantisme Français*, 102, 1956, pp 121-36).
1047 ———	Bucer et la réforme réligieuse'. (*Bulletin de la Societé de l'histoire du Protestantisme Français*, 102, 1956, pp 193-230).
1048 Metzger, B. M.	'The Geneva Bible of 1560'. (*Theology Today*, 17, 1960, pp 339-52).
1049 ———	'The influence of the Codex Bezae upon the Geneva Bible of

1050 Meyer, C. S.   1560'. (*New Testament Studies*, 8, 1961-2, pp 72-7).
'Henry VIII burns Luther's books, 12 May 1521'. (*Journal of Ecclesiastical History*, 9, 1958, pp 173-87).

1051 Miles, L.   'The Platonic source of *Utopia's* 'minimum religion' '. (*Renaissance News*, 9, 1956, pp 83-90).

1052 ———   'With a coal? The composition of Thomas More's *Dialogue of comfort*'. (*Philological Quarterly*, 45, 1966, pp 437-42).

1053 ———   'The *Dialogue of comfort* and More's execution. Some comments on literary purpose'. (*Modern Languages Review*, 61, 1966, pp 556-60).

1054 ———   'More's *Dialogue of comfort* as a first draft'. (*Studies in Philology*, 63, 1966, pp 126-34).

1055 Miriam-Joseph, Sister   '*Hamlet*, a christian tragedy'. (*Studies in Philology*, 59, 1962, pp 119-40).

1056 Møller, J. G.   'The beginnings of puritan covenant theology'. (*Journal of Ecclesiastical History*, 14, 1963, pp 46-67).

1057 Morán, A.   'El episcopado en el anglicanismo' (*Miscelánea Comillas*, 34-5, 1960, pp 207-38).

1058 Moreau, G.   'Contribution a l'histoire du *Livre des martyrs*'. (*Bulletin de la Societé de l'histoire du Protestantisme Français*, 103, 1957, pp 173-99).

1059 Moreau, J.   'Introduction à la lecture des *Hymnes* de Spenser'. (*Revue de Théologie et de Philosophie*, 3 series 14, 1964, pp 65-83).

1060 Morgan, W. T.   'An examination of churchwardens' accounts, and of some disputes concerning them before the consistory court of St. David's'. II. (*Journal of the Historical Society*

1061 ——— *of the Church in Wales*, 8, 1958, pp 58-81).
'Disciplinary cases against churchwardens in the consistory courts of St. David's'. (*Journal of the Historical Society of the Church in Wales*, 10, 1960, pp 17-42).

1062 Morris, R. C. 'Thomas More and the early church fathers' (*Traditio*, 24, 1968, pp 379-407).

1063 Morrissey, T. J. 'The strange affair of Matthew Hartegan, S. J., 1644-5'. (*Irish Theological Quarterly*, 37, 1970, pp 159-72).

1064 Mosse, G. L. 'Puritanism reconsidered'. (*Archiv für Reformationsgeschichte*, 55, 1964, pp 37-48).

1065 Mueller, J. M. 'The exegesis of experience. Dean Donne's *Devotions upon emergent occasions*'. (*Journal of English and German Philology*, 67, 1968, pp 1-19).

1066 Murilla, E. L. '*Paradise regained*. Observations on its meaning'. (*Studia Neophilologica*, 27, 1955, pp 179-91).

1067 Murphy, M. 'John Foxe, martyrologist and 'editor' of Old English'. (*English Studies*, 49, 1968, pp 516-23).

1068 Murray, P. 'Shakespeare, The religious aspect'. (*Irish Ecclesiastical Record*, 107, 1967, pp 143-57).

1069 Murray, W. A. 'What was the soul of the apple?' [concerns the *metempsychosis* of Donne] (*Review of English Studies*, new series 10, 1959, pp 141-55.

1070 Myers, J. N. L. 'Thomas James, *Concordantiae sanctorum Patrum* (1607)'. (*The Bodleian Library Record*, 5, 1955, pp 212-17).

1071 Nash, M. C. 'The fate of the English Cistercian abbots in the reign of Henry VIII'. (*Cîteaux*, 16, 1965, pp 97-113).

1072 New, J. F. H. 'The Whitgift-Cartwright controversy'. (*Archiv für Reformationsgeschichte*, 59, 1968, pp 203-12).

1073 Newmeyer, E. — 'Beza and Milton, New light on the temptation of learning' (*Bulletin of the New York Public Library*, 66, 1962, pp 485-98).

1074 Novarr, D. — 'The dating of Donne's *La Corona*'. (*Philological Quarterly*, 36, 1957, pp 259-65).

1075 Oakley, F. — 'Jacobean political theology. The absolute and ordinary powers of the King'. (*Journal of the History of Ideas*, 29, 1968, pp 323-46).

1076 O'Dwyer, M. — 'Recusant fines in Essex 1583-1593' (*The Month*, 206, 1958, pp 28-37).

1077 Ogden, H. V. S. — 'The crisis of *Paradise Lost* reconsidered'. (*Philological Quarterly*, 36, 1957, pp 1-19).

1078 Ornstein, R. — 'Donne, Montaigne and natural law'. (*Journal of English and German Philology*, 55, 1956, pp 213-29).

1079 Opie, J. — 'The Anglicizing of John Hooper'. (*Archiv für Reformationsgeschichte*, 59, 1968, pp 150-77).

1080 O'Rourke, W. J. — 'St. John Fisher's defence of the holy priesthood'. (*Heythrop Journal*, 8, 1967, pp 260-92).

1081 Owen, H. G. — 'Parochial curates in Elizabethan London' (*Journal of Ecclesiastical History*, 10, 1959, pp 66-73).

1082 ——— 'The episcopal visitation. Its limits and limitations in Elizabethan London'. (*Journal of Ecclesiastical History*, 11, 1960, pp 179-85).

1083 ——— 'Lecturers and lectureships in Tudor London'. (*Church Quarterly Review*, 162, 1961, pp 63-76).

1084 ——— 'A nursery of Elizabethan nonconformity [The parish of the Minories, London] 1567-1572'. (*Journal of Ecclesiastical History*, 17, 1966, pp 65-76).

1085 Pacchi, A. — 'Ruggero Bacone e Roberto Grossatesta in un inedito hobbesiano del 1634'. (*Rivista critica di storia della filosofia*, 20, 1965, pp 499-502).

1086 Padberg, R.   'Der Sinn der *Utopie* des Thomas Morus. Fragen der politischen Verantwortung des Christen am Vorabend der Reformation'. (*Theologie und Glaube*, 57, 1967, pp 28-47).

1087 Pallet, J.   'La correspondance inédite de Martin Bucer'. (*Archiv für Reformationsgeschichte*, 46, 1955, pp 213-21).

1088 Parks, G. B.   'The Parma letters and the dangers to Cardinal Pole'. (*Catholic Historical Review*, 46, 1960, pp 299-317).

1089 Parmiter, G. de C.   'The indictment of St. Thomas More'. (*Downside Review*, 75, 1957, pp 149-66).

1090 ———   'St. Thomas More and the oath'. (*Downside Review*, 78, 1959-60, pp 1-13).

1091 ———   'Tudor indictments illustrated by the indictment of St. Thomas More'. (*Recusant History*, 6, 1961 pp 141-56).

1092 ———   'A note on some aspects of the royal supremacy of Henry VIII'. (*Recusant History*, 10, 1969-70, pp 183-92).

1093 Patrides, C. A.   'The 'Protevangelium' in Renaissance theology and *Paradise Lost*'. (*Studies in English literature 1500-1900*, 3, 1963, pp 19-30).

1094 ———   'Milton and Arianism'. (*Journal of the History of Ideas*, 25, 1964, pp 423-29).

1095 Paul, J. E.   'The last Abbots of Reading and Colchester'. (*Bulletin of the Institute of Historical Research*, 33, 1960, pp 115-21).

1096 ———   'The last Abbot of Reading'. (*The Month*, new series 25, 1961, pp 69-81).

1097 Pauley, W. C. de   'Richard Baxter surveyed'. (*Church Quarterly Review*, 164, 1963, pp 32-43).

1098 Paulsen, A. — '*Utopia*, a humanist document'. (*Reality*, 11, 1963, pp 76-92).

1098a Pearl, V. — See 1125

1099 Pennington, D. H. — 'Cromwell and the historians' (*History Today*, 8, 1958, pp 598-605).

1100 Peters, R. — 'The administration of the archdeaconry of St. Albans, 1580-1625'. (*Journal of Ecclesiastical History*, 13, 1962, pp 61-75).

1101 ——— 'Some catholic opinions of King James VI and I' (*Recusant History*, 10, 1969-70, pp 292-303).

1102 Peters, W. A. M. — 'St. Ignatius in England'. (*The Month*, new series 16, 1956, pp 21-9).

1103 ——— 'Richard Whitford and St. Ignatius' visit to England'. (*Archivum Historicum Societatis Jesu*, 25, 1956, pp 328-50).

1104 Peterson, D. L. — 'John Donne's Holy Sonnets and the Anglican doctrine of contrition'. (*Studies in Philology*, 56, 1959, pp 504-18).

1105 Petti, A. G. — 'Peter Philips composer and organist (1561-1628)'. (*Recusant History*, 4, 1957, pp 48-60).

1106 ——— 'Richard Verstegan and catholic martyrologies of the later Elizabethan period' (*Recusant History*, 5, 1959, pp 64-90).

1107 ——— 'Stephen Vallenger, 1541-1591'. (*Recusant History*, 6, 1962, pp 248-64).

1108 Pimlott, J. A. R. — 'Christmas under the puritans'. (*History Today*, 10, 1960, pp 832-39).

1109 Pineas, R. — 'Erasmus and More. Some contrasting theological opinions'. (*Renaissance News*, 13, 1960, pp 298-300).

1110 ——— 'Thomas More's use of humour as a weapon of religious controversy'. (*Studies in Philology*, 58, 1961, pp 97-114).

1111 ——— 'Sir Thomas More's controversy with Christopher St. German'.

1112 ——— (*Studies in English Literature, 1500-1900*, 1, 1961, pp 49-62.
'William Tyndale's influence on John Bale's polemical use of history'. (*Archiv für Reformationsgeschichte*, 53, 1962, pp 79-96).

1113 ——— 'John Bale's nondramatic works of religious controversy'. (*Studies in the Renaissance*, 9, 1962, pp 218-33).

1114 ——— 'William Tyndale's use of history as a weapon of religious controversy'. (*Harvard Theological Review*, 55, 1962, pp 121-41).

1115 ——— 'The English morality play as a weapon of religious controversy'. (*Studies in English Literature, 1500-1900*, 2, 1962, pp 157-80).

1116 ——— 'William Tyndale's polemical use of the Scriptures'. (*Nederlands archief voor Kerkgeschiedenis*, 45, 1962, pp 65-78).

1117 ——— 'More versus Tyndale. A study of controversial technique'. (*Modern Language Quarterly*, 24, 1963, pp 144-50).

1117a ——— 'William Tyndale; controversialist.' (*Studies in Philology*, 60, 1963, pp 117-32).

1118 ——— 'Thomas More's *Utopia* and Protestant polemics'. (*Renaissance News*, 17, 1964, pp 197-201).

1119 ——— 'Robert Barnes polemical use of history'. (*Bibliothèque d'humanisme et renaissance*, 26, 1964, pp 55-69).

1120 ——— 'Thomas Becon as a religious controversialist'. (*Nederlands archief voor Kerkgeschiedenis*, 46, 1965, pp 206-20).

1121 ——— 'Thomas More's controversy with Simon Fish'. (*Studies in English Literature, 1500-1900*, 7, 1967, pp 15-28).

1122 Pinnington, J.	'Moravian and Anglican. A new look at the circumstances surrounding the arrival of the Renewed Brethren in England'. (*Bulletin of the John Rylands Library,* 52, 1969-70, pp 200-17).
1123 Pouligo, R.	'Cromwell et la dictature puritaine' (*L'Information historique,* 19, 1957, pp 100-4).
1124 ———	'Cromwell et la dictature puritaine' II.(*L'Information historique,* 19, 1957, pp 139-46).
1125 'Presbytarians, Independents and Puritans'.	The Independents: a reappraisal in history; by B. Worden. Exorcist or historian: the danger of ghost hunting; by V. Pearl. The Presbyterian Independents exorcised; a brief comment; by D. Underdown. Presbyterians and Independents; some comments; by G. Yule. Presbyterians, Independents and Puritans; a voice from the past; by J. H. Hexter. A rejoinder by S. Foster. (*Past and Present,* 47, 1970, pp 116-46).
1126 Purvis, J. S.	'The registers of archbishops Lee and Holgate'. (*Journal of Ecclesiastical History,* 13, 1962, pp 186-94).
1127 Quinn, D. B.	'John Donne's principles of biblical exegesis'. (*Journal of English and German Philology,* 61, 1962, pp 313-29).
1128 Rabb, T. K.	'Puritanism and the rise of experimental science in England'. (*Cahiers d'histoire Mondiale,* 7, 1962, pp 46-67).
1129 ———	'Sir Edwin Sandys and the parliament of 1604'. (*American Historical Review,* 69, 1963-4, pp 646-70).
1129a ———	See 1181.
1130 Ratcliff, E. C.	'The liturgical work of archbishop Cranmer'. (*Journal of Ecclesiastical History,* 7, 1956, pp 189-203).

1131 Rayner, C. G. and Rayner, S. F. 'Christopher Gibbons, "that famous musitian"'. (*Musica disciplina*, 24, 1970, pp 151-71).

1132 Reesing, J. 'The materiality of God in Milton's *de doctrina christiana*'. (*Harvard Theological Review*, 50, 1957, pp 159-73).

1133 Regina, G. 'Formazione storica e ideologica della Chiesa Anglicana'. (*La Scuola Cattolica*, 84, 1956, pp 99-130).

1134 Reynolds, E. E. 'English spiritual writers V: St. John Fisher'. (*The Clergy Review*, 44, 1959, pp 193-200).

1135 ——— 'Recusants in the province of York' (1596).(*The Month*, new series. 27, 1962, pp 227-37).

1136 Rice, H. A. L. 'Thomas Cranmer, 1489-1556, archbishop of Canterbury' (*History Today*, 6, 1956, pp 478-85).

1137 Richardson, C. C. 'Cranmer and the analysis of Eucharistic doctrine'. (*Journal of Theological Studies*, new series 16, 1965, pp 421-37).

1138 Rigler, G. H. 'Milton's treatment of Satan in *Paradise Lost*'. (*Neophilologus*, 43, 1958, pp 309-22).

1139 Ringler, W. 'Lydgate's *Serpent of Division* of 1559, edited by John Stow'. (*Bibliographical Studies*, 14, 1961, pp 201-3).

1140 Ritter, G. A. 'Divine right und Prärogative der englischen Könige, 1603-1640'. (*Historische Zeitschrift*, 196, 1963, pp 584-625).

1141 Roberts, J. R. 'The influence of the *Spiritual exercises* of St. Ignatius on the nativity poems of Robert Southwell'. (*Journal of English and German Philology*, 59, 1960, pp 450-6).

1142 Rogers, D. '*The catholic moderator*. A French reply to Bellarmine, and its English author Henry Constable'. (*Recusant History*, 5, 1960, pp 224-35).

1143	Rohr, J. von	'Covenant and assurance in Early English Puritanism' (*Church History*, 34, 1965, pp 195-203).
1144	Rooke, G. H.	'Dom William Ingram and his account book 1504-1533'. (*Journal of Ecclesiastical History*, 7, 1956, pp 30-44).
1145	Rosenblatt, J. P.	'Celestial entertainment in Eden. Book V of *Paradise Lost*.' (*Harvard Theological Review*, 62, 1969, pp 411-27).
1146	Rosenthal, J. T.	'Richard Duke of York. A XVth century layman and the church'. (*Catholic Historical Review*, 50, 1964-5, pp 171-87).
1147	Ross, D. S.	'Hooper's alleged authorship of *A brief and clear confession of the Christian faith*.' (*Church History*, 39, 1970, pp 18-29).
1148	Rossi, P.	'Sul carattere non utilitaristico della filosofia di F. Bacone'. (*Rivista critica di storia della filosofia*, 12, 1957, pp 22-41).
1149	Roth, C.	'Sir Thomas Bodley, Hebraist'. (*The Bodleian Library record*, 7, 1962-7. pp 242-57).
1150	Roth, F.	'Sources for a history of the English Austin Friars, III; The fifteenth century, IV; The sixteenth century'. (*Augustiniana*, 10, 1960, pp 341-402; 403-64).
1151	———	'Sources for a history of the English Austin Friars'. (*Augustiniana*, 11, 1961, pp 465-572).
1152	———	'A history of the English Austin Friars'. (*Augustiniana*, 12, 1962, pp 93-122).
1153	———	'A history of the English Austin Friars'. (*Augustiniana*, 12, 1962, pp 391-442).
1154	———	'A history of the English Austin Friars'. (*Augustiniana*, 13, 1963, pp 515-51).
1155	———	'A history of the English Austin

		Friars.(*Augustiniana*, 14, 1964, pp 163-215).
1156	———	'A history of the English Austin Friars'. (*Augustiniana*, 14, 1964, pp 670-710).
1157	———	'A history of the English Austin Friars'. (*Augustiniana*, 15, 1965, pp 175-236).
1158	———	'A history of the English Austin Friars'. (*Augustiniana*, 15, 1965, pp 567-628).
1159	———	'A history of the English Austin Friars'. (*Augustiniana*, 16, 1966, pp 204-63).
1160	———	'A history of the English Austin Friars'. (*Augustiniana*, 16, 1966, pp 446-519).
1160a	———	'A history of the English Austin Friars'. (*Augustiniana*, 17, 1967, pp 84-166).
1161	Rott, J.	'Le sort des papiers et de la bibliothèque de Bucer en Angleterre'. (*Revue d'historie et de philosophie religieuses*, 46, 1966, pp 346-67).
1162	Rowse, A. L.	'Sir Nicholas Throgmorton' (*History Today*, 12, 1962, pp 125-31).
1163	Rueger, Z.	'Gerson, the concilar movement and the right of resistance 1642-4'. (*Journal of the History of Ideas*, 25, 1964, pp 467-86).
1164	Rusche, H.	'Prophecies and propaganda, 1641-1651'. (*English Historical Review*, 84, 1969, pp 752-70).
1165	Russell, C. S. R.	'Arguments for religious unity in England, 1530-1650'. (*Journal of Ecclesiastical History*, 18, 1967, pp 201-26).
1166	———	'The authorship of the bishop's diary of the House of Lords in 1641' (*Bulletin of the Institute of Historical Research*, 41, 1968, pp 229-36).
1167	Russell, G. H.	'Vernacular instruction of the laity in the later middle ages in England.

Some texts and notes'. (*Journal of Religious History*, 2, 1962, pp 98-119).

1168 Sachs, A. 'The religious despair of *Dr. Faustus*'. (*Journal of English and German Philology*, 63, 1964, pp 625-47).

1169 Sandham, G. P. 'An English Jesuit dramatist; Fr. Joseph Simeon, 1593-1671'. (*The Month*, new series 24, 1960, pp 308-13).

1170 Sawada, P. A. 'Two anonymous Tudor treatises on the general council'. (*Journal of Ecclesiastical History*, 12, 1961, pp 197-214).

1171 Sayers, J. 'Canterbury proctors at the court of *audientia litterarum contradictarum*'. (*Traditio*, 22, 1966, pp 311-45).

1172 Scarisbrick, J. J. 'The pardon of the clergy 1531'. (*Cambridge Historical Journal*, 12, 1956, pp 22-39).

1173 ——— 'Clerical Taxation in England 1485-1547'. (*Journal of Ecclesiastical History*, 11, 1960, pp 41-54).

1174 ——— 'Henry VIII and the Vatican library'. (*Bibliothèque d'humanisme et renaissance*, 24, 1962, pp 211-16).

1175 Schmidt, A. J. 'A treatise on England's perils, 1578'. (*Archiv für Reformationsgeschichte*, 46, 1955, pp 243-49).

1176 ——— 'Thomas Wilson, Tudor scholar-statesman' (1523/4-1581). (*Huntington Library Quarterly*, 20, 1956-7, pp 205-7).

1177 Schoeck, R. J. 'The use of St. John Chrysostom in XVIth century controversy: Christopher St. German and Sir Thomas More in 1533'. (*Harvard Theological Review*, 54, 1961, pp 21-7).

1178 ——— 'The *chronica chronicorum* of Sir Thomas More, and Tudor historians'. (*Bulletin of the Institute of Historical Research*, 35, 1962, pp 84-6).

1179 ——— 'Canon law in England on the eve of the Reformation'. (*Medieval Studies*, 25, 1963, pp 125-47).

1180 ——— 'Recent studies in the English Renaissance'. (*Studies in English literature, 1500-1900*, 10, 1970, pp 215-50).

1181 'Science, religion and society in the XVIth and XVIIth centuries'. 1. William Harvey (no parliamentarian, no heretic) and the idea of monarchy, by C. Hill. 2. Puritanism and science. Problems of definition, by H. F. Kearney. 3. Religion and the rise of modern science, by T. K. Rabb. (*Past and Present*, 31, 1965, pp 97-126).

1182 Scott, K. L. 'A mid-XVth century English illuminating shop and its customers'. (*Journal of the Warburg and Courtauld Institutes*, 31, 1968, pp 170-196).

1183 Sellin, P. R. 'Milton's epithet "agonistes" '. (*Studies in English Literature, 1500-1900*, 4, 1964, pp 137-62).

1184 Selwyn, D. G. 'A neglected edition of Cranmer's Catechism'. (*Journal of Theological Studies*, new series 15, 1964, pp 76-91).

1185 Shanahan, D. 'The death of Thomas More, secular priest, great grandson of St. Thomas More'. (*Recusant History*, 7, 1963, pp 23-32).

1186 Shapiro, I. A. 'Walton and the occasion of Donne's devotions'. (*Review of English Studies*, new series 9, 1958, pp 18-22).

1187 Shorrocks, D. M. M. 'Probate jurisdication within the diocese of Canterbury'. (*Bulletin of the Institute of Historical Research*, 31, 1958, pp 186-95).

1188 Shriver, F. 'Orthodoxy and diplomacy. James I and the Vorstius affair'. (*English Historical Review*, 85, 1970, pp 449-74).

1189 Simon, J. 'The reformation and English education'. (*Past and Present*, 11, 1957, pp 48-65).

1190 ——— 'The social origins of Cambridge Students 1603-1640'. (*Past and Present*, 26, 1963, pp 58-67).

1191 Sirluck, E. 'Miltons political thought. The first cycle'. (*Modern Philology*, 61, 1963-4, pp 209-24).

1192 Sitwell, G. 'Leander Jones's mission to England 1634-5'. (*Recusant History*, 5, 1960, pp 132-82).

1193 Skinner, Q. 'History and ideology in the English revolution'. (*Historical Journal*, 8, 1965, pp 151-78).

1194 ——— 'The ideological context of Hobbes' political thought'. (*Historical Journal* 9, 1966, pp 286-317).

1195 Slights, C. 'Ingenious piety: Anglican casuistry of the XVIIth century'. (*Harvard Theological Review*, 63, 1970, pp 409-32).

1196 Smith, L. B. 'Henry VIII and the protestant triumph' (*American Historical Review*, 71, 1965-6, pp 1237-64).

1197 Smyth, C. 'Little Gidding and Leighton Bromswold'. (*Church Quarterly Review*, 165, 1964, pp 290-305).

1198 Snow, V. F. 'Parliamentary reapportionment proposals in the Puritan revolution' (*English Historical Review*, 74, 1959, pp 409-42).

1199 Solt, L. F. 'Anti-intellectualism in the Puritan revolution'. (*Church History*, 24, 1956, pp 306-16).

1200 ——— 'Revolutionary Calvinist parties in England under Elizabeth I and Charles I'. (*Church History*, 27, 1958, pp 234-9).

1201 ——— 'Puritanism and democracy in the New model army'. (*Archiv für Reformationsgeschichte*, 50, 1959, pp 234-52).

1202 ——— 'The fifth monarchy men. Politics

1203 Spalding, J. C.   and the millenium'. (*Church History*, 30, 1961, pp 314-24).

'Sermons before parliament, 1641-9, as a public puritan diary'. (*Church History*, 36, 1967, pp 24-35).

1204 ——— 'The *Reformatio legum ecclesiasticarum* of 1552 and the furthering of discipline in England'. (*Church History*, 39, 1970, pp 162-71).

1205 ——— and Brass, M. F. 'Reduction of episcopacy as a means to unity in England 1640-1662'. (*Church History*, 30, 1961, pp 414-32).

1206 Sprunger, K. L. 'Ames, Ramus and the method of puritan theology'. (*Harvard Theological Review*, 59, 1966, pp 133-51).

1207 Stanwood, P. G. 'Patristic and contemporary borrowing in the Caroline divines'. (*Renaissance Quarterly*, 23, 1970, pp 421-9).

1208 Stapleton, L. 'The theme of virtue in Donne's verse epistles'. (*Studies in Philology*, 55, 1958, pp 187-200).

1209 ——— 'Milton's conception of time in *The Christian doctrine*'. (*Harvard Theological Review*, 57, 1964, pp 9-21).

1210 Stassen, G. 'Anabaptist influence in the origin of the particular baptists'. (*Mennonit Quarterly Review*, 36, 1962, pp 322-48).

1211 Steadman, J. M. 'Una and the clergy. The ass symbol in *The Faerie Queene*'. (*Journal of the Warburg and Courtauld Institutes*, 21, 1958, pp 134-7).

1212 ——— 'Milton and the patristic tradition. The quality of hellfire'. (*Anglia*, 76, 1958, pp 116-28).

1213 ——— 'Heroic value and the divine image in *Paradise Lost*'. (*Journal of the Warburg and Courtauld Institutes*, 22, 1959, pp 88-105).

1214 ——— ' "Faithful champion" the theological basis of Milton's hero of faith'. (*Anglia,* 77, 1959, pp 12-28).

1215 ——— 'Recognition in the fable of *Paradise Lost*'. (*Studia Neophilologica,* 31, 1959, pp 159-73).

1216 ——— 'The God of *Paradise Lost* and *Divina Commedia*'. (*Archiv für das Studium der neueren Sprachen,* 195, 1959, pp 273-89).

1217 ——— 'Tradition and innovation in Milton's 'sin'. The problem of literary indebtedness'. (*Philological Quarterly,* 39, 1960, pp 93-103).

1218 ——— 'Miracle and the epic marvellous in *Paradise Lost*'. (*Archiv für das Studium der neueren Sprachen,* 198, 1961, pp 289-303).

1219 ——— 'The 'suffering servant' and Milton's heroic norm (in *Paradise Regained*)'. (*Harvard Theological Review,* 54, 1961, pp 29-43).

1220 ——— 'Milton and the *argumentum paris.* Biblical exegesis and rhetoric'. (*Archiv für das Studium der neueren Sprachen,* 202, 1965-6, pp 347-60).

1221 Stephenson, A. A. 'Anglican orders. II: The argument of Gregory Dix. III: The ordinal of 1552' (*The Month,* new series 14, 1955, pp 78-86; 152-9).

1223 Stewart, B. S. 'The cult of the royal martyr' [Charles I]. (*Church History,* 38, 1969, pp 175-87).

1224 Stone, L. 'The educational revolution in England, 1560-1640'. (*Past and Present,* 28, 1964, pp 41-80).

1225 Strohl, H. 'L'activité scientifique de Bucer' (*Revue d'histoire et de philosophie religieuses,* 36, 1956, pp 121-35).

1226 Surtis, P. 'Natural law in Richard Hooker (c. 1554-1600)'. (*Irish Theological Quarterly,* 35, 1968, pp 173-85).

1227 Surtz, E.	'The setting for More's plea for Greek in *Utopia*' (*Philological Quarterly*, 35, 1956, pp 353-65).
1228 ———	'John Fisher and the scholastics'. (*Studies in Philology*, 55, 1958, pp 136-53).
1229 Sylvester, R. S.	'Cavendish's *Life of Wolsey*. The artistry of a Tudor biographer'. (*Studies in Philology*, 57, 1960, pp 44-71).
1230 ———	'John Constable's poems to Thomas More'. (*Philological Quarterly*, 42, 1963, pp 525-31).
1231 Talbot, C. H.	'Marmaduke Huby, abbot of Fountains, 1495-1526' (*Analecta sacri ordinis Cisterciensis*, 20, 1964, pp 165-84).
1232 Tashiro, T. T.	'English poets, Egyptian onions, and the protestant view of the Eucharist'. (*Journal of the History of Ideas*, 30, 1969, pp 563-78).
1233 Tate, W. E.	'The episcopal licencing of schoolmasters in England'. (*Church Quarterly Review*, 157, 1956, pp 426-32).
1234 Taylor, T. F.	'The Douai defence'. (*Recusant History*, 10, 1969, pp 176-80).
1235 Tellechea Idigoras, J. I.	'Bartolomé Carranza y la restauración católica inglesa 1554-1558'. (*Anthologia Annua*, 12, 1964, pp 159-282).
1236 Thomas, H.	'*Jacob and Esau*, 'rigidly calvinistic'?' (*Studies in English Literature, 1500-1900*, 9, 1969, pp 199-213).
1237 Thomas, K.	'Women and the Civil War Sects'. (*Past and Present*, 13, 1958, pp 42-62).
1238 ———	'Another Digger broadside' (*Past and Present*, 42, 1969, pp 57-68).
1239 Thomas, R.	'Presbyterians in transition'. (*Historical Journal*, 60, 1961-2, pp 195-204).
1240 Thomson, J. A. F.	'Tithe disputes in later medieval London'. (*English Historical Review*, 78, 1963, pp 1-17).

1241 ——— 'Piety and charity in late medieval London'. (*Journal of Ecclesiastical History*, 16, 1965, pp 178-95).

1242 Thorndike, L. 'Some tracts on comets 1456-1500'. (*Archives Internationales d'histoire des sciences*, 11, 1958, pp 225-50).

1243 Torrance, T. F. 'Kingdom and church in the thought of Martin Butzer' (*Journal of Ecclesiastical History*, 6, 1955, pp 48-59).

1244 Trappes-Lomax, T. B. 'The family of Poyntz and its catholic associations'. (*Recusant History*, 6, 1961, pp 68-79).

1245 ——— 'The parentage and family of the martyr Bl. John Wall, O.F.M.' (*Recusant History*, 6, 1961-2, pp 195-200).

1246 Trattner, W. I. 'God and expansion in Elizabethan England. John Dee, 1527-1583'. (*Journal of the History of Ideas*, 25, 1964, pp 17-34).

1247 Trevor-Roper, H. 'La revolution anglaise de Cromwell'. (*Annales*, 10, 1955, pp 331-40).

1248 Trinterud, L. J. 'A reappraisal of William Tyndale's debt to Martin Luther'. (*Church History*, 31, 1962, pp 24-45).

1249 Tucci, R. 'L'anglicanesimo, de fenomeno insulare a movimento mondiale'. (*La Civiltà Cattolica*, 4, 1959, pp 363-78).

1250 Tuve, R. 'George Herbert and *caritas*'. (*Journal of the Warburg and Courtauld Institutes*, 22, 1959, pp 303-31).

1251 ——— 'Sacred 'parody' of love poetry and Herbert'. (*Studies in the Renaissance*, 8, 1961, pp 249-90).

1252 Ullman, W. 'Thomas Becket's miraculous oil'. [coronation oil 14th-17th century] (*Journal of Theological Studies*, new series 8, 1957, pp 129-33).

1252a Underwood, D. See 1125.

1253 Upcott, J.   'Regnans in excelsis, 1558-1570-1588. Note on *Regnans in excelsis* by E. I. Watkin; further note by Th. Colwey'. (*Istina*, 8, 1960, pp 327-44).

1254 Van Der Wall, G. A.   'Motieven in Thomas Morus' Utopia'. (*Tijdschrift voor filosofie*, 27, 1965, pp 419-75).

1255 Vann, R. T.   'Quakerism and the social structure in the Interregum'. (*Past and Present*, 43, 1969, pp 71-91).

1256 Verleyden, A. L. E.   'Une correspondance inédite adressée par les familles protestantes des Pays Bas a leurs coreligionnaires d'Angleterre (11 Nov. 1569-25 Fev. 1570)'. (*Bulletin de la Commission royale d'histoire*, 120, 1955, pp 95-257).

1257 Vinay, V.   'Riformatori e lotte contadine. Scritti e polemiche relative alla ribellione dei contadini nella Cornovaglia e nel Devonshire sotto Edoardo VI'. (*Rivista di storia e letteratura religiosa*, 3, 1967, pp 203-51).

1258 Walker, J.   'William Chillingworth'. (*Journal of Ecclesiastical History*, 6, 1955, pp 175-89).

1259 Walker, R. B.   'Lincoln cathedral in the reign of Queen Elizabeth I'. (*Journal of Ecclesiastical History*, 11, 1960, pp 186-201).

1260 ———   'The growth of puritanism in the county of Lincoln in the reign of Queen Elizabeth I'. (*Journal of Religious History*, 1, 1961, pp 148-59).

1261 Walne, P.   'Parish registers and the registration of births, marriages and deaths in England and Wales'. (*Archivum*, 8, 1958, pp 79-87).

1262 Walsh, E. and Forster, A. M. C.   'The recusancy of the Brandlings' (*Recusant History*, 10, 1969, pp 35-64).

1263 Walzer, M. — 'Puritanism as a revolutionary ideology'. (*History and Theory*, 3, 1963, pp 59-90).

1264 Wardell, J. W. — 'The recusants of the Friarage, Yarm, Yorkshire'. (*Recusant History*, 8, 1965, pp 158-65).

1265 Warren, E. B. — 'The life and works of Robert Fayrfax'. (*Musica disciplina*, 11, 1957, pp 134-52).

1266 ——— 'The masses of Robert Fayrfax' (*Musica disciplina*, 12, 1958, pp 145-76).

1267 ——— 'Robert Fayrfax, Motets and settings of the *Magnificat*'. (*Musica disciplina*, 15, 1961, pp 113-43).

1268 Watson, A. G. — 'Christopher and William Carye, collectors of monastic manuscripts and 'John Carye' '. (*The Library*, 5 series, 20, 1965, pp 135-42).

1269 Wayment, H. G. — 'The use of engravings in the design of the Renaissance windows in King's College Chapel, Cambridge'. (*Burlington Magazine*, 100, 1958, pp 378-88).

1270 Webber, J. — 'The prose styles of John Donne's *Devotions upon emergent occasions*'. (*Anglia*, 79, 1962, pp 138-52).

1271 ——— 'Celebration of word and world in Lancelot Andrewes' style'. (*Journal of English and German Philology*, 64, 1965, pp 255-69).

1272 Wedgwood, C. V. — 'The causes of the English Civil War. A new analysis'. (*History Today*, 5, 1955, 670-76).

1273 ——— 'The Covenanters in the first Civil War'. (*Scottish Historical Review*, 39, 1960, pp 1-15).

1274 Welch, C. E. — 'An ecclesiastical precedent book from St. Asaph'. (*Journal of the Historical Society of the Church in Wales*, 11, 1961, pp 9-24).

1275 Welsby, P. A. — 'Lancelot Andrewes and the nature of Kingship'. (*Church Quarterly Review*, 156, 1955, pp 400-8).

1276	West, R. H.	'The Christianness of *Othello*'. (*Shakespeare Quarterly*, 15, 1964, pp 333-43).
1277	Westland, J.	'The orthodox Christian framework of Marlowe's *Faustus*'. (*Studies in English Literature 1500-1900*, 3, 1963, pp 191-205).
1278	Whatmore, L. E.	'The venerable William Pike, layman'. (*Recusant History*, 9, 1967-8, pp 258-63).
1279	Wheeler, T.	'The purpose of Bacon's *History of Henry VII*'. (*Studies in Philology*, 54, 1957, pp 1-13).
1280	White, B. R.	'The organisation of the particular baptists, 1644-1660'. (*Journal of Ecclesiastical History*, 17, 1966, pp 209-26).
1281	————	'The doctrine of the Church in the particular Baptist Confession of 1644'. (*Journal of Theological Studies*, new series 19, 1968, pp 570-90).
1282	White, H. C.	'The contemplative element in Robert Southwell'. (*Catholic Historical Review*, 48, 1962-3, pp 1-11).
1283	Whitlock, B. W.	'Ye curious schooler in Christendom' [Letter of Edward Alleyn to John Donne.] (*Review of English Studies*, new series 6, 1955, pp 365-71).
1284	————	'Donne's university years'. (*English Studies*, 42, 1962, pp 1-20).
1285	Whitney, D. A.	'London puritanism. The Haberdasher's Company'. (*Church History*, 32, 1963, pp 298-321).
1286	Wickert, M.	'Miltons Entwürfe zu einem Drama vom Sündenfall' (*Anglia*, 73, 1955, pp 171-206).
1287	Willey, B.	'Robert Herrick 1591-1674' (*Church Quarterly Review*, 156, 1955, pp 248-55).
1288	Williams, D. A.	'London Puritanism. The parish of St. Stephen's Coleman Street'. (*Church Quarterly Review*, 160, 1959, pp 464-82).

1289 Williams, G. H. — 'Translatio studii. The puritans' conception of their first university in New England, 1636'. (*Archiv für Reformationsgeschichte*, 57, 1966, pp 152-81).

1290 Williams, J. A. — 'Katherine Gawen, papist', (*The Month*, new series 29, 1963, pp 169-75).

1290a Williams, P. — See 696.

1291 Wilson, E. M. — 'Spanish and English religious poetry of the XVIIth century' (*Journal of Ecclesiastical History*, 9, 1958, pp 38-53).

1292 Wilson, J. F. — 'Comment on 'two roads to the puritan millenium' ' (*Church History*, 32, 1963, pp 339-43).

1293 Woodman, A. V. — 'The Buckinghamshire and Oxfordshire rising of 1549' (*Oxoniensia*, 22, 1957, pp 78-84).

1294 Woodward, G. W. O. — 'The role of parliament in the Henrician reformation' (*Schweizer Beiträge zur allgemeinen Geschichte*, 16, 1958, pp 56-65).

1295 ——— 'The exemption from suppression of certain Yorkshire priories'. (*English Historical Review*, 76, 1961, pp 385-401).

1296 ——— 'A speculation in monastic lands' (*English Historical Review*, 79, 1964, pp 778-83).

1297 Woolff, C. G. — 'Literary reflections of the puritan character' (*Journal of the History of Ideas*, 29, 1968, pp 13-32).

1298 Woolrych, A. H. — 'The good old cause and the fall of the Protectorate'. (*Catholic Historical Journal*, 13, 1957, pp 133-61).

1299 ——— 'The collapse of the great rebellion'. (*History Today*, 8, 1958, pp 606-15).

1300 ——— 'The calling of Barebones parliament'. (*English Historical Review*, 80, 1965, pp 492-573).

1300a Worden, B. — See 1125.

1301 Yost, J. K. — 'German protestant humanism and

	the early English reformation. Richard Taverner and official translation'. (*Bibliothèque d'humanisme et renaissance*, 32, 1970, pp 613-25).
1302 ———	'Taverner's use of Erasmus and the protestantisation of English humanism'. (*Renaissance Quarterly*, 23, 1970, pp 266-76).
1303 Yule, G.	'Theological developments in Elizabethan Puritanism'. (*Journal of Religious History*, 1, 1960-1, pp 16-25).
1303a ———	See 1125.
1304 Zagorin, P.	'The English Revolution 1640-1660'. (*Cahiers d'histoire Mondiale*, 2, 1954-5, pp 668-81).
1305 Zinnhabler, R.	'Heinrich VIII und die Reformation in England'. (*Theologische praktische Quartalschrift*, 118, 1970, pp pp 241-8).
1306 Zwiwerblowky, R. J.	'Milton and the *conjectura cabbalistica*'. (*Journal of the Warburg and Courtauld Institutes*, 18, 1955, pp 90-113).

SECTION 4. SOCIETY PUBLICATIONS

1307 Abernathy, G. R. Jnr.   *The English presbyterians and the Stuart Restoration 1648-1663* [Transactions of the American Philosophical Soc. new series 15, fasc 2] (Philadelphia 1965).

1308 Allmand, C. T.   'Some effects of the last phase of the Hundred Year's War upon the maintenance of clergy.' (*Studies in Church History*, 3, Leyden 1966, pp 179-90).

1309 Aveling, H.   *Post reformation catholicism in East Yorkshire 1558-1790* (York, East Yorkshire Local History Society, 1960).

1310 ———   *The catholic recusants of the West Riding of Yorkshire, 1538-1790* [Proceedings of the Leeds Philosophical and Literary Society. Literary and historical section, 10, no 6] (Leeds 1963).

1311 ———   'Some aspects of Yorkshire catholic recusant history 1558-1791.' (*Studies in Church History*, 4, Leyden 1967, pp 98-121).

1312 ———   *Catholic recusancy in the city of York, 1558-1791* [Catholic Record Society. Monograph series, 2] (London 1970).

1313 ——— and Pantin, W. A.   *The letter book of Robert Joseph, monk-scholar of Evesham and Gloucester college, Oxford, 1530-33* [Oxford Historical Society, new series 19] (Oxford 1967).

1314 Avery, D.   *Poverty and philanthropy in Tottenham in the XVIth and XVIIth centuries* (London, Central Reference Library, Edmonton hundred Historical Society, 1963).

1315 ———   *Popish recusancy in the Elizabethan hundred of Edmonton* (London,

1316 Babbage, S. B.	Edmonton hundred Historical Society, 1968). *Puritanism and Richard Bancroft.* [Church historical society] (London 1962).
1317 Barnes, T. G.	'County politics and a puritan *cause célèbre*: Somerset church ales 1633'. (*Transactions of the Royal Historical Society*, 5 series 9, 1959, pp 103-22).
1318 Bell, M. and Schumaker, W.	'The fallacy of the fall in *Paradise Lost*'. (*Publications of the Modern Language Association*, 70, 1955, pp 1185-203).
1319 Bill, P. A.	*The Warwickshire parish clergy in the later middle ages* (Stratford upon Avon, Dugdale Society, 1967).
1320 Blake, N. F.	*The history of Reynard the Fox translated from the Dutch original by William Caxton* [Early English Text Society, no 263] (London 1970).
1321 Bowers, F.	'Adam, Eve and the fall in *Paradise Lost*' (*Publications of the Modern Language Association*, 84, 1969, pp 264-73).
1322 Bowker, M.	*An episcopal court book for the diocese of Lincoln, 1514-1520* (Lincoln, Record Society, 1967).
1323 Bowler, H.	*Recusant roll no. 2(1593-94). An abstract in English with an explanatory introduction.* [Catholic Record Society publications, 57] (London 1965).
1324 Brett, P.	'Edward Paston (1550-1630): A Norfolk gentleman and his musical collection' (*Transactions of the Cambridge Bibliographical Society*, 4, i, 1964, pp 51-69).
1325 Cargill-Thompson, W. D. J.	'The two editions of Thomas Bilson's *True difference between Christian subjection and unchristian rebellion*'. (*Transactions of the*

1326 ———   *Cambridge Bibliographical Society*, 2, ii, 1955, pp 299-303).
'The sixteenth century editions of *A supplication unto King Henry the Eighth* by Robert Barnes DD: a footnote to the history of the royal supremacy'. (*Transactions of the Cambridge Bibliographical Society*, 3, ii, 1960, pp 133-43).

1327 Carlson, L. M.   'A corpus of Elizabethan Nonconformist writings'. (*Studies in Church History*, 2, London, 1965, pp 297-309).

1328 Cirkett, A. F.   *English wills 1498-1526* (Bedfordshire Historical Society, Luton Museum, 1957).

1329 Clair, J. A.   'Donne's *The Canonization*'. (*Publications of the Modern Language Association*, 80, 1965, pp 300-2).

1330 Clark, F.   *The catholic church and Anglican orders* (London, Catholic Truth Society, 1962).

1331 Collins, A. J.   *Manuale ad usum percelebris Ecclesie Sarisburiensis*. From the edition printed at Rouen in 1543, compared with those of 1506 (London), 1516 (Rouen), 1523 (Antwerp), and 1526 (Paris). [Henry Bradshaw Society Fasc 91] (Chichester 1960).

1332 Collinson, P.   'The Elizabethan Puritans and the foreign Reformed Churches in London'. (*Proceedings of the Huguenot Society of London*, 20, 1963-4, pp 528-68).

1333 ———   'The beginnings of English sabbatarianism'. (*Studies in Church History*, 1, London 1964, pp 207-21).

1334 ———   'The role of women in the English reformation illustrated by the life and friendships of Anne Locke'.

1335 ——

1336 Cross, M. C.

1337 Crow, J. and Wilson, F. P.

1338 Darlington, I.

1339 Davis, J. F.

1340 Denney, A. H.

1341 Dickens, A. G.

1342 ——

1343 ——

1344 ——

1345 —— and Newton, J.

1346 Dobson, R. B.

(*Studies in Church History*, 2, London 1965, pp 258-72).
'Episcopacy and reform in England in the later XVIth century' (*Studies in Church History*, 3, Leyden 1966, pp 91-125).
The letters of Sir Francis Hastings 1574-1609 [Somerset Record Society, Fasc 69] (Yeovil 1969).
Jacob and Esau (1568) [Malone Society reprints] (London 1956).
London consistory court wills, 1429-1547 (London Record Society, 1968).
'Lollard survival and the textile industry in the South East of England'. (*Studies in Church History*, 3, Leyden 1966, pp 191-201).
The Sibton abbey estates. Select documents 1325-1509 (Ipswich, Suffolk Record Society, 1960).
'Wilfred Holme of Huntington, Yorkshire's first protestant poet (d. 1538)'. (*Yorkshire Archaeological Journal*, 39, 1956, pp 119-36).
Clifford letters of the XVIth century [Surtees Society, 172] (Durham 1962).
'The writers of Tudor Yorkshire'. (*Transactions of the Royal Historical Society*, 5 series, 13, 1963, pp 49-76).
'Secular and religious motivations in the Pilgrimage of Grace'. (*Studies in Church History*, 4, Leyden, 1967, pp 39-64).
'Further light on the scope of Yorkshire recusancy in 1604' (*Yorkshire Archaeological Journal*, 38, 1955, 524-8).
'Richard Bell, prior of Durham (1464-1468) and bishop of Carlisle

1347 Dobson, C. S. A.

1348 Doyle, A. I.

1348a ———
1349 Du Boulay, F. R. H.

1350 Dunning, R. W.

1351 Dunstan, G. R.

1352 ———

1353 Elton, G. R.

1354 ———

1355 Emmison, F. G.

(1478-1495)' (*Transactions of the Cumberland and Westmorland Antiquarian and Archaeological Society*, new series 65, 1965, pp 182-221).

Oxfordshire Protestation returns (London, Oxfordshire Record Society, 1955).

'Borley and the Waldegraves in the sixteenth century'. (*Transactions of the Essex Archaeological Society*, 24, pp 17-31).

See 1417.

Diocesis Cantuariensis registrum Thome Bourgchier, pars prima et secunda [Canterbury and York society 54] (London 1957).

'The Wells consistory court in the XVth century' (*Proceedings of the Somersetshire archaeological and natural history society*, 106, 1961-2, pp 46-61).

The register of Edmund Lacy, bishop of Exeter 1420-1455. Registrum commune. Vol. II [The Canterbury and York society 132] (Torquay 1966).

The register of Edmund Lacy, bishop of Exeter, 1420-1455. Registrum commune, Vol. III [The Canterbury and York society, 134] (Torquay 1967).

'Reform by statute: Thomas Starkey's *Dialogue* and Thomas Cromwell's policy'. (*Proceedings of the British Academy*, 54, 1968, pp 165-88).

'The political creed of Thomas Cromwell' (*Transactions of the Royal Historical Society*, 5 series. 6, 1956, pp 69-92).

Wills at Chelmsford, Essex and East Hertfordshire 1400-1619; and

England and Wales

		1620-1720, 2 vols (London, British Record Society, 1958-61).
1356	Ernstberger, A.	'Englands Ansichten zur Weltlage, 1641-2' [*Sitzungsherichte der Bayerischen Akademie der Wissenschaften*, Phil-hist, Kl, 1961 Fasc 6] (Munich 1961).
1356a	Fines, J.	See 1359.
1357	Flesseman Van Leer, E.	'Richard Hooker, Anglicanisme en Protestantisme' (*Kerk en Theologie*, 6, 1955, pp 234-42).
1358	Fletcher, J. M. and McConica, J. K.	'A sixteenth century inventory of the library of Corpus Christi College, Cambridge'. (*Transactions of the Cambridge Bibliographical Society*, 3, iii, 1961, pp 187-200).
1359	——— and Fines, J.	'Nicholas Harpesfield's note of Cranmer's recantation'. (*Transactions of the Cambridge Bibliographical Society*, 4, iv, 1967, pp 310-2).
1360	Forster, A. M. C.	'Durham entries on the Recusants Rolls 1636-7' [Surtees Society 175, *Miscellanea Vol. III*, pp 123-202] (Durham 1965).
1361	Gibson, J. W. and Harvey, B. F.	*Index to Wills proved in the peculiar court of Banbury 1542- 1858* [Oxfordshire Record Society] (Oxford 1959).
1361a	Gifford, D. H.	See 1398.
1362	Gifford, W.	'Time and place in Donne's sermons' (*Publications of the Modern Language Association*, 83, 1967, pp 388-98).
1363	Haigh, C.	*The last days of the Lancashire monasteries and the Pilgrimage of Grace* [Remains historical and literary connected with the Palatine counties of Lancaster and Chester, 3 series, 17] (Manchester, Chetham Society, 1969).
1364	Haines, R. M.	'Some arguments in favour of plurality in the Elizabethan church'. (*Studies in Church History*, 5, Leyden 1969, pp 166-92).

1365 Hall, B.   'Puritanism. The problem of definition'. (*Studies in Church History*, 2, London 1965, pp 283-96).

1366 Hanham, A.   *Churchwarden's accounts of Ashburton, 1479-1580* (Exeter, Devon and Cornwall Record Society, 1970).

1366a Harvey, B. F.   See 1361.

1367 Hattaway, M.   'Marginalia by Henry VIII in his copy of *The Bokes of Soloman*'. (*Transactions of the Cambridge Bibliographical Society*, 4, ii, 1965, pp 166-70).

1368 Hill, C.   'Puritans and "the dark corners of the land" '. (*Transactions of the Royal Historical Society*, 5 series, 13, 1963, pp 77-102).

1369 Hodgett, G. A. J.   *The state of the ex-religious and former chantry priests in the diocese of Lincoln, 1547-1575*. From returns in the exchequer. [Lincolnshire Record Society 53] (Lincoln 1959).

1370 Hoskins, W. G.   'English provincial towns in the early 16th century'. (*Transactions of the Royal Historical Society*, 5 series, 6, 1956, pp 1-19).

1371 Hudleston, C. R.   *The registers of Morland, Vol. I; 1538-1742*. (Kendal, Cumberland and Westmorland Antiquarian Society, 1957).

1372 Hughes, M. Y.   'Some of Donne's "ecstasies" '. (*Publications of the Modern Language Association*, 75, 1960, pp 509-18).

1373 Huntley, F. L   'Macbeth and the background of Jesuitical equivocation'. (*Publications of the Modern Language Association*, 79, 1964, pp 390-400).

1374 Hurstfield, J.   'Church and state, 1558-1612. The task of the Cecils'. (*Studies in Church History*, 2, London, 1965, pp 119-40).

1375	Jackson, W. A.	*Records of the court of the Stationers' company 1602-1640.* (London, Bibliographical Society, 1957).
1376	Jacob, E. F.	'Archbishop John Stafford' (*Transactions of the Royal Historical Society*, 5 series. 12, 1962, pp 1-23).
1377	James, M. R.	'The history of Lambeth Palace Library'. (*Transactions of the Cambridge Bibliographical Society*, 3, i, 1959, pp 1-32).
1378	Jordan, W. K.	*The forming of the charitable institutions of the West of England. A study in the changing pattern of social aspiration in Bristol and Somerset 1480-1660.* [Transactions of the American Philosophical Society, new series 50, fasc 8] (Philadelphia 1960).
1379	————	*Social institutions in Kent, 1480-1660. A study of the changing pattern of social aspirations.* [Archaeologia Cantiana, fasc 75] (Ashford, Kent Archaeological Society, 1961).
1380	————	*The social institutions of Lancashire. A study of the changing pattern of aspiration in Lancashire 1480-1660* (Manchester, The Chetham Society, 1962).
1381	Kelly, M.	'The submission of the clergy'. (*Transactions of the Royal Historical Society*, 5 series, 15, 1965, pp 97-119).
1382	Kenny, A.	*The responsa scholarum of the English College, Rome. 1st part: 1598-1621* [Catholic Record Society, 54-5] (London 1962-3).
1383	Kenshaw, I.	*Bolton priory rentals and ministers' accounts, 1473-1539* [Yorkshire Archaeological Society. Record series, 132] (Leeds 1970).

1384 Kingsford, C. L.   *The Grey Friars of London* [British Society of Franciscan studies] (new ed London 1966).

1385 Lefroy, E. J.   'Joseph Justus Scaliger, 1540-1609'. (*Proceedings of the Huguenot Society of London*, 20, 1963-4, pp 485-98).

1386 Lewalski, B. K.   '*Samson Agonistes* and the 'tragedy' of the Apocalypse'. (*Publications of the Modern Language Association*, 75, 1970, pp 1050-62).

1387 Lloyd Jukes, H. A.   'Peter Gunning, 1613-1684: scholar, churchman, controversialist'. (*Studies in Church History*, 1, London, 1964, pp 222-32).

1388 ———   'Digory Wheare's contribution to the study and teaching of ecclesiastical history in England in the XVIIth century'. (*Studies in Church History*, 5, Leyden 1969, pp 193-203).

1389 Loades, D. M.   'The authorship and publication of *The Copy of a letter sent by John Bradforth to the Earls of Arundel etc.*' (*Transactions of the Cambridge Bibliographical Society*, 3, ii, 1960, pp 155-60).

1390 ———   'The Press under the early Tudors'. (*Transactions of the Cambridge Bibliographical Society*, 4, i, 1964, pp 29-50).

1391 ———   'The collegiate churches of County Durham at the time of the dissolution'. (*Studies in Church History*, 4, Leyden 1967, pp 65-75).

1392 ———   *The papers of George Wyatt, Esq. of Boxley Abbey in the county of Kent, son and heir of Sir Thomas Wyatt, the younger.* [Camden Society, 4 series 5] (London, Royal Historical Society, 1968).

1393 Lockyer, R.   *Thomas Wolsey, late Cardinal. His life and death written by George*

1394 Loomie, A. J.   *Cavendish his gentleman usher* (London, The Folio Society, 1962). *Toleration and diplomacy. The religious issue in Anglo-Spanish relations 1603-1605.* [Transactions of the American Philosophical Society, new series 3, Fasc 6] (Philadelphia 1963).

1395 Lovatt, R.   '*The Imitation of Christ* in late Medieval England'. (*Transactions of the Royal Historical Society*, 5 series, 18, 1968, pp 97-121).

1396 Manning, R. B.   'Anthony Browne, 1st viscount Montague. The influence in county politics of an Elizabethan Catholic nobleman'. (*Sussex Archaeological Collection*, 106, 1968, pp 103-12).

1396a McConica, J. K.   See 1358.

1397 Masters, B. R. and Ralph, E.   *The Church book of St. Ewen's, Bristol, 1454-1584.* (Bristol, Bristol and Gloucester Archaeological Society, 1968).

1398 Mellows, W. T. and Gifford, D. H.   *Elizabethan Peterborough* [Peterborough Tudor Documents III] (Lamport Hall, Northamptonshire Record Society, 1956).

1399 Mulgrew, M. L.   *Parish register of St. Mary, Castlegate, York*, fasc 1 1604-1704 (Claremont, Leeds, Yorkshire Archaeological Society, 1970).

1400 Nattrass, M.   'Witch posts and early dwellings in Cleveland'. (*Yorkshire Archaeological Journal*, 39, 1956, pp 136-46).

1400a Newton, J.   See 1345.

1401 Norton, F. J.   'The library of Bryan Rowe, Vice-Provost of King's College'. (*Transactions of the Cambridge Bibliographical Society*, 2, iv, 1957, 339-52).

1401a Ralph, E.   See 1397.

1402 Ornstein, R.   'Marlowe and God. The tragic theology of *Dr. Faustus*'. (*Publications of the Modern Language Association*, 83, 1968, pp 1378-85).

1403 Owen, D. M. — 'Synods in the diocese of Ely in the later middle ages and the XVIth century' (*Studies in Church History*, 3, Leyden 1966, pp 217-22).

1404 ——— *The records of the Established Church in England excluding parochial records* [Archives and the user, 1] (Cambridge, British Records Association, 1970).

1404a Pantin, W. A. — See 1313.

1405 Parker, T. M. — 'Arminianism and Laudianism in XVIIth century England'. (*Studies in Church History*, 1, London, 1964, pp 20-34).

1406 Patrides, C. A. — 'Milton and the Protestant theory of the atonement' (*Publications of the Modern Language Association*, 74, 1959, pp 7-13).

1407 Pearl, V. — 'The "Royal independents" in the English civil war'. (*Transactions of the Royal Historical Society*, 5 series, 18, 1968, pp 69-96).

1408 Peckham, W. D. — *The acts of the Dean and Chapter of the Cathedral church of Chichester, 1545-1692* (Lewes, Sussex Record Society, 1959).

1409 Peters, R. — 'The notion of "the church" in the writings attributed to King James VI and I'. (*Studies in Church History*, 3, Leyden 1966, pp 223-31).

1410 Petti, A. G. — *The letters and despatches of Richard Verstegen* [Catholic Record Society, 52] (London, 1959).

1411 Porter, H. C. — 'The nose of wax. Scripture and the spirit from Erasmus to Milton'. (*Transactions of the Royal Historical Society*, 5 series, 14, 1964, pp 155-74).

1412 Purvis, J. S. — 'The literacy of the later Tudor clergy in Yorkshire' (*Studies in Church History*, 5, Leyden 1969, pp 147-65).

1413 Renold, P. — *The Wisbech stirs 1595-8*

1414 ———	*Letters of William Allen and Richard Barrett 1572-1598.* [Catholic Record Society, record series, 58] (Oxford 1967).
1415 Rhodes, D. E.	'Provost Argentine of Kings and his books'. (*Transactions of the Cambridge Bibliographical Society*, 2, ii, 1955, pp 205-15).
1416 Sabin, A.	*Registers of the church of St. Augustine the Less, Bristol 1577-1700* (Bristol and Gloucestershire Archaeological Society, 1956).
1416a Schumaker, W.	See 1318.
1417 Stanwood, P. G. and Doyle, A. I.	'Cosin's Correspondence'. (*Transactions of the Cambridge Bibliographical Society*, 5, i, 1969, pp 74-8).
1418 Stueher, M. St.	'The balanced diction of Hooker's Polity'. (*Publications of the Modern Language Association*, 71, 1956, pp 808-26).
1419 Styles, D.	*Ministers accounts of the collegiate church of St. Mary, Warwick, 1432-1485* (London, Dugdale Society, 1969).
1420 Sylvester, R. S.	*George Cavendish. The life and death of Cardinal Wolsey* [Early English Text Society] (London 1959).
1421 Talbot, C. H.	*Miscellanea – Recusant records* [Catholic Record Society, 53] (Newport 1961).
1422 ———	*Letters from the English abbots to the chapter at Citeaux, 1442-1521*, [Camden Society, 4 series, 4] (London, Royal Historical Society, 1967).
1423 Telfer, W.	*Faversham abbey and its last abbot, John Castock* (2 ed Faversham, The Faversham Society, 1966).
1424 Thomson, J. A. F.	'John Foxe and some sources for Lollard history. Notes for a critical

[Catholic Record Society, 51] (London 1958).

	appraisal'. (*Studies in Church History*, 2, London 1965, pp 251-57).
1425 Thwaite, H.	*Abstracts of Abbotside wills, 1552-1688* [Yorkshire Archaeological Society, Record series, 130] (Leeds 1968).
1426 Tildesley, N. W.	*Bushbury parish register 1560-1812* [Staffordshire parish register Society] (Willenhall, Staffs 1958).
1427 Tyler, P.	'The status of the Elizabethan parochial clergy'. (*Studies in Church History*, 4, Leyden, 1967, pp 76-97).
1428 Webb, J.	*Poor relief in Elizabethan Ipswich* (Ipswich, Suffolk Record Society, 1967).
1428a Wilson, F. R.	See 1337.
1429 Woodward, D. H.	'Thomas Fuller, the protestant divines, and Plagiary yet speaking'. (*Transactions of the Cambridge Bibliographical Society*, 4, iii, 1966, pp 201-24).
1430 Youings, J.	*Devon Monastic Lands. Calendars of particulars for grants 1536-1558* [Devon and Cornwall Record Society, new series, 1] (Exeter 1955).

SECTION 5. REVIEW ARTICLES (listed under reviewers)

(The numbers in column three refer to sections 1, 2 and 4 of this bibliography).

1431	Abbot, I. R.	304	*American Historical Review*, 61, 1955-6, pp 619-20.
1432	Abel, D.	484	*History Today*, 7, 1957, pp 344-5.
1433	——	485	*History Today*, 12, 1962, pp 368-9.
1434	Adams, B. B.	36	*Journal of English and German Philology*, 68, 1969, pp 503-6.
1435	Albright, R. W.	123	*Journal of Modern History*, 38, 1966, pp 66-7.
1436	Aldama, A. M. de	72	*Archivum Historicum Societatis Jesu*, 29, 1960, pp 419-20.
1437	Alexander, P.	177	*Renaissance News*, 17, 1964, pp 234-5.
1438	Allen, D. C.	521	*Modern Philology*, 54, 1956-7, pp 138-9.
1439	——	472	*Modern Language News*, 72, 1957, pp 382-5.
1440	——	679	*Modern Language News*, 72, 1957, pp 387-8.
1441	——	459	*Modern Language News*, 74, 1959, pp 751-3.
1442	Anglo, S.	618	*Renaissance News*, 23, 1960, pp 157-62.
1443	——	548	*Review of English Studies*, new series 14, 1963, pp 186-9.
1444	Anon	215	*Recusant History*, 8, 1965, pp 2-7.
1445	——	337	*Recusant History*, 8, 1965, pp 8-11.
1446	——	724	*Recusant History*, 8, 1966, pp 285-7.
1447	Antheunis, L.	337	*Revue d'histoire ecclésiastique*, 59, 1964, pp 949-51.
1448	Arthos, J.	170	*Renaissance News*, 15, 1962, pp 247-8.

1449	Ashley, L. R. N.	443	*Bibliothèque d'humanisme et renaissance*, 29, 1967, pp 495-7.
1450	——	545	*Bibliothèque d'humanisme et renaissance*, 30, 1968, pp 426-8.
1451	——	156	*Bibliothèque d'humanisme et renaissance*, 32, 1970, pp 476-9.
1452	Ashley, M.	585	*History Today*, 17, 1967, p 639.
1453	Ashmarth, M.	482	*Ephemerides Liturgicae*, 81, 1967, pp 505-6.
1454	Ashton, R.	285	*History*, 46, 1961, pp 136-9.
1455	——	54	*Economic History Review*, 2 series, 23, 1970, pp 392-5.
1456	Aston, M.	574	*History*, 53, 1968, pp 56-8.
1457	Aubert, R.	683	*Revue d'histoire ecclésiastique*, 60, 1965, pp 661-2.
1458	Auerbach, E.	380	*Burlington Magazine*, 106, 1964, pp 343-5.
1459	Aveling, H.	664	*Journal of Ecclesiastical History*, 20, 1969, pp 351-4.
1460	——	214	*Historical Journal*, 13, 1970, pp 172-3.
1461	Ayers, R. W.	442	*Renaissance Quarterly*, 23 1970, pp 339-42.
1462	Aylmer, G. E.	651	*History*, 44, 1959, pp 61-3.
1463	——	447	*Economic History Review*, 2 series, 14, 1961-2, pp 346-9.
1464	——	285	*Economic History Review*, 2 series, 15, 1962-3, pp 155-6.
1465	——	230	*English Historical Review*, 81, 1966, pp 783-9.
1466	Babin, M.	509	*Comparative Literature*, 18, 1966, pp 269-72.
1467	Bainton, R. H.	206	*American Historical Review*, 62, 1956-7, pp 612-13.
1468	——	123	*Journal of Ecclesiastical History*, 16, 1965, pp 243-4.
1469	——	39	*Church History*, 38, 1969, pp 123-4.
1470	Bakelants, L.	254.	*Latomus*, 15, 1956, p 615.
1471	——	128	*Latomus*, 23, 1963, pp 870-2.

1472 Baker, S. A. — 327 *Journal of English and German Philology*, 65, 1966, pp 723-7.

1473 Balfour-Melville, E. W. M. — 606 *Scottish Historical Review*, 35, 1956, pp 158-60.

1474 Ballust, La Sala — 458 *Hispania*, 23, 1963, pp 136-8.

1475 Bamber, J. E. — 113 *The Month*, new series 20, 1958, pp 182-4.

1476 Barber, A. E. — 560 *Journal of English and German Philology*, 65, 1966, pp 318-30.

1477 Barnes, T. G. — 586 *Journal of Modern History*, 37, 1965, pp 77-9.

1478 Barrois, G. A. — 565 *Theology Today*, 18, 1961, pp 108-110.

1479 Barroll, J. L. — 239 *Modern Languages Review*, 56, 1961, pp 99-100.

1480 Battenhouse, R. W. — 633 *Journal of the Bible and Religion*, 26, 1958, pp 149-50.

1481 ——— 70 *Church History*, 29, 1960, pp 362-3.

1482 ——— 510 *Renaissance News*, 16, 1963, pp 142-4.

1483 Baumer, F. L. — 206 *Journal of Modern History*, 30, 1958, pp 49-50.

1484 Bebis, C. S. — 626 *Greek Orthodox Theological Review*, 9, 1963-4, pp 285-9.

1485 Beckinsale, B. W. — 364 *History*, 55, 1970, p 256.

1486 Beer, J. B. — 487 *Modern Languages Review*, 60, 1965, pp 434-5.

1487 Beller, E. A. — 207 *American Historical Review*, 62, 1956-7, pp 383-4.

1488 Bennett, J. — 142 *Modern Languages Review*, 56, 1961, pp 588-90.

1489 ——— 265 *Modern Languages Review*, 58, 1963, pp 98-100.

1490 ——— 411 *Modern Languages Review*, 64, 1969, pp 873-5.

1491 Bennett, G. V. — 609 *Journal of Ecclesiastical History*, 10, 1959, pp 250-1.

1492 ——— 212 *Journal of Theological Studies*, new series 10, 1959, pp 448-50.

1493 ——— 305 *Church Quarterly Review*, 161, 1960, pp 500-1.

1494	———	39	*Journal of Theological Studies*, new series 20, 1969, pp 697-700
1495	Bense, W. F.	561	*Journal of English Studies*, 6, 1969, pp 100-2.
1496	Bernard Maitre, H.	360	*Bibliothèque d'humanisme et renaissance*, 32, 1970, pp 480-1.
1497	Berry, L. E.	111	*Journal of English and German Philology*, 67, 1968, pp 306-8.
1498	Bertraund, R. O.	419	*Arbor*, 39, 1958, pp 134-6.
1499	Bevington, D. M.	560	*Modern Philology*, 64, 1966, pp 335-7.
1500	Blakiston, N.	269	*Antiquaries Journal*, 42, 1962, pp 268-70.
1501	———	554	*Burlington Magazine*, 110, 1967, pp 49-50.
1502	Bock, H.	199	*Historische Zeitschrift*, 188, pp 173-7.
1503	Bony, A. H.	345	*Modern Languages Review*, 64, 1969, pp 388-90.
1504	Booty, J. E.	561	*Theological Studies*, 29, 1968, pp 335-7.
1505	———	445	*Theological Studies*, 30, 1969, pp 136-8.
1506	———	214	*Theological Studies*, 30, 1969, pp 506-7.
1507	Boseworth, G. H.	369	*Church Quarterly Review*, 159, 1958, pp 460-2.
1508	Bourde, A. J.	35	*Révue Historique*, 229, 1963, pp 443-6.
1509	———	83	*Revue Historique*, 229, 1963, pp 446-50.
1510	———	470	*Revue Historique*, 229, 1963, pp 459-63.
1511	———	458	*Revue Historique*, 229, 1963, pp 473-6.
1512	Bowker, M.	526	*Historical Journal*, 10, 1967, pp 468-70.
1513	———	512	*Journal of Ecclesiastical History*, 21, 1970, pp 187-9.
1514	Boyle, L. E.	434	*Medium Aevum*, 33, 1964, pp 227-30.
1515	———	37	*Review of English Studies*, new series 17, 1966, pp 308-9.

1516 Bradley, R. I. 1323 *Catholic Historical Review,* 54, 1968-9, pp 156-7.
1517 Bradner, L. 678 *Modern Language News,* 73, 1958, pp 58-60.
1518 ——— 239 *Modern Language News,* 75, 1960, pp 707-8.
1519 Breen, Q. 206 *Church History,* 26, 1957, pp 386-7.
1520 Breward, I. 39 *Journal of Religious History,* 5, 1968-9, pp 271-3.
1521 Brinkley, R. F. 265 *Renaissance News,* 15, 1962, pp 346-8.
1522 Brockunier, S. H. 392 *American Historical Review,* 73, 1967-8, pp 1614-15.
1523 Broderick, J. F. 304 *Theological Studies,* 17, 1956, pp 112-14.
1524 ——— 439 *Theological Studies,* 29, 1968, pp 548-9.
1525 Brodrick, J. 419 *The Month,* new series 19, 1958, pp 175-6.
1526 ——— 420 *The Month,* new series 22, 1959, pp 229-32.
1527 Brook, V. J. K. 201 *Journal of Theological Studies,* new series 15, 1964, pp 441-3.
1528 ——— 40 *Journal of Theological Studies,* new series 15, 1964, pp 443-5.
1529 ——— 94 *Journal of Theological Studies,* new series 19, 1968, pp 374-6.
1530 Brooke, C. N. L. 622 *Journal of Ecclesiastical History,* 15, 1964, pp 111-12.
1531 Brooke, R. B. 642 *Journal of Theological Studies,* new series 18, 1967, pp 260-2.
1532 Brooks, F. W. 232 *History,* 42, 1957, pp 147-8.
1533 Brown, A. 466 *Review of English Studies,* new series 10, 1959, pp 80-2.
1534 Brunner, K. 589 *Anglia,* 78, 1960, pp 372-5.
1535 ——— 72 *Historische Zeitschrift,* 192, 1961, pp 695-7.
1536 ——— 178 *Historische Zeitschrift,* 197, 1963, pp 699-701.
1537 ——— 170 *Erasmus,* 15, 1963, pp 147-50.
1538 ——— 2 *Erasmus,* 16, 1964, pp 230-3.
1539 Brush, J. W. 7 *Renaissance Quarterly,* 21, 1968, pp 67-70.

1540 Buchanan, J. N.   230 *Canadian Historical Review,* 47, 1966, pp 383-5.

1541 Bühler, C. F.   183 *Speculum,* 30, 1955, pp 648-9.

1542 ———   645 *Renaissance News,* 13, 1960, pp 154-7.

1543 Bullaugh, V. L.   105 *Renaissance News,* 14, 1961, pp 181-3.

1544 Bunce, J. E.   636 *Catholic Historical Review,* 42, 1957, pp 514-16.

1545 Burns, J. H.   486 *History Today,* 19, 1969, pp 60-1.

1546 Bush, D.   199 *Modern Language News,* 71, 1956, pp 306-9.

1547 Butterworth, R.   256 *The Heythrop Journal,* 2, 1961, pp 76-8.

1548 Byard, M. M.   619 *Renaissance Quarterly,* 23, 1970, pp 487-9.

1549 Cafiero, L.   612 *Rivista critica di storia della filosofia,* 16, 1961, pp 225-7.

1550 Cameron, J. K.   294 *Journal of Ecclesiastical History,* 19, 1968, pp 262-3.

1551 ———   486 *Scottish Historical Review,* 48, 1969, pp 184-6.

1552 Campagnola, S. à   367 *Laurentianum,* 3, 1962, p 530.

1553 Campbell, M.   140 *Renaissance News,* 14, 1961, pp 272-4.

1554 Carey, J.   348 *Renaissance Quarterly,* 20, 1967, pp 373-7.

1555 Cargill-Thompson, W. D. J.   300 *Journal of Theological Studies,* new series 20, 1969, pp 344-6.

1556 Carlson, L. H.   427 *Church History,* 34, 1965, pp 90-1.

1557 ———   348 *Church History,* 36, 1967, pp 99-100.

1558 Carsten, F. L.   469 *Historische Zeitschrift,* 183, 1957, pp 404-5.

1559 ———   144 *Historische Zeitschrift,* 183, 1957, pp 648-9.

1560 ———   12 *Historische Zeitschrift,* 190, 196 pp 655-7.

1561 Carter, A. H.   617 *Renaissance News,* 12, 1959, pp 117-19.

1562 ———	549	*Renaissance News*, 12, 1959, pp 280-2.
1563 Chadwick, O.	353	*Journal of Ecclesiastical History*, 10, 1959, pp 248-50.
1564 ———	284	*Journal of Theological Studies*, new series 11, 1960, pp 213-16.
1565 ———	105	*Journal of Ecclesiastical History*, 11, 1960, pp 247-8.
1566 Chambers, A. B.	70	*Modern Language News*, 75, 1960, pp 434-6.
1567 Chauviré, R.	144	*Revue Historique*, 217, 1957, pp 134-6.
1568 ———	423	*Revue Historique*, 217, 1957, pp 139-41.
1569 ———	469	*Revue Historique*, 217, 1957, pp 360-1.
1570 ———	606	*Revue Historique*, 217, 1957, pp 362-3.
1571 ———	446	*Revue Historique*, 217, 1957, pp 365-7.
1572 Cheney, C. R.	688	*English Historical Review*, 87, 1962, pp 713-14.
1573 Chibnall, M.	304	*Economic History Review*, 2 series 8, 1955-6, pp 477-50.
1574 Chrimes, S. B.	296	*History*, 41, 1956, pp 213-14.
1575 ———	269	*History*, 48, 1963, pp 18-27.
1576 Clancy, T. H.	1410	*Archivum Historicum Societatis Iesu*, 29, 1960, pp 176-7.
1577 ———	284	*The Month*, new series 23, 1960, pp 118-20.
1578 ———	598	*Heythrop Journal*, 8, 1967, pp 92-4.
1579 ———	455	*Manuscripta*, 12, 1968, pp 112-13.
1580 Clark, D. L.	169	*Journal of English and German Philology*, 56, 1957, pp 633-6.
1581 Clark, F.	485	*Heythrop Journal*, 4, 1963, pp 192-4.
1582 ———	626	*Heythrop Journal*, 5, 1964, pp 92-4.

1583 Clebsch, W. A. 344 *Bibliothèque d'humanisme et renaissance,* 28, 1966, pp 774-5.

1584 Coates, W. H. 141 *Journal of Modern History,* 32, 1960, pp 385-6.

1585 Coleman, D. C. 284 *Economic History Review,* 2 series 13, 1960-1, pp 113-15.

1586 ——— 228 *Economic History Review,* 2 series 14, 1961-2, pp 559-62.

1587 Colledge, E. 589 *Modern Languages Review,* 56, 1961, pp 400-1.

1588 Collinson, P. 59 *Journal of Ecclesiastical History,* 13, 1962, pp 244-5.

1589 ——— 181 *History,* 48, 1963, pp 69-71.
1590 ——— 586 *Renaissance News,* 18, 1965, pp 240-1.

1591 ——— 435 *Journal of Ecclesiastical History,* 18, 1967, pp 103-4.

1592 ——— 28 *Journal of Ecclesiastical History,* 18, 1967, pp 104-5.

1593 Cone, C. B. 86 *Manuscripta,* 10, 1966, pp 51-2.

1594 Conrad, N. 566 *Zeitschrift der Savigny – Stiftung für Rechtsgeschichte: Germanistische Abteilung,* 75, 1958, pp 395-8.

1595 Cooper, J. P. 354 *Renaissance News,* 18, 1965, pp 133-5.

1596 ——— 585 *History,* 55, 1970, pp 114-16.
1597 Cope, J. I. 521 *Modern Language News,* 71, 1956, pp 529-32.

1598 ——— 532 *Renaissance News,* 13, 1960, pp 250-2.

1599 Corish, P. J. 692 *Irish Historical Studies,* 10, 1957, pp 328-33.

1600 Costello, D. T. 105 *Manuscripta,* 5, 1961, pp 108-9.

1601 Cottle, B. 589 *Review of English Studies,* new series 12, 1961. pp 182-3.

1602 Cowan, I. B. 94 *Scottish Historical Review,* 47, 1968, pp 89-90.

1603 ——— 486 *English Historical Review,* 85, 1970, pp 579-81.

1604 Craig, H. 618 *Speculum,* 34, 1959, pp 702-5.

1605 Crane, D. J.   348 *Durham University Journal,* 59, 1966-7, p 44.

1606 Cranston, M.   468 *History Today,* 15, 1965, pp 207-9.

1607 Crawford, C.   480 *The Month,* new series 41, 1969, pp 314-16.

1608 Crehan, J.   131 *Clergy Review,* new series 44, 1959, pp 418-24.

1609 Cross, M. C.   214 *Journal of Ecclesiastical History,* 20, 1969, pp 350-1.

1610 ———   520a *Durham University Journal,* 1970-71, pp 147-8.

1611 Cuddihy, M.   86 *Thought,* 40, 1965, pp 305-7.

1612 ———   348 *Thought,* 42, 1967, pp 153-5.

1613 Cuming, G. J.   543 *Journal of Theological Studies,* new series 19, 1968, pp 681-3.

1614 Cunningham, T. W.   559 *Catholic Historical Review,* 45, 1959-60, pp 64-5.

1615 ———   458 *Catholic Historical Review,* 45, 1959-60, pp 194-5.

1616 ———   479 *Catholic Historical Review,* 51, 1965-6, pp 94-6.

1617 Curry, J. V.   177 *Thought,* 29, 1964, pp 122-4.

1618 Curtin, B.   367 *Studia Hibernica,* 4, 1964, pp 249-51.

1619 Curtis, M.   100 *Isis,* 51, 1960, pp 112-13.

1620 Dahmus, J. H.   304 *Church History,* 25, 1956, pp 286-7.

1621 ———   269 *Manuscripta,* 7, 1963, pp 41-2.

1622 Daiches, D.   199 *Review of English Studies,* new series 8, 1957, pp 305-7.

1623 Dallor, G. W.   444 *Bibliotheca sacra,* 122, 1965, pp 278-9.

1624 Daly, G.   496 *Augustiniana,* 18, 1968, pp 165-9.

1625 Dannenfeldt, K. H.   222 *Renaissance Quarterly,* 20, 1967, pp 492-3.

1626 Danner, H. W.   219 *Studia Neophilologica,* 42, 1970, pp 459-63.

1627 Dauphin, H.   641 *Revue d'histoire ecclésiastique,* 57, 1956, p 1138.

1628 ———   116 *Revue d'histoire ecclésiastique,* 52, 1957, pp 315-16.

1629 ———   172 *Revue d'histoire ecclésiastique,* 53, 1958, pp 355-6.

1630	281	*Revue d'histoire ecclésiastique,* 53, 1958, pp 526-9.
1631	419	*Revue d'histoire ecclésiastique,* 53, 1958, pp 894-8.
1632	1369	*Revue d'histoire ecclésiastique,* 54, 1959, pp 1111-12.
1633	82	*Revue d'histoire ecclésiastique,* 54, 1959, pp 110-11.
1634	121	*Revue d'histoire ecclésiastique,* 55, 1960, pp 193-8.
1635	152	*Revue d'histoire ecclésiastique,* 55, 1960, p 343.
1636	420	*Revue d'histoire ecclésiastique,* 55, 1960, pp 590-2.
1637	550	*Revue d'histoire ecclésiastique,* 55, 1960, pp 776.
1638	122	*Revue d'histoire ecclésiastique,* 55, 1960, pp 994-6.
1639	476	*Revue d'histoire ecclésiastique,* 56, 1961, pp 343-4.
1640	305	*Revue d'histoire ecclésiastique,* 56, 1961, pp 538-44.
1641	537	*Revue d'histoire ecclésiastique,* 57, 1962, pp 336-7.
1642	688	*Revue d'histoire ecclésiastique,* 57, 1962, p 714.
1643	373	*Revue d'histoire ecclésiastique,* 58, 1963, p 1082.
1644	217	*Revue d'histoire ecclésiastique,* 59, 1964, pp 741-2.
1645	269	*Revue d'histoire ecclésiastique,* 60, 1965, pp 549-52.
1646	533	*Revue d'histoire ecclésiastique,* 60, 1965, pp 696-7.
1647	26	*Revue d'histoire ecclésiastique,* 61, 1966, pp 1024-5.
1648	367	*Revue d'histoire ecclésiastique,* 61, 1966, pp 1025-7.
1649	622	*Revue d'histoire ecclésiastique,* 62, 1967, pp 112-15.
1650	574	*Revue d'histoire ecclésiastique,* 62, 1967, pp 672-3.
1651	490	*Revue d'histoire ecclésiastique,* 62, 1967, pp 677-8.

1652	———	644	*Revue d'histoire ecclésiastique*, 63, 1968, pp 315-16.
1653	———	308	*Revue d'histoire ecclésiastique*, 63, 1968, pp 1127.
1654	———	496	*Revue d'histoire ecclésiastique*, 64, 1969, pp 230-2.
1655	———	486	*Revue d'histoire ecclésiastique*, 64, 1969, pp 656-8.
1656	Davies, C. S. L.	117	*History*, 49, 1964, pp 352-3.
1657	———	512	*History*, 54, 1969, pp 31-48.
1658	———	9	*History*, 54, 1970, pp 250-1.
1659	Davies, G.	636	*American Historical Review*, 62, 1965-7, pp 118-9.
1660	Davis, H. F.	131	*Clergy Review*, new series 44, 1959, pp 407-17.
1661	Dawley, P. M.	383	*Church History*, 30, 1961, pp 117-18.
1662	Deanesley, M.	574	*Journal of Ecclesiastical History*, 17, 1966, pp 265-6.
1663	Delaissé, L. M. J.	645	*Scriptorium*, 16, 1962, pp 352-5.
1664	Delcourt, M.	560	*Latomus*, 25, 1966, pp 305-9.
1665	Delius, W.	309	*Theologische Literaturzeitung*, 88, 1963, pp 768-70.
1666	———	270	*Trierer theologische Zeitschrift*, 89, 1964, pp 438-9.
1667	———	418	*Trierer theologische Zeitschrift*, 90, 1965, pp 764-5.
1668	———	579	*Trierer theologische Zeitschrift*, 92, 1967, pp 523-4.
1669	Derrett, J. D. M.	480	*Clergy Review*, new series 54, 1969, pp 401-3.
1670	De Villiers, E.	636	*History*, 42, 1957, pp 55-6.
1671	Dickens, A. G.	61	*Journal of Ecclesiastical History*, 11, 1960, p 270.
1672	———	363	*English Historical Review*, 77, 1962, pp 331-2.
1673	———	483	*Journal of Ecclesiastical History*, 14, 1963, pp 99-101.
1674	———	626	*Past and Present*, 27, 1964, pp 123-5.
1675	———	89	*Journal of Theological Studies*, new series 17, 1966, pp 227-9.
1676	———	260	*English Historical Review*, 81, 1966, pp 583-4.

1677 ———	344	*History*, 52, 1967, pp 77-8.
1678 ———	435	*English Historical Review*, 82, 1967, pp 382-3.
1679 ———	574	*Medium Aevum*, 36, 1967, pp 299-301.
1680 Donaldson, G.	636	*English Historical Review*, 72, 1957, pp 117-20.
1681 Donner, N. W.	560	*Studia Neophilologica*, 38, 1966, pp 366-70.
1682 ———	443	*English Studies*, 49, 1968, pp 164-6.
1683 Donno, E. S.	423	*Renaissance News*, 9, 1956, pp 226-8.
1684 Doyle, A. I.	423	*Review of English Studies*, new series 9, 1958, pp 300-2.
1685 Drake, G.	418	*Church History*, 25, 1966, pp 116-17.
1686 Du Boulay, F. R. H.	269	*Journal of Ecclesiastical History*, 13, 1962, pp 237-9.
1687 ———	642	*English Historical Review*, 82, 1967, pp 376-7.
1688 Dubief, H.	230	*Revue d'histoire moderne et contemporaine*, 13, 1966, pp 163-5.
1689 Dufort, J. M.	1330	*Sciences Ecclésiastiques*, 15, 1963, pp 302-3.
1690 Du Four, R.	427	*Catholic Historical Review*, 50, 1964-5, pp 577-8.
1691 Dugmore, C. W.	146	*Journal of Ecclesiastical History*, 12, 1961, pp 245-7.
1692 ———	485	*Journal of Ecclesiastical History*, 13, 1962, pp 239-41.
1693 ———	540	*Journal of Ecclesiastical History*, 14, 1963, pp 101-3.
1694 ———	40	*History*, 49, 1964, pp 71-2.
1695 ———	89	*Journal of Ecclesiastical History*, 17, 1966, pp 129-30.
1696 ———	261	*Journal of Ecclesiastical History*, 21, 1970, pp 267-8.
1697 Durner, H. W.	559	*Review of English Studies*, new series 10, 1959, pp 301-3.
1698 Dwyer, J. G.	337	*Catholic Historical Review*, 51, 1965-6, pp 99-100.

1699	———	331	*Catholic Historical Review,* 54, 1968-9, pp 370-2.
1700	Dwyer, J. J.	116	*Clergy Review,* 41, 1956, pp 534-7.
1701	———	144	*The Month,* new series 15, 1956, pp 251-2.
1702	———	224	*Clergy Review,* new series 40, 51, 1966, pp 75-6.
1703	———	512	*The Month,* new series 23, 1968, pp 159-60.
1704	Edwards, F.	35	*The Month,* new series 23, 1960, pp 34-44.
1705	———	205	*The Month,* new series 24, 1960, pp 54-6.
1706	———	526	*The Month,* new series 25, 1960, pp 250-1.
1707	Edwards, J. G.	622	*English Historical Review,* 80, 1965, pp 340-2.
1708	Edwards, K.	90	*English Historical Review,* 85, 1970, pp 567-9.
1709	Ellis, K. L.	297a	*Durham University Journal,* 59, 1966-7, p 44.
1710	Elton, G. R.	412	*Cambridge Historical Journal,* 13, 1957, pp 187-9.
1711	———	458	*Archiv für Reformationsgeschichte,* 50, 1959, pp 283-4.
1712	———	284	*Historical Journal,* 3, 1960, pp 89-92.
1713	———	1420	*History,* 45, 1960, pp 49-50.
1714	———	285	*Historical Journal,* 4, 1961, pp 229-30.
1715	———	363	*Journal of Theological Studies,* new series 12, 1961, pp 148-50.
1716	———	383	*Journal of Ecclesiastical History,* 12, 1961, pp 109-10.
1717	———	181	*Historical Journal,* 5, 1962, pp 203-5.
1718	———	483	*English Historical Review,* 79, 1964, pp 111-14.
1719	———	1310	*Journal of Theological Studies,* new series 16, 1965, pp 254-6.
1720	———	435	*Journal of Theological Studies,* new series 17, 1966, pp 512-14.

1721	——	344	*Historical Journal*, 10, 1967, pp 137-8.
1722	——	222	*Historical Journal*, 11, 1968, pp 187-9.
1723	——	94	*Historical Journal*, 11, 1968, pp 586-8.
1724	——	512	*Historical Journal*, 12, 1969, pp 158-63.
1725	——	288	*Historical Journal*, 12, 1969, pp 702-6.
1726	——	343	*Journal of Modern History*, 42, 1970, pp 129-31.
1727	——	408	*Historical Journal*, 13, 1970, pp 343-5.
1728	——	522	*Historical Journal*, 13, 1970, pp 803-5.
1729	Emery, R. W.	304	*Speculum*, 31, 1956, pp 386-8.
1730	Enno von Gelder, H. A.	606	*Tijdschrift voor geschiedenis*, 69, 1956, pp 113-14.
1731	——	266	*Tijdschrift voor geschiedenis*, 70, 1957, pp 394-5.
1732	——	419	*Tijdschrift voor geschiedenis*, 71, 1958, pp 268-9.
1733	——	12	*Tijdschrift voor geschiedenis*, 72, 1959, pp 146-8.
1734	——	607	*Tijdschrift voor geschiedenis*, 73, 1960, pp 124-6.
1735	——	626	*Tijdschrift voor geschiedenis*, 78, 1965, pp 335-7.
1736	——	123	*Tijdschrift voor geschiedenis*, 79, 1966, pp 204-5.
1737	——	585	*Tijdschrift voor geschiedenis*, 82, 1969, pp 421-3.
1738	Espiner-Scott, J.	254	*Revue de Littérature comparée*, 34, 1960, pp 317-20.
1739	Ettlinger, L. D.	554	*History*, 55, 1970, pp 251-2.
1740	Evenett, H. O.	367	*Journal of Religious History*, 3, 1964-5, pp 181-3.
1741	Everitt, A.	1379	*Economic History Review*, 2 series 15, 1962, pp 376-7.
1742	Eusden, J. D.	353	*Renaissance News*, 13, 1960, pp 41-3.
1743	Fairclough, A. B. R.	587	*History Today*, 8, 1958, pp 659-60.

1744 Fairweather, E. R. 565 *Church History,* 30, 1961, pp 114-15.
1745 Farmer, H. 304 *Revue d'histoire ecclésiastique,* 51, 1956, pp 589-92.
1746 ——— 305 *Collectanea Ordinis Cisterciensium Reformatorum,* 22, 1960, pp 324-6.
1747 Ferguson, A. B. 526 *Renaissance News,* 19, 1966, pp 250-2.
1748 ——— 560 *Journal of the History of Ideas,* 29, 1968, pp 303-10.
1849 Ferguson, J. W. 486 *Renaissance Quarterly,* 23, 1970, pp 84-6.
1750 Ferguson, W. K. 419 *American Historical Review,* 63, 1957-8, pp 648-51.
1751 Fink, Z. S. 539 *Historical Journal,* 4, 1961, pp 323-4.
1752 Finlayson, M. G. 54 *Canadian Historical Review,* 50, 1969, pp 330-2.
1753 Fischer, H. 548 *Anglia,* 79, 1961, pp 484-7.
1754 Fisher, B. 676 *Catholic Historical Review,* 48, 1962-3, pp 249-51.
1755 ——— 586 *Catholic Historical Review,* 50, 1964-5, pp 574-5.
1756 Fixler, M. 92 *Church History,* 27, 1958, pp 278-9.
1757 ——— 510 *Church History,* 31, 1962, pp 369-70.
1758 ——— 443 *Review of English Studies,* new series 19, 1968, pp 439-40.
1759 ——— 156 *Review of English Studies,* new series 20, 1969, pp 499-501.
1760 Fletcher, H. 254 *Journal of English and German Philology,* 56, 1957, pp 266-8.
1761 Foreville, R. 580 *Revue d'histoire de l'Église de France,* 42, 1956, pp 69-71.
1762 Foster, E. R. 284 *Journal of Modern History,* 32, 1960, pp 152-3.
1763 Frank, J. 513 *Renaissance News,* 11, 1958, pp 37-9.
1764 Fraser, R. A. 548 *Journal of English and*

1765	Friedmann, R.	626	*German Philology*, 63, 1964, pp 337-41. *Church History*, 31, 1962, pp 464-6.
1766	Gabrielli, V.	639	*Rivista storica italiana*, 76, 1964, pp 813-23.
1767	——	230	*Rivista storica italiana*, 79, 1967, pp 271-6.
1768	——	512	*Rivista storica italiana*, 81. 1969, pp 190-8.
1769	Galbraith, V. H.	304	*English Historical Review*, 72, 1957, pp 104-6.
1770	——	305	*English Historical Review*, 76, 1961, pp 98-102.
1771	Gardner, H.	356	*Journal of English and German Philology*, 63, 1964, pp 780-4.
1772	Gardner, L. R.	305	*Journal of Religious History*, 1, 1960, pp 117-9.
1773	——	524	*Journal of Religious History*, 3, 1964-5, pp 361-3.
1774	Garner, R.	453	*Journal of English and German Philology*, 61, 1962, pp 184-6.
1775	——	411	*Modern Philology*, 66, 1968-9, pp 366-8.
1776	Gawlick, G.	560	*Anglia*, 85, 1967, pp 95-9.
1777	George, C. H.	40	*Archiv für Reformationsgeschichte*, 55, 1964, pp 131-2.
1778	Genzel, P.	678	*Zentralblatt für Bibliothekswesen*, 72, 1958, pp 350-4.
1779	——	645	*Zentralblatt für Bibliothekswesen*, 73, 1959, pp 213-16.
1780	Giblin, C.	367	*Archivum Franciscanum Historicum*, 57, 1964, pp 234-7.
1781	Gilbert, F.	468	*American Historical Review*, 71, 1965-6, pp 170-2.
1782	Gottfried, R.	493	*Modern Language News*, 71, 1956, pp 444-7.
1783	Gough, J. W.	468	*English Historical Review*, 81, 1966, pp 356-8.

1784 Grace, W. J. 509 *Modern Philology*, 65, 1967-8, pp 379-81.
1785 Greene, R. L. 548 *Medium Aevum*, 31, 1962, pp 220-2.
1786 Greenleaf, W. H. 230 *Historical Journal*, 8, 1965, pp 413-15.
1787 Grimm, H. J. 420 *American Historical Review*, 64, 1958-9, pp 619-21.
1788 Grundy, J. 345 *Review of English Studies*, new series 19, 1968, pp 310-11.
1789 Guggisberg, H. R. 80a *Bibliothèque d'humanisme et renaissance*, 28, 1966, pp 759-60.
1790 ——— 560 *Historische Zeitschrift*, 207, 1968, pp 114-16.
1791 ——— 230 *Historische Zeitschrift*, 207, 1968, pp 178-81.
1792 Gundersheimer, W. L. 326 *Bibliothèque d'humanisme et renaissance*, 31, 1969, pp 255-6.
1793 Gurth, D. J. 512 *Canadian Historical Review*, 50, 1969, pp 458-9.
1794 Gwynn, A. 305 *Theological Studies*, 21, 1960, pp 670-3.
1795 Habernicht, R. E. 240 *Renaissance Quarterly*, 21, 1968, pp 216-19.
1796 Hageman, H. G. 206 *Theology Today*, 15, 1958, pp 279-81.
1797 Hall, A. R. 230 *History*, 50, 1965, pp 332-7.
1798 Hall, B. 425 *Journal of Ecclesiastical History*, 10, 1959, pp 111-12.
1799 ——— 420 *Journal of Theological Studies*, new series 11, 1960, pp 110-17.
1800 ——— 94 *Journal of Ecclesiastical History*, 20, 1969, pp 144-6.
1801 Hall, G. D. G. 336 *Journal of Ecclesiastical History*, 20, 1969, pp 341-2.
1802 Hall, V. 210 *Renaissance News*, 12, 1959, pp 35-6.
1803 Haller, W. 44 *Modern Language News*, 71, 1956, pp 607-9.
1804 ——— 563 *Renaissance News*, 9, 1956, pp 219-21.

1805	———	207	*Church History*, 26, 1957, pp 295-6.
1806	———	353	*Church History*, 28, 1959, pp 438-9.
1807	———	532	*Church History*, 29, 1960, pp 364-5.
1808	———	598	*American Historical Review*, 71, 1965-6, pp 953-4.
1809	Hammermayer, L.	95	*Historisches Jahrbuch*, 81, 1962, pp 495-6.
1810	Hammerstein, N.	367	*Historische Zeitschrift*, 203, 1966, pp 398-9.
1811	Hankins, J. E.	177	*Shakespeare Quarterly*, 15, 1964, pp 231-3.
1812	Hanlon, J. D.	122	*Catholic Historical Review*, 46, 1960-1, pp 193-8.
1813	Hannah, W.	563	*The Month*, new series 16, 1956, pp 244-6.
1814	Harbison, E. H.	262	*Theology Today*, 13, 1956, pp 429-30.
1815	———	232	*Renaissance News*, 10, 1957, pp 38-40.
1816	———	419	*Renaissance News*, 11, 1958, pp 120-2.
1817	Hardison, O. B.	179	*Modern Philology*, 65, 1967-8, pp 67-70.
1818	Harièr, R.	575	*Modern Language Quarterly*, 26, 1965, pp 612-14.
1819	Harlow, C. G.	348	*Review of English Studies*, new series 20, 1969, pp 82-3.
1820	Hastings, A.	88	*Downside Review*, 75, 1957, pp 181-5.
1821	Hastings, M.	243	*Speculum*, 39, 1964, pp 317-20.
1822	Hassinger, E.	144	*Archiv für Reformationsgeschichte*, 50, 1959, pp 135-7.
1823	Havran, M. J.	313	*Catholic Historical Review*, 49, 1963-4, pp 549-50.
1824	———	229	*Catholic Historical Review*, 51, 1965-6, pp 104-6.
1825	———	224	*Manuscripta*, 10, 1966, pp 49-51.

1826	———	74	*Catholic Historical Review*, 54, 1968-9, pp 154-5.
1827	———	75	*Catholic Historical Review*, 55, 1969-70, pp 104-6.
1828	Hay, D.	387	*English Historical Review*, 71, 1956, pp 146-7.
1829	———	679	*English Historical Review*, 73, 1958, pp 289-90.
1830	———	92	*History*, 43, 1958, pp 47-8.
1831	———	421	*Renaissance Quarterly*, 22, 1969, pp 373-6.
1832	Heath, P.	42	*English Historical Review*, 84, 1969, pp 793-5.
1833	Heltzel, V. B.	493	*Renaissance News*, 9, 1956, pp 158-60.
1834	Hennell, M.	63	*Church Quarterly Review*, 165, 1964, pp 522-3.
1835	Hexter, J. H.	651	*American Historical Review*, 64, 1958-9, pp 362-3.
1836	———	420	*English Historical Review*, 74, 1959, pp 693-6.
1837	Highfield, J. R. L.	304	*Journal of Ecclesiastical History*, 7, 1956, pp 254-5.
1838	———	90	*Medium Aevum*, 39, 1970, pp 70-3.
1839	Hill, C.	199	*English Historical Review*, 71, 1956, pp 286-8.
1840	———	363	*History*, 46, 1961, pp 53-4.
1841	———	418	*Canadian Historical Review*, 45, 1964, pp 334-6.
1842	———	94	*Economic History Review*, 2 series 20, 1967, pp 389-91.
1843	———	253	*Economic History Review*, 2 series 20, 1967, pp 557-8.
1844	———	316	*History and Theory*, 6, 1967, pp 117-27.
1845	———	585	*Economic History Review*, 2 series 21, 1968, pp 183-5.
1846	Hill, R. M. T.	304	*History*, 41, 1956, pp 207-8.
1847	Hilling, N.	566	*Archiv für Katholisches Kirchenrecht*, 128, 1957-8, pp 284-5.
1848	———	567	*Archiv für Katholisches*

			Kirchenrecht, 128, 1957-8, pp 284-5.
1849	Hinnebusch, W. A.	305	*Manuscripta*, 5, 1961, pp 54-6.
1850	———	496	*Speculum*, 43, 1968, pp 537-9.
1851	Hinton, R. W. K.	96	*Historical Journal*, 5, 1962, pp 205-8.
1852	Hirsch, E. F.	206	*Review of Religion*, 22, 1957-8, pp 182-5.
1853	Hirsch, R.	679	*Renaissance News*, 10, 1957, pp 202-4.
1854	Hoar, G. A.	2	*Manuscripta*, 7, 1963, pp 182-4.
1855	Hockey, F.	146	*Revue d'histoire ecclésiastique*, 56, 1961, pp 720-1.
1856	———	1340	*Revue d'histoire ecclésiastique*, 56, 1961, pp 339-41.
1857	———	483	*Revue d'histoire ecclésiastique*, 58, 1963, pp 214-15.
1858	———	338	*Revue d'histoire ecclésiastique*, 60, 1965, pp 166-73
1859	———	642	*Revue d'histoire ecclésiastique*, 61, 1966, pp 704-5.
1860	———	81	*Revue d'histoire ecclésiastique*, 61, 1966, pp 1021-3.
1861	———	526	*Revue d'histoire ecclésiastique*, 61, 1966, pp 1023-4.
1862	———	1422	*Revue d'histoire ecclésiastique*, 63, 1968, pp 1118-19.
1863	———	512	*Revue d'histoire ecclésiastique*, 64, 1969, pp 485-8.
1864	Hodge, A.	12	*History Today*, 7, 1957, pp 791-2.
1865	———	614	*History Today*, 14, 1964, pp 591-3.
1866	Hodgins, M. M.	226	*Church Quarterly Review*, 158, 1957, pp 250-2.
1867	Hodgkinson, T.	614	*Burlington Magazine*, 107, pp 259, 60.
1868	Hohl, C. L.	489	*Catholic Historical Review*, 48, 1962-3, pp 78-9.
1869	———	37	*Manuscripta*, 9, 1965, pp 180-1.
1870	Holmes, G. A.	338	*Economic History Review*, 2 series 17, 1964-5, pp 404-7.

1871	Holmes, M.	43	*History Today*, 15, 1965, pp 284-5.
1872	Höltgen, K. J.	245	*Anglia*, 80, 1962, pp 199- 204.
1873	———	453	*Anglia*, 80, 1962, pp 342-6.
1874	———	30	*Anglia*, 81, 1963, pp 489-96.
1875	Holtzman, W.	304	*Historische Zeitschrift*, 182, 1956, pp 426-8.
1876	Homan, S. R.	544	*Journal of English and German Philology*, 67, 1968, pp 699-702.
1877	Hood, F.	199	*Church Quarterly Review*, 157, 1956, pp 230-3.
1878	Hope, N. V.	383	*Theology Today*, 18, 1961, pp 240-2.
1879	Hopper, S. R.	176	*Theology Today*, 19, 1962, pp 131-3.
1880	Hornberger, T.	654	*American Literature*, 41, 1969, pp 431-2.
1881	Horton, D.	424	*Theology Today*, 14, 1957, pp 439-41.
1882	Hoskins, W. G.	232	*Economic History Review*, 2 series 10, 1957-8, pp 142-4.
1883	Hough, G.	251a	*Durham University Journal*, 49, 1956-7, pp 37-8.
1884	Hudson, W. S.	199	*Journal of Religion*, 35, 1955, pp 260-1.
1885	Huelin, G.	262	*Church Quarterly Review*, 157, 1956, pp 505-6.
1886	———	1398	*Church Quarterly Review*, 158, 1957, p 386.
1887	Hugenholtz, F. W. M.	304	*Tijdschrift voor Geschiedenis*, 68, 1955, pp 376-7.
1888	Hughes, M. Y.	588	*Modern Language News*, 73, 1958, pp 527-32.
1889	———	311	*Modern Language News*, 76, 1961, pp 551-6.
1890	———	176	*Modern Language News*, 76, 1961, pp 650-3.
1891	Hughes, P.	692	*Catholic Historical Review*, 44, 1958, pp 176-8.
1892	———	305	*American Historical Review*, 66, 1960-1, pp 134-5.
1893	———	383	*Catholic Historical Review*, 47, 1961-2, pp 373-4.

1894	Hulme, H.	199	*American Historical Review*, 61, 1955-6, pp 113-14.
1895	———	636	*Journal of Modern History*, 29, 1957, pp 50-1.
1896	———	412	*Journal of Modern History*, 30, 1958, pp 236-40.
1897	Hunter, W. B.	562	*Modern Language News*, 72, 1957, pp 620-2.
1898	Hurstfield, J.	420	*Historical Journal*, 3, 1960, pp 92-3.
1899	———	353	*English Historical Review*, 75, 1960, pp 122-4.
1900	———	146	*English Historical Review*, 77, 1962, pp 727-31.
1901	Husain, I.	460	*Philological Quarterly*, 42, 1963, pp 570-5.
1902	Jacob, E. F.	692	*Journal of Ecclesiastical History*, 8, 1957, pp 248-9.
1903	———	419	*History*, 44, 1959, pp 53-4.
1904	———	305	*Historical Journal*, 3, 1960, pp 194-7.
1905	Jacquot, F.	158	*Revue d'historie des sciences et leurs applications*, 19, 1966, pp 70-3.
1906	James, M. E.	420	*Durham University Journal*, 53, 1960-1, pp 20-4.
1907	———	512	*Durham University Journal*, 62, 1969-70, pp 46-9.
1908	Jedin, H.	435	*Erasmus*, 18, 1966, pp 691-5.
1909	Jenkins, C.	304	*Church Quarterly Review*, 155, 1956, pp 77-80.
1910	———	1349	*Journal of Ecclesiastical History*, 9, 1958, pp 96-7.
1911	———	352	*Journal of Theological Studies*, new series 9, 1958, pp 187-9.
1912	John, E.	371	*Downside Review*, 79, 1961, pp 73-6.
1913	Johnson, E. R.	254	*Modern Philology*, 54, 1956, pp 273-5.
1914	Jones, E. D.	622	*Journal of the Historical Society of the Church in Wales*, 13, 1963, pp 20-6.
1915	Jones, J. R.	18	*Durham University Journal*, 53, 1960-1, pp 37-8.

1916 Jones, W. J. 468 *Canadian Historical Review*, 47, 1966, pp 71-3.
1917 Jordan, W. K. 226 *American Historical Review*, 63, 1956-7, pp 613-14.
1918 ——— 305 *Renaissance News*, 14, 1961, pp 24-5.
1919 Judson, M. A. 462 *American Historical Review*, 73, 1967-8, pp 134-5.
1920 Kamen, H. 421 *History*, 54, 1969, pp 270-2.
1921 Kearney, H. F. 606 *Irish Historical Studies*, 60, 1954-5, pp 475-6.
1922 ——— 229 *American Historical Review*, 70, 1964-5, pp 118-19.
1923 Kearney, E. W. 296 *Catholic Historical Review*, 43, 1957-8, pp 505-6.
1924 Kelly, N. 154 *The Clergy Review*, new series 44, 1959, pp 63-8.
1925 Kemp, E. 338 *Journal of Ecclesiastical History*, 16, 1965, pp 237-8.
1926 Kenyon, J. P. 228 *History Today*, 11, 1961, p 581.
1927 ——— 447 *Historical Journal*, 5, 1962, p 93-4.
1928 Ker, N. R. 645 *Medium Aevum*, 29, 1960, pp 144-7.
1929 Kermode, F. 44 *Review of English Studies*, new series 8, 1957, pp 201-3.
1930 ——— 450 *Modern Languages Review*, 56, 1961, pp 407-8.
1931 Kilbourn, W. 601 *Journal of Modern History*, 30, 1958, pp 393-4.
1932 Kinser, S. 421 *Canadian Historical Review*, 50, 1969, pp 221-3.
1933 Kluxen, H. 420 *Historische Zeitschrift*, 191, 1960, pp 372-3.
1934 Knight, M. 204 *Church Quarterly Review*, 158, 1957, pp 240-2.
1935 Knowles, E. B. 429 *Renaissance News*, 13, 1960, pp 166-7.
1936 ——— 337 *Renaissance News*, 17, 1964, pp 35-7.
1937 Knowles, D. 144 *Catholic Historical Journal*, 12, 1956, pp 92-4.

1938	———	123	*English Historical Review*, 81, 1966, pp 384-5.
1939	———	642	*Journal of Ecclesiastical History*, 17, 1966, pp 263-4.
1940	———	496	*English Historical Review*, 83, 1968, pp 564-6.
1941	Knox, D. B.	391	*Journal of Religious History*, 4, 1966-7, pp 352-4.
1942	Koenigsberger, H. G.	419	*English Historical Review*, 73, 1958, pp 679-85.
1943	Krodel, G. G.	574	*Historische Zeitschrift*, 205, 1967, pp 683-4.
1944	Landau, P.	336	*Historische Zeitschrift*, 210, 1970, pp 405-7.
1945	Lane, F. C.	419	*Journal of Economic History*, 19, 1959, pp 146-8.
1946	Lapeyre, H.	337	*Revue Historique*, 234, 1965, pp 460-1.
1947	Latham, R. C.	100	*English Historical Review*, 75, 1960, pp 350-2.
1948	———	302	*Journal of Ecclesiastical History*, 21, 1970, pp 364-5.
1949	Lawson, W.	26	*The Month*, new series 30, 1963, pp 353-9.
1950	Lea, K. M.	70	*Review of English Studies*, new series 12, 1961, pp 75-7.
1951	———	532	*Review of English Studies*, new series 12, 1961, pp 204-7.
1952	———	170	*Review of English Studies*, new series 14, 1963, pp 294-7.
1953	———	257	*Review of English Studies*, new series 15, 1964, pp 321-3.
1954	———	615	*Review of English Studies*, new series 16, 1965, pp 61-3.
1955	Lecler, J.	199	*Recherches de science religieuse*, 52, 1964, pp 640-2.
1956	———	626	*Recherches de science religieuse*, 52, 1964, pp 640-2.
1957	———	139	*Recherches de science religieuse*, 57, 1969, pp 298-300.
1958	———	463	*Études*, 1970, pp 628-9.
1959	Le Compte, E. S.	163	*Renaissance News*, 17, 1964, pp 133-5.

1960	Lefebvre, G.	226	*Revue Historique*, 217, 1957, pp 363-5.
1961	Leff, G.	92	*Past and Present*, 13, 1958, pp 89-95.
1962	Lehmberg, S. E.	1336	*American Historical Review*, 76, 1970-71, p 147.
1963	Levine, M.	439	*American Historical Review*, 73, 1967-8, p 807.
1964	Leishman, J. B.	646	*Review of English Studies*, new series 9, 1958, pp 82-5.
1965	———	353	*Review of English Studies*, new series 11, 1960, pp 73-5.
1966	———	142	*Review of English Studies*, new series 13, 1962, pp 303-10.
1967	Lewalski, B. K.	521	*Review of Religion*, 21, 1957, pp 198-202.
1968	———	557	*Modern Philology*, 61, 1963-4, pp 122-3.
1969	———	168	*Church History*, 35, 1966, pp 244-5.
1970	Liermann, H.	295	*Zeitschrift der Savigny-Stiftung für Rechtsgeschichte: Kanonistische Abteilung*, 75, 1958, pp 504-6.
1971	Loades, D. M.	626	*Durham University Journal*, 61, 1968-9, pp 42-3.
1972	———	681	*Durham University Journal*, 61, 1968-9, pp 166-7.
1973	———	343	*Durham University Journal*, 63, 1970-71, pp 146-7.
1974	Loane, M. L.	89	*Journal of Religion*, 46, 1966, pp 74-5.
1975	———	574	*Journal of Religion*, 46, 1966, pp 410-11.
1976	Logan, F. D.	269	*Catholic Historical Review*, 48, 1962, pp 419-20.
1977	Lohse, B.	485	*Zeitschrift für Kirchengeschichte*, 73, 1962, pp 395-8.
1978	Loomie, A. J.	586	*Thought*, 39, 1964, pp 633-4.
1979	———	512	*Thought*, 44, 1969, pp 148-50.
1980	Lovelace, R.	187	*Church History*, 39, 1970, pp 556-7.

1981 Lucki, E. 419 *Journal of Modern History*, 30, 1958, pp 241-2.

1982 Luman, R. 305 *Journal of Religion*, 42, 1962, pp 69-70.

1983 ——— 626 *Journal of Religion*, 44, 1964, pp 164-6.

1984 Lunn, D. R. 221 *Heythrop Journal*, 10, 1969, pp 440-1.

1985 Lynch, J. E. 336 *The Jurist*, 29, 1969, pp 225-8.

1986 Lyon, B. 483 *Manuscripta*, 7, 1963, pp 38-41.

1987 McCabe, J. H. 509 *Thought*, 42, 1967, pp 291-2.

1988 MacCaffrey, I. G. 450 *Modern Language News*, 76, 1961, pp 647-50.

1989 ——— 175 *Modern Language Quarterly*, 27, 1966, pp 477-80.

1990 ——— 438 *Renaissance Quarterly*, 23, 1970, pp 203-6.

1991 MacCaffrey, W. T. 412 *History*, 42, 1957, pp 232-4.

1992 ——— 161 *American Historical Review*, 63, 1957-8, pp 1039-40.

1993 ——— 501 *History*, 47, 1962, pp 307-8.

1994 ——— 512 *American Historical Review*, 74, 1968-9, pp 592-4.

1995 MacCormack, J. R. 215 *Canadian Historical Review*, 44, 1963, pp 248-9.

1996 McConica, J. K. 526 *Heythrop Journal*, 9, 1968, pp 224-5.

1997 McDermott, E. 161 *Catholic Historical Review*, 44, 1958, pp 178-9.

1998 MacDougall, D. J. 229 *Canadian Historical Review*, 46, 1965, pp 257-9.

1999 MacFarlane, K. B. 692 *English Historical Review*, 73, 1958, pp 675-9.

2000 MacFarlane, L. J. 304 *The Month*, new series 15, 1956, pp 115-17.

2001 McGrath, P. 74 *The Month*, new series 34, 1965, pp 124-5.

2001 ——— 331 *The Month*, new series 35, 1966, pp 58-9.

2002 ——— 444 *The Month*, new series 36, 1966, pp 278-9.

2003 ——— 75 *The Month*, new series 36, 1966, p 345.

2004	———	15	*The Month,* new series 37, 1967, pp 186-7.
2005	———	363	*The Month,* new series 39, 1967, pp 254-5.
2006	———	357	*History,* 55, 1970, pp 256-7.
2007	Mackie, J. D.	636	*Scottish Historical Review,* 36, 1957, pp 52-8.
2008	McKisack, M.	122	*Past and Present,* 17, 1960, pp 93-5.
2009	———	574	*Journal of Theological Studies,* new series 17, 1966, pp 505-7.
2010	McLean, G. R. D.	485	*Church Quarterly Review,* 164, 1963, pp 103-4.
2011	MacLear, J. F.	333	*Church History,* 30, 1961, pp 368-9.
2012	———	215	*Church History,* 32, 1963, pp 101-2.
2013	———	80a	*Church History,* 35, 1966, pp 368-9.
2014	McClelland, V. A.	23	*Clergy Review,* 53, 1968, pp 565-7.
2015	McLelland, T. C.	540	*Church History,* 31, 1962, pp 368-9.
2016	McNamee, M. B.	354	*Manuscripta,* 10, 1966, pp 48-9.
2017	McNeil, J. T.	181	*Theology Today,* 18, 1961, pp 374-6.
2018	———	334	*Church History,* 34, 1965, pp 217-18.
2019	———	89	*Church History,* 34, 1965, pp 356-7.
2020	McNulty, R.	488	*Renaissance Quarterly,* 21, 1968, pp 73-8.
2021	McShane, E. D.	420	*Catholic Historical Review,* 45, 1959-60, pp 189-91.
2022	Madsen, W. G.	327	*Modern Philology,* 65, 1967-8, pp 251-3.
2023	Major, J. M.	321	*Journal of English and German Philology,* 61, 1962, pp 375-7.
2024	Malatesta, E.	502	*Gregorianum,* 49, 1968, pp 211-13.
2025	Manley, F.	385	*Renaissance Quarterly,* 20, 1967, pp 252-3.

2026 Manning, B. 229 *English Historical Review*, 81, 1966, pp 358-60.

2027 Manuel, F. E. 560 *History and Theory*, 6, 1967, pp 127-30.

2028 Marc'hadour, G. 161 *Clergy Review*, new series 45, 1960, pp 11-23.

2029 ——— 1420 *Clergy Review*, new series 45, 1960, pp 11-23.

2030 ——— 615 *Revue Belge de philologie et d'historie*, 44, 1966, pp 279-81.

2031 Marenco, F. 526 *Rivista storica italiana*, 80, 1968, pp 386-95.

2032 Margolin, J. C. 573 *Bibliothèque d'humanisme et renaissance*, 26, 1964, pp 622-3.

2033 ——— 585 *Bibliothèque d'humanisme et renaissance*, 29, 1967, pp 279-80.

2034 ——— 360 *Les Etudes Philosophiques*, 2, 1970, pp 237-8.

2035 Martin, L. C. 627 *Review of English Studies*, new series 16, 1965, pp 69-70.

2036 Martinelli, R. 48 *Studi Urbinati*, 37, 1963, pp 314-18.

2037 Mathew, D. 72 *The Month*, new series 23, 1960, pp 306-8.

2038 ——— 105 *English Historical Review*, 76, 1961, pp 102-4.

2039 Mattingly, G. 470 *American Historical Review*, 66, 1960-1, pp 135-7.

2040 May, G. 364 *Erasmus*, 22, 1970, pp 782-4.
2041 Mehl, D. 443 *Anglia*, 86, 1968, pp 229-32.
2042 ——— 327 *Anglia*, 86, 1969, pp 229-32.
2043 Mertner, E. 507 *Anglia*, 79, 1961, pp 498-500.
2044 Mertzbacher, F. 336 *Archiv für Katholisches Kirchenrecht*, 137, 1968, pp 647-53.

2045 Metzger, H. 254 *Anglia*, 75, 1957, pp 478-82.
2046 Meyer, C. S. 444 *Church History*, 36, 1967, pp 89-90.

2047 Meyer, J. R. 135 *Journal of the American Academy of Religion*, 38, 1970, pp 107-9.

2048	Miles, L.	262	*Renaissance News,* 11, 1958, pp 133-8.
2049	———	270	*Philological Quarterly,* 43, 1964, pp 138-41.
2050	———	270	*Modern Languages Review,* 59, 1964, pp 257-9.
2051	Miller, E. H.	510	*Journal of English and German Philology,* 62, 1963, pp 805-6.
2052	Mitchell, A. A.	231	*History Today,* 20, 1970, pp 823-5.
2053	Mitchell, G.	88	*Irish Theological Quarterly,* 24, 1957, pp 102-5.
2054	Moeller, B.	344	*Erasmus,* 18, 1966, pp 757-60.
2055	Mols, R.	560	*Nouvelle Revue Théologique,* 88, 1966, pp 315-16.
2056	Monter, E. W.	585	*Bibliothèque d'humanisme et renaissance,* 31, 1969, pp 207-10.
2057	Morrall, J. B.	269	*Irish Historical Studies,* 13, 1962, pp 667-8.
2058	Morris, B.	586	*Journal of the History of Philosophy,* 6, 1968, pp 398-400.
2059	Morris, C.	420	*History,* 47, 1962, pp 64-6.
2060	———	42	*Medium Aevum,* 38, 1969, pp 220-2.
2061	Mosse, G. L.	153	*American Historical Review,* 64, 1958-9, pp 150-1.
2062	———	146	*Church History,* 30, 1961, pp 238-9.
2063	———	181	*American Historical Review,* 67, 1961-2, pp 106-8.
2064	Myers, A. R.	269	*History Today,* 12, 1962, p 140.
2065	Nadel, G. H.	178	*History and Theory,* 3, 1963, pp 255-61.
2066	Napier, C. J. L.	88	*Ephermerides theologicae Lovanienses,* 33, 1957, pp 381-2.
2067	Narr, W. D.	435	*Historische Zeitschrift,* 206, 1968, pp 443-5.
2068	Neill, K.	351	*Catholic Historical Review,* 44, 1958-9, pp 505-6.

2069	Neill, S.	23	*Journal of Ecclesiastical History,* 20, 1969, pp 159-62.
2070	Nelson, W.	70	*Renaissance News,* 13, 1960, pp 36-8.
2071	Nevo, R.	167	*Review of English Studies,* new series 17, 1966, pp 91-4.
2072	Newhall, R. A.	269	*American Historical Review,* 67, 1961-2, pp 1008-9.
2073	Newman, J.	547	*Renaissance News,* 12, 1959, pp 286-7.
2074	Nicholl, D.	122	*The Month,* new series 23, 1960, pp 308-10.
2075	Nicholson, R.	688	*Scottish Historical Review,* 43, 1963, pp 104-6.
2076	Norling, B.	636	*Review of Politics,* 19, 1957, pp 244-7.
2077	Norris, D.	512	*Dublin Review,* 517, 1968, pp 222-4.
2078	Novotny, A.	385	*Erasmus,* 19, 1967, pp 515-17.
2079	———	561	*Erasmus,* 20, 1968, pp 54-7.
2080	———	455	*Erasmus,* 21, 1969, pp 564-6.
2081	Nugent, D. G.	561	*Manuscripta,* 12, 1968, pp 114-15.
2082	Nuttall, G. F.	400	*Journal of Ecclesiastical History,* 9, 1958, pp 110-11.
2083	———	626	*Journal of Ecclesiastical History,* 15, 1964, pp 113-16.
2084	———	229	*Journal of Ecclesiastical History,* 16, 1965, pp 247-8.
2085	———	443	*Journal of Theological Studies,* new series 18, 1967, pp 525-8.
2086	———	253	*Journal of Ecclesiastical History,* 19, 1968, pp 129-30.
2087	———	198	*Journal of Ecclesiastical History,* 20, 1969, pp 357-9.
2088	O'Connell, M. R.	181	*Catholic Historical Review,* 47, 1961-2, pp 524-5.
2089	———	485	*Catholic Historical Review,* 48, 1962-3, pp 386-8.
2090	———	201	*Catholic Historical Review,* 50, 1964-5, pp 575-7.
2091	———	86	*Catholic Historical Review,* 50, 1964-5, pp 578-80.

2092	———	586	*Manuscripta*, 10, 1966, pp 52-3.
2093	O'Dwyer, M.	476	*Catholic Historical Review*, 47, 1961-2, pp 370-2.
2094	Offler, H. S.	336	*Journal of Theological Studies*, new series 20, 1969, pp 683-5.
2095	O'Kelly, B.	485	*Renaissance News*, 16, 1963, pp 128-30.
2096	Ong, W. J.	254	*Renaissance News*, 9, 1956, pp 206-11.
2097	Oppel, H.	559	*Anglia*, 76, 1958, pp 554-7.
2098	O'Rourke, W. J.	561	*Heythrop Journal*, 10, 1969, pp 64-6.
2099	O'Sullivan, J. F.	622	*Speculum*, 38, 1963, pp 508-11.
2100	O'Sullivan, W.	308	*Irish Historical Studies*, 16, 1968-9, pp 215-19.
2101	Owen, D.	42	*Historical Journal*, 12, 1969, pp 367-9.
2102	Pagnoul, A. M.	26	*Revue Belge de philologie et d'histoire*, 44, 1966, pp 654-7.
2103	Pallet, J. V.	60	*Bibliothèque d'humanisme et renaissance*, 27, 1965, pp 745-7.
2104	Pantin, W. A.	305	*The Dublin Review*, 484, 1960, pp 163-9.
2105	Parker, T. M.	122	*Journal of Ecclesiastical History*, 10, 1959, pp 241-2.
2106	———	353	*History*, 44, 1959, pp 57-8.
2107	———	453	*Church Quarterly Review*, 160, 1959, pp 266-8.
2108	———	305	*Journal of Ecclesiastical History*, 11, 1960, pp 242-5.
2109	———	131	*Journal of Theological Studies*, new series 12, 1961, pp 134-46.
2110	———	363	*Church Quarterly Review*, 162, 1961, pp 123-9.
2111	———	181	*Church Quarterly Review*, 163, 1962, pp 253-5.
2112	———	59	*History Today*, 13, 1963, p 135.
2113	———	485	*History*, 47, 1963, pp 66-7.
2114	———	123	*History*, 51, 1966, pp 214-15.

2115 —— 42 *Journal of Theological Studies* new series 19, 1968, pp 678-80.

2116 Parker, W. R. 169 *Modern Languages Review,* 72, 1957, pp 447-51.

2117 Parks, G. B. 247 *Renaissance News,* 18, 1965, pp 145-7.

2118 —— 80a *Renaissance News,* 19, 1966, pp 245-7.

2119 Pascal, R. 520 *Modern Languages Review,* 60, 1965, pp 593-4.

2120 Passmore, W. 337 *Downside Review,* 82, 1964, pp 262-4.

2121 —— 586 *Downside Review,* 82, 1964, pp 373-4.

2122 —— 224 *Downside Review,* 83, 1965, pp 189-91.

2123 —— 74 *Downside Review,* 83, 1965, pp 280-5.

2124 —— 435 *Downside Review,* 84, 1966, pp 339-41.

2125 —— 222 *Downside Review,* 86, 1968, pp 197-200.

2126 —— 23 *Downside Review,* 86, 1968, pp 280-5.

2127 —— 486 *Downside Review,* 87, 1969, pp 226-8.

2128 —— 1363 *Downside Review,* 88, 1970, pp 83-5.

2129 —— 30 *Renaissance News,* 16, 1963, pp 242-5.

2130 Patrides, C. A. 487 *Journal of English and Germanic Philology,* 64, 1965, pp 586-9.

2131 —— 175 *Review of English Studies,* new series 18, 1967, pp 330-2.

2132 —— 438 *Review of English Studies,* new series 21, 1970, pp 212-15.

2133 Pearl, V. 267 *History,* 55, 1970, p 263.

2134 Peipenburg, W. W. 412 *Canadian Historical Review,* 39, 1958, pp 52-4.

2135 —— 226 *Canadian Historical Review,* 39, 1958, pp 57-9.

2136 —— 227 *Canadian Historical Review,* 41, 1960, pp 58-61.

2137	Pelikan, J.	206	*Journal of Religion*, 37, 1957, p 128.
2138	Pendry, E. D.	136	*Modern Languages Review*, 65, 1970, pp 867-8.
2139	Pennington, D. H.	1347	*English Historical Review*, 71, 1956, p 490.
2140	———	206	*History Today*, 6, 1956, pp 711-12.
2141	———	226	*History*, 42, 1957, pp 236-8.
2142	———	390	*History Today*, 8, 1958, p 287.
2143	———	227	*History Today*, 9, 1959, pp 211-13.
2144	———	607	*History Today*, 9, 1959, pp 211-13.
2145	———	97	*History*, 46, 1961, pp 57-8.
2146	———	477	*History Today*, 11, 1961, pp 512-14.
2147	———	96	*History Today*, 12, 1962, pp 441-3.
2148	———	421	*English Historical Review*, 86, 1970, pp 1360-3.
2149	Petti, A. G.	430	*History*, 46, 1961, pp 248-9.
2150	Pettit, N.	198	*Catholic Historical Review*, 56, 1970-1, pp 164-7.
2151	Pilkington, R.	599	*The Wiseman Review*, 492, 1962, pp 193-5.
2152	Pincin, C.	468	*Giornale storico della letteratura italiana*, 142, 1963, pp 107-10.
2153	Pontifex, D.	221	*Downside Review*, 87, 1969, pp 314-15.
2154	Porter, H. C.	105	*Historical Journal*, 3, 1960, pp 197-9.
2155	———	485	*Journal of Theological Studies*, new series 14, 1963, pp 538-40.
2156	———	270	*Journal of Theological Studies*, new series 15, 1964, pp 437-9.
2157	———	37	*Journal of Ecclesiastical History*, 16, 1965, pp 103-4.
2158	———	344	*Canadian Historical Review*, 48, 1967, pp 382-4.
2159	———	526	*History*, 55, 1970, pp 11-12.
2160	———	94	*History*, 55, 1970, pp 460-2.
2161	Potter, G. R.	105	*Church Quarterly Review*, 161, 1960, pp 396-7.

2162 Post, G. 260 *American Journal of Legal History,* 9, 1965, pp 368-71.

2163 Poulot, É. 50 *Archives de Sociologie des Religions,* 14, 1962, pp 163-4.

2164 Powicke, M. R. 188 *American Historical Review,* 61, 1955-6, pp 382-4.

2165 Price, F. D. 1408 *English Historical Review,* 76, 1961, pp 711-12.

2166 ——— 140 *Scottish Historical Review,* 42, 1963, pp 66-8.

2167 Price, J. M. 286 *Journal of Economic History,* 23, 1963, pp 108-9.

2168 Procaccio, G. 468 *Rivista storica italiana,* 77, 1965, pp 975-82.

2169 Quinn, D. B. 668 *Irish Historical Studies,* 12, 1961, pp 283-8.

2170 ——— 146 *Irish Historical Studies,* 12, 1961, pp 288-92.

2171 ——— 145 *Irish Historical Studies,* 12, 1961, pp 288-92.

2172 ——— 140 *Irish Historical Studies,* 13, 1962-3, pp 382-5.

2173 Quinn, J. 486 *Theological Studies,* 31, 1970, pp 197-9.

2174 Rabb, T. K. 421 *American Historical Review,* 75, 1969-70, pp 478-81.

2175 Raby, F. J. E. 37 *Journal of Theological Studies,* new series 16, 1965, pp 250-2.

2176 Radinowicz, M. A. 509 *Renaissance Quarterly,* 20, 1967, pp 517-19.

2177 Ramsey, P. 419 *Economic History Review,* 2 series 12, 1960, pp 456-62.

2178 ——— 420 *Economic History Review,* 2 series 12, 1960, pp 456-62.

2179 Rapp, F. 642 *Revue d'histoire et de philosophie religieuses,* 48, 1968, pp 74-5.

2180 Rau, F. 526 *Historische Zeitschrift,* 207, 1968, pp 175-8.

2181 Rayez, A. 367 *Revue d'ascétique et de mystique,* 42, 1966, pp 100-2.

2182 Rea, W. F. 12 *The Month,* new series 19, 1958, pp 17-22.

2183 Read, C. 144 *American Historical Review*, 61, 1955-6, pp 950-2.
2184 ——— 412 *American Historical Review*, 63, 1957-8, pp 963-5.
2185 ——— 35 *Journal of Modern History*, 32, 1960, pp 154-5.
2186 Reed, A. W. 423 *Modern Languages Review*, 52, 1957, pp 412-13.
2187 Reeves, M. 92 *Medium Aevum*, 28, 1959, pp 225-9.
2188 Reidy, M. F. 239 *Catholic Historical Review*, 46, 1960-1, pp 482-3.
2189 Ribner, I. 62 *Journal of English and German Philology*, 61, 1962, pp 172-6.
2190 Rice, E. F. 559 *Archiv für Reformationsgeschichte*, 51, 1960, pp 112-13.
2191 ——— 270 *Renaissance News*, 17, pp 107-10.
2192 Richardson, C. C. 135 *Church History*, 38, 1969, pp 540-2.
2193 Richardson, H. G. 269 *English Historical Review*, 77, 1962, pp 268-70.
2194 Robbins, C. 271 *Renaissance News*, 12, 1959, pp 287-90.
2195 Roberts, J. R. 348 *Journal of English and German Philology*, 66, 1967, pp 254-7.
2196 ——— 345 *Journal of English and German Philology*, 68, 1969, pp 290-4.
2197 Robeyns, A. 37 *Bulletin de théologie ancienne et médiévale*, 9, 1964, pp 576-7.
2198 Robins, H. F. 104 *Journal of English and German Philology*, 57, 1958, pp 135-6.
2199 Robinson, M. R. 226 *Journal of Economic History*, 18, 1958, pp 98-100.
2200 Robson, W. W. 450 *Review of English Studies*, new series 13, 1962, pp 198-200.
2201 Rogers, E. F. 559 *Modern Language News*, 74, 1959, pp 340-5.

2202	———	560	*Catholic Historical Review,* 53, 1967-8, pp 446-7.
2203	Roots, I.	314	*History,* 55, 1970, p 264.
2204	Rose, E.	94	*Canadian Historical Review,* 49, 1968, pp 434-5.
2205	Ross, C. D.	129	*English Historical Review,* 74, 1959, pp 493-4.
2206	———	1349	*English Historical Review,* 74, 1959, pp 493-4.
2207	Ross, K. N.	601	*Church Quarterly Review,* 159, 1958, pp 601-2.
2208	Rossiter, A. P.	1337	*Modern Languages Review,* 52, 1957, pp 413-15.
2209	Rossiter, H.	419	*Historische Zeitschrift,* 187, 1959, pp 144-7.
2210	Rotondo, R.	626	*Rivista storica italiana,* 78, 1966, pp 103-39.
2211	Rouse, R. H.	270	*Speculum,* 39, 1964, pp 704-6.
2212	Rowse, A. L.	178	*History Today,* 12, 1962, pp 889-91.
2213	———	181	*English Historical Review,* 78, 1965, pp 326-7.
2214	———	512	*History Today,* 18, 1968, pp 585-7.
2215	———	322	*History Today,* 20, 1970, p 515.
2216	Rubini, F.	270	*Bibliothèque d'humanisme et renaissance,* 26, 1964, pp 284-7
2217	Rupp, G.	458	*Historical Journal,* 2, 1959, pp 83-5.
2218	———	122	*History,* 45, 1960, pp 141-3.
2219	———	626	*Journal of Theological Studies,* new series 15, 1964, pp 204-8.
2220	Russell, N. H.	1375	*English Historical Review,* 74, 1958, pp 491-2.
2221	St. Anthonis, S. à	434	*Collectanaea Franciscana,* 32, 1962, pp 174-5.
2222	Salmon, J. H. M.	300	*Journal of Religious History,* 4, 1966-7, pp 164-7.
2223	Saunders, J. J.	59	*Journal of Religious History,* 2, 1963, pp 259-61.
2224	Scaduto, M.	337	*Archivum Historicum Societatis Iesu,* 34, 1965, pp 145-8.

2225	———	86	*Archivum Historicum Societatis Iesu*, 35, 1966, pp 253-5.
2226	———	224	*Archivum Historicum Societatis Iesu*, 35, 1966, pp 255-6.
2227	Scheerder, J.	464	*Revue d'histoire ecclésiastique*, 56, 1961, pp 1131-2.
2228	Schepers, B. M.	565	*The Thomist*, 23, 1960, pp 607-12.
2229	Schlatter, R.	458	*Journal of Modern History*, 33, 1961, pp 59-60.
2230	Schmitter, D. M.	181	*Renaissance News*, 14, 1961, pp 301-3.
2231	Schnith, K.	269	*Historisches Jahrbuch*, 83, 1964, pp 403-5.
2232	———	243	*Historisches Jahrbuch*, 84, 1965, pp 153-5.
2233	Schoeck, R. J.	100	*The New Scholasticism*, 33, 1959, pp 387-90.
2234	———	239	*Renaissance News*, 13, 1960, pp 175-7.
2235	———	178	*Renaissance News*, 16, 1963, pp 224-6.
2236	———	676	*Journal of English and German Philology*, 62, 1963, pp 369-72.
2237	———	307	*Catholic Historical Review*, 49, 1963-4, pp 229-30.
2238	———	123	*Thought*, 40, 1965, pp 610-12.
2239	———	260	*Catholic Historical Review*, 52, 1966-7, pp 407-8.
2240	Schulin, E.	652	*Historische Zeitschrift*, 211, 1970, pp 754-6.
2241	Schultz Herbrüggen, H.	128	*Renaissance News*, 18, 1965, pp 137-9.
2242	———	168	*Modern Philology*, 63, 1965-6, pp 357-9.
2243	———	615	*Theologische Revue*, 63, 1967, pp 394-5.
2244	Schweibert, E. G.	59	*Renaissance News*, 16, 1963, pp 222-4.
2245	Schweinitz, K. de	284	*American Historical Review*, 65, 1959-60, pp 362-3.

2246	———	285	*American Historical Review*, 66, 1960-1, pp 719-20.
2247	Schweizer, J.	543	*Theologische Zeitschrift*, 24, 1968, pp 291-3.
2248	Scott-Moncrieff, G.	137	*The Month*, new series 43, pp 63-4.
2249	Seaver, P. S.	214	*Journal of Modern History*, 42, 1970, pp 236-40.
2250	Selwyn, D. G.	60	*Journal of Theological Studies*, new series 17, 1966, pp 229-32.
2251	Shapiro, I. A.	18	*Review of English Studies*, new series 13, 1962, pp 301-3.
2252	Shawcross, J. T.	443	*Renaissance Quarterly*, 20, 1967, pp 515-17.
2253	Shepherd, M. H.	60	*Journal of Religion*, 45, 1965, pp 353-4.
2254	Shils, I.	207	*Journal of Modern History*, 29, 1957, pp 122-3.
2255	Sillem, A.	565	*Revue d'histoire ecclésiastique*, 55, 1960, p 1151.
2256	Silverstein, T.	400	*Renaissance News*, 12, 1959, pp 45-7.
2257	Simms, J. G.	367	*Irish Historical Studies*, 14, 1964, pp 71-2.
2258	Simon, I.	18	*Revue Belge de philologie et d'histoire*, 39, 1961, pp 490-2.
2259	———	114	*Revue Belge de philologie et d'histoire*, 40, 1962, pp 283-6.
2260	Simon, M.	417	*Revue d'histoire et de philosophie religieuses*, 43, 1963, pp 172-92.
2261	Simpson, A.	199	*Review of Religion*, 20, 1956, pp 192-6.
2262	———	232	*Church History*, 26, 1957, pp 294-5.
2263	Sirluck, E.	199	*Modern Philology*, 53, 1955-6, pp 278-80.
2264	———	241	*Modern Philology*, 53, 1955-6, pp 280-2.
2265	———	521	*Church History*, 26, 1957, pp 189-92.
2266	———	176	*Modern Philology*, 59, 1961-2, pp 68-9.

2267	Skinner, Q.	560	*Past and Present,* 38, 1967, pp 153-68.
2268	Slavin, A. J.	344	*Renaissance News,* 19, 1966, pp 247-50.
2269	———	283	*History,* 55, 1970, pp 458-9.
2270	Smalley, B.	92	*English Historical Review,* 74, 1959, pp 101-3.
2271	Smith, A. G. R.	343	*History,* 55, 1970, p 254.
2272	Smith, L. B.	144	*Journal of Ecclesiastical History,* 7, 1956, pp 258-9.
2273	Smylie, J. H.	565	*Catholic Historical Review,* 46, 1960-1, pp 340-1.
2274	Smyth, C.	609	*Church Quarterly Review,* 160, 1959, pp 390-3.
2275	———	1316	*Church Quarterly Review,* 164, 1963, pp 386-7.
2276	———	37	*Church Quarterly Review,* 165, 1964, pp 495-501.
2277	———	524	*Church Quarterly Review,* 166, 1965, pp 362-5.
2278	———	344	*Church Quarterly Review,* 167, 1966, pp 364-5.
2279	Solt, L. F.	1307	*American Historical Review,* 71, 1965-6, pp 557-8.
2280	Southern, R. W.	304	*Journal of Theological Studies,* new series 8, 1957, pp 190-4.
2281	———	305	*Journal of Theological Studies,* new series 13, 1962, pp 469-75.
2282	Southgate, W. M.	40	*Journal of Ecclesiastical History,* 15, 1964, pp 256-8.
2283	———	214	*Journal of Modern History,* 42, 1970, pp 240-2.
2284	Sparkes, A. W.	233	*Journal of Religious History,* 3, 1964-5, pp 363-6.
2285	Sperani, C.	682	*Renaissance Quarterly,* 23, 1970, pp 459-61.
2286	Stacpoole, A.	1422	*Downside Review,* 86, 1968, pp 317-19.
2287	Steadman, J. M.	56	*Modern Language Quarterly,* 22, 1961, pp 403-5.
2288	———	441	*Philological Quarterly,* 40, 1961, pp 159-60.

2289 ——— 257 *Journal of English and German Philology*, 63, 1964, pp 516-21.

2290 ——— 647 *Archiv für das Studium der neueren Sprachen*, 201, 1964, pp 218-21.

2291 ——— 370 *Renaissance News*, 18, 1965, pp 164-7.

2292 ——— 168 *Modern Languages Review*, 63, 1968, pp 940-2.

2293 ——— 509 *Journal of English and German Philology*, 68, 1969, pp 515-17.

2294 Stearns, R. P. 612 *American Historical Review*, 64, 1958-9, pp 364-5.

2295 ——— 178 *Journal of Modern History*, 36, 1964, pp 54-5.

2296 ——— 187 *American Historical Review*, 85, 1969-70, pp 2049-50.

2297 Stein, A. 370 *Modern Language Quarterly*, 26, 1965, pp 586-600.

2298 Sternfeld, F. W. 208 *Renaissance News*, 10, 1957, pp 148-51.

2299 Stevenson, D. L. 481 *Renaissance News*, 17, 1964, pp 345-8.

2300 Stone, L. 226 *Economic History Review*, 2 series 11, 1959, pp 518-19.

2301 ——— 284 *History*, 44, 1959, pp 257-60.

2302 ——— 285 *English Historical Review*, 77, 1962, pp 327-9.

2303 ——— 140 *English Historical Review*, 77, 1962, pp 532-4.

2304 Strand, K. A. 642 *Renaissance News*, 19, 1966, pp 369-71.

2305 Straus, G. 626 *Historische Zeitschrift*, 198, 1964, pp 119-23.

2306 Strong R. 396 *Burlington Magazine*, 106, 1964, p 346.

2307 Stroup, T. B. 348 *Modern Philology*, 65, 1967-8 pp 297-9.

2308 Stupperich, R. 626 *Archiv für Reformationsgeschichte*, 56, 1965, pp 128-30.

2309 Summers, J. H. 450 *Journal of English and*

2310	Surtz, E.	239	*Journal of English and German Philology*, 61, 1962, pp 181-4.
2311	———	2	*Journal of English and German Philology*, 59, 1960, pp 732-4.
2312	Susso, G.	419	*Renaissance News*, 16, 1963, pp 17-21.
2313	Sutherland, D. W.	336	*Rivista storica italiana*, 70, 1958, pp 593-5.
2314	Svendsen, K.	450	*Speculum*, 45, 1970, pp 145-7.
2315	Syfret, R. H.	562	*Renaissance News*, 45, 1961, pp 200-3.
2316	Sykes, N.	132	*Review of English Studies*, new series 9, 1958, pp 322-4.
2317	———	226	*Church Quarterly Review*, 158, 1957, pp 382-3.
2318	———	131	*English Historical Review*, 73, 1958, pp 294-8.
2319	Sylvester, R. S.	321	*Journal of Ecclesiastical History*, 10, 1959, pp 246-8.
2320	Tabacco, G.	336	*Renaissance News*, 14, 1961, pp 178-81.
2321	Tavard, G. H.	89	*Studia monastica*, 3 series 9, 1968, pp 1224-5.
2322	Taylor, T. F.	100	*Catholic Historical Review*, 52, 1966-7, pp 257-8.
2323	Telle, E. V.	139	*Church Quarterly Review*, 160, 1959, pp 506-11.
2324	Tellecha Idigoras, J. I.	4	*Renaissance Quarterly*, 21, 1968, pp 553-5.
2325	Teter, L. E.	135	*Revista Española de derecho canónico*, 21, 1966, pp 624-5.
2326	Thielmans, M. R.	620	*Theological Studies*, 29, 1968, pp 975-7.
2327	Thomas, K.	326	*Le Moyen Age*, 75, 1969, pp 184-6.
2328	Thompson, C. R.	559	*Review of English Studies*, new series 20, 1969, pp 80-1.
2329	Thomson, S. H.	574	*Renaissance News*, 12, 1959, pp 203-8.
2330	Thomson, G. S.	493	*Speculum*, 41, 1966, pp 774-5.
			English Historical Review, 72, 1957, pp 318-20.

2331	Trapp, J. B.	560	*Renaissance News*, 19, 1966, pp 373-5.
2332	Trautz, F.	269	*Historische Zeitschrift*, 196, 1963, pp 702-6.
2333	———	495	*Theologische Literaturzeitung*, 88, 1963, pp 598-9.
2334	———	996	*Theologische Literaturzeitung*, 94, 1969, pp 921-3.
2335	Trevor-Roper, H.	140	*Journal of Ecclesiastical History*, 12, 1961, pp 247-9.
2336	———	146	*Journal of Theological Studies*, new series 12, 1961, pp 376-9.
2337	———	230	*History and Theory*, 5, 1966, pp 61-82.
2338	———	285	*Economic History Review*, 2 series 14, 1961-2, pp 138-40.
2339	Trimble, W. R.	304	*Catholic Historical Review*, 42, 1956, pp 192-3.
2340	———	226	*Catholic Historical Review*, 43, 1957-8, pp 487-8.
2341	———	206	*Review of Politics*, 20, 1958, pp 659-63.
2342	———	215	*Mid-America*, 44, 1962, pp 250-2.
2343	———	1421	*Catholic Historical Review*, 48, 1962-3, pp 79-80.
2344	———	224	*Journal of Modern History*, 38, 1966, pp 73-4.
2345	———	418	*Catholic Historical Review*, 52, 1966-7, pp 122-3.
2346	———	123	*Catholic Historical Review*, 52, 1966-7, pp 255-6.
2347	———	526	*Review of Politics*, 30, 1968, pp 107-9.
2348	———	54	*Mid-America*, 51, 1969, pp 68-9.
2349	Trinterud, L. J.	458	*Church History*, 29, 1960, pp 361-2.
2350	———	181	*Church History*, 30, 1961, pp 489-91.
2351	———	123	*Church History*, 34, 1965, pp 468-9.
2352	Tucker, M. J.	222	*American Historical Review*, 73, 1967-8, pp 272-3.

2353	Tucker, S. I.	589	*Journal of English and German Philology*, 60, 1961, pp 317-21.
2354	Tuve, R.	254	*Modern Language News*, 73, 1958, pp 206-11.
2355	Underdown, D. E.	207	*English Historical Review*, 72, 1957, pp 543-4.
2356	———	652	*American Historical Review*, 75, 1969-70, pp 2047-9.
2357	Van de Perre, H.	190	*De Gulden Passer*, 35, 1957, pp 252-3.
2358	Vann, R. T.	598	*History and Theory*, 7, 1968, pp 102-14.
2359	Villapodierna, I. à	367	*Collectanea Franciscana*, 34, 1964, pp 210-12.
2360	Vincitorio, G. L.	601	*Catholic Historical Review*, 44, 1958-9, pp 186-8.
2361	———	215	*Catholic Historical Review*, 48, 1962-3, pp 391-2.
2362	Walker, R. B.	451	*Journal of Religious History*, 3, 1964, pp 95-7.
2363	———	123	*Journal of Religious History*, 4, 1966-7, pp 161-4.
2364	Wall, E. F.	1413	*Catholic Historical Review*, 45, 1959-60, pp 386-7.
2365	Wallace, J.	96	*Journal of the History of Ideas*, 24, 1962, pp 150-4.
2366	———	370	*Journal of English and German Philology*, 26, 1965, pp 586-600.
2367	Walsh, J.	564	*Heythrop Journal*, 3, 1962, pp 190-2.
2368	———	323	*Revue d'histoire ecclésiastique*, 63, 1968, pp 1122-3.
2369	———	664	*The Month*, new series 43, 1970, pp 187-9.
2370	Walzer, M.	181	*History and Theory*, 2, 1962, pp 89-96.
2371	Warrilow, J.	576	*Revue d'histoire ecclésiastique*, 57, 1962, p 1134.
2372	Watkin, E. I.	319	*Downside Review*, 293, pp 421-4.
2373	Webber, J.	320	*Journal of English and German Philology*, 65, 1966, pp 336-9.

2374	Wendel, F.	626	*Revue d'histoire et de philosophie religieuses*, 42, 1962, pp 366-8.
2375	Wernham, R. B.	469	*English Historical Review*, 72, 1957, pp 505-7.
2376	———	412	*English Historical Review*, 75, 1960, pp 124-8.
2377	———	470	*English Historical Review*, 76, 1961, pp 501-3.
2378	Weske, D. B.	642	*Speculum*, 42, 1967, pp 768-9.
2379	Wheeler, B. M.	503	*Journal of the Bible and Religion*, 26, 1958, pp 259-60.
2380	Wheeler, G.	599	*Theological Studies*, 23, 1962, pp 678-80.
2381	White, H. C.	453	*Modern Philology*, 60, 1962-3, pp 64-6.
2382	———	37	*American Historical Review*, 70, 1964-5, pp 431-3.
2383	———	201	*Renaissance News*, 18, 1965, pp 46-52.
2384	———	30	*Journal of English and German Philology*, 64, 1965, pp 305-9.
2385	Whiteman, A.	256	*Journal of Theological Studies*, new series 14, 1963, pp 239-42.
2386	Wiatt, W. H.	575	*Journal of English and German Philology*, 65, 1966, pp 164-7.
2387	Wicksteed, S.	305	*Cîteaux*, 12, 1961, pp 99-101
2388	Wieselgren, O.	420	*Historisk Tidskrift*, 2 series 23, 1960, pp 359-61.
2389	Wigan, B.	290	*Church Quarterly Review*, 163, 1962, pp 370-2.
2390	Wiles, R. M.	525	*Renaissance News*, 11, 1958, pp 276-7.
2391	Wilkinson, B.	269	*Speculum*, 38, 1963, pp 639-41.
2392	Wilkinson, W. W. J.	206	*Catholic Historical Review*, 43, 1957, pp 340-2.
2393	Willan, T. S.	226	*Journal of Economic History*, 8, 1957, pp 111-12.
2394	Willey, B.	244	*Journal of Theological Studies*, new series 14, 1963, pp 237-9.

2395 Williams, A. 563 *Journal of Theological Studies,* new series 8, 1957, pp 208-11.
2396 Williams, D. 348 *Studia Neophilologica,* 38, 1966, pp 370-2.
2397 Williams, Glanmor 140 *History,* 46, 1961, pp 246-8.
2398 ——— 331 *Archiv für Reformationsgeschichte,* 59, 1968, pp 279-81.
2399 Williams, J. A. 1309 *The Dublin Review,* 484, 1960, pp 186-8.
2400 Williams, P. 146 *History,* 46, 1961, pp 244-6.
2401 ——— 140 *Economic History Review,* 2 series 14, 1961-2, pp 141-4.
2402 ——— 27 *Durham University Journal,* 56, 1963-4, p 44.
2403 Williamson, C. F. 265 *Studia Neophilologica,* 34, 1962, pp 341-4.
2404 ——— 627 *Studia Neophilologica,* 36, 1964, pp 189-91.
2405 Willis, G. G. 103 *Journal of Ecclesiastical History,* 21, 1970, pp 84-5.
2406 Wilson, C. 284 *English Historical Review,* 75, 1960, pp 685-7.
2407 ——— 228 *Historical Journal,* 5, 1962, pp 80-92.
2408 Wilson, E. C. 70 *Modern Philology,* 57, 1959-60, pp 269-71.
2409 Wolgast, E. 462 *Erasmus,* 20, 1968, pp 761-4.
2410 Wood, T. 294 *Journal of Theological Studies,* new series 20, 1969, pp 348-51.
2411 Wood-Legh, K. L. 42 *Downside Review,* 86, 1968, pp 315-16.
2412 Woodward, G. W. O. 1363 *Journal of the History of Religion,* 6, 1970-1, pp 79-80.
2413 Woolfe, B. P. 483 *Annali della fondazione italiana per la storia amminstrativa,* 2, 1965, pp 660-6.
2414 Woolrych, A. H. 313 *History,* 49, 1964, pp 74-5.
2415 Wright, B. A. 402 *Modern Languages Review,* 51, 1956, pp 422-3.
2416 ——— 109 *Review of English Studies,* new series 8, 1957, pp 78-94.

2417 Wright, J. N. 131 *The Month,* new series 22, 1959, pp 110-13.

2418 Wright, L. B. 668 *American Historical Review,* 65, 1959-60, pp 364-5.

2419 Yoder, J. H. 626 *Theology Today,* 20, 1963, pp 432-3.

2420 Youings, J. 305 *Economic History Review,* 2 series 13, 1960-1, pp 285-8.

2421 Zagorin, P. 586 *American Historical Review,* 70, 1964-5, pp 434-5.

2422 ——— 230 *American Historical Review,* 71, 1965-6, pp 951-3.

2423 Zuck, L. H. 420 *Church History,* 29, 1960, pp 99-100.

SECTION 6. COMPLETED THESES

2424 Abernathy, G. R. Jnr. — The English Presbyterians and the Stuart Restoration. (University of Texas); Ph.D, 1955.

2425 Addy, J. — Ecclesiastical discipline in the county of York 1559-1714, with especial reference to the Archdeacon's court. (University of Leeds); M.A., 1960.

2426 Alexander, G. M. V. — The life and career of Edmund Bonner, bishop of London, until his deprivation in 1549. (University of London); Ph.D, 1960.

2427 Allen, G. R. — The Lancashire recusants in the reigns of James I and Charles I, with special reference to the part they played in the Civil War. (University of Durham); M.A., 1958.

2428 Andriette, E. A. — The Counties of Devon and Exeter in the Civil War period 1640-1646. (University of Wisconsin); Ph.D, 1968.

2429 Anglin, J. P. — The court of the Archdeacon of Essex 1571-1609. An institutional and social study. (University of California) [Los Angeles]; Ph.D, 1965.

2430 Austin, Sister Mary Teresita — The political, economic and social aspects of Edward VI's reign, as seen through the sermons and letters of Hugh Latimer. (Michigan State University); Ph.D, 1961.

2431 Bevilacqua, A. J. — Procedure in the ecclesiastical courts of the Church of England, with its historical antecedents in Roman and decretal law. (Pont. University Gregoriana Diss. juris can.); 1956.

2432 Blackwood, B. G. — Social and religious aspects of the history of Lancashire 1635-55. (University of Oxford); B.Litt., 1956.

2433 Bohi, M. J. — Nathanial Ward, Pastor Ingeniosus 1580?-1652. (University of Illinois); Ph.D, 1959.

2434 Bossy, J. A. — Elizabethan Catholicism, the link with France. (University of Cambridge); Ph.D, 1961.

2435 Bostick, T. P. — English foreign policy 1528-1534. The diplomacy of the divorce. (University of Illinois); Ph.D, 1967.

2436 Breward, I. — The life and theology of William Perkins. (University of Manchester); Ph.D, 1963.

2437 Brooks, P. N. — Thomas Cranmer's doctrine of the sacraments. (University of Cambridge); Ph.D, 1960.

2438 Brown, M. C. — The Anglican doctrine of the church during the 17th century. (University of Durham); M.A., 1957.

2439 Brundage, J. A. — The compoti of the Bursars of Whalley Abbey, Lancashire, 1508-1536. (Fordham University); Ph.D, 1955.

2440 Capp, B. S. — The fifth monarchy men; an analysis of their origins, activities, ideas and composition. (University of Oxford); D. Phil., 1970.

2441 Cargill-Thompson, W. D. J. — The two regiments; a study of the development of the theory of the relations of church and state during the reformation, with particular reference to England. (University of Cambridge); Ph.D, 1960.

2442 Carlson, A. P. — The bishops and the Queen. A study of Puritan episcopal activity in early Elizabethan England, 1558-1566. (Princeton University); Ph.D, 1962.

2443 Carroll, P. N. — Puritanism and the wilderness. The intellectual significance of the New England frontier 1629-1675. (Northwestern University); Ph.D, 1968.

2444 Cassidy, I. — The episcopate of William Cotton, bishop of Exeter 1598-1621, with special reference to the state of the clergy and the administration of the

		ecclesiastical courts. (University of Oxford); B.Litt., 1963.
2445	Chalmers, C. D.	The archdeaconry of Leicester 1558-1625. (University of Leeds); M.A., 1963.
2446	Clancy, T. H.	Political thought of the Counter Reformation in England 1572-1615; a study of the Allen-Parsons party. (University of London) [Faculty of Economics]; Ph.D, 1960.
2447	Clouse, R. G.	The influence of John Henry Alstead on English Millenarian thought in the 17th century. (State University of Iowa); Ph.D, 1963.
2448	Cohen, A.	The Kingdom of God in Puritan thought. A study of the English puritan quest for the fifth monarchy. (Indiana University); Ph.D, 1961.
2449	Collinson, P.	The puritan classical movement in the reign of Elizabeth I. (University of London); Ph.D, 1957.
2450	Corley, J. M.	Some Elizabethan controversies about the church and the ministry. (University of Durham); M.Litt., 1960.
2451	Cosgrove, J. D.	The recusant gentry in Lancashire 1570-1642. (University of Manchester); M.A., 1964.
2452	Crowley, W. S.	Erastianism in England 1640-1662. (The University of Iowa); Ph.D, 1966.
2453	Daeley, J. I.	The episcopal administration of Matthew Parker, archbishop of Canterbury 1559-75. (University of London); Ph.D, 1967.
2454	Davidson, A.	Roman catholicism in Oxfordshire from the later Elizabethan period to the civil war. (University of Bristol); Ph.D, 1970.
2455	Davis, E. L.	The revolution in English foreign policy 1618-1624; a study in the growth of Puritan influence. (Harvard University); Ph.D, 1959.
2456	Davis, J. F.	Heresy and Reformation in the

	south east of England 1520-1559. (University of Oxford); D.Phil., 1968.
2457 Day, S. R.	Archbishop Richard Bancroft 1544-1610. (University of Oxford); D.Phil., 1956.
2458 Denholm, A. T.	Thomas Hooker, puritan teacher, 1586-1647. (The Hartford Seminary Foundation); Ph.D, 1961.
2459 Dewar, M. W.	How far was the Westminster Assembly of Divines representative of seventeenth century Anglican theology? (University of Belfast); Ph.D, 1960.
2460 Dietel, W. M.	Puritanism and Anglicanism. A study of theological controversy in Elizabethan England. (Yale University); Ph.D, 1958.
2461 Eastwood, C. C.	An investigation of the doctrine of the priesthood of all believers from the reformation to the present day. (University of London); Ph.D, 1957.
2462 Edwards, A. J.	The *sede vacante* administration of Archbishop Thomas Cranmer 1533-53. (University of London); M.Phil., 1968.
2463 Egan, W. J.	The rule of faith in St. Thomas More's controversy with William Tyndale, 1528-1533.(Pont. University Gregoriana Dissert. in Fac. theology), 1960.
2464 Elkin, R. E.	The interactions between the Irish rebellion and the English Civil Wars. (University of Illinois); Ph.D, 1961.
2465 Ellis, I. P.	Edwin Sandys and the settlement of religion in England 1558-88. (University of Oxford); B.Litt., 1962.
2466 Emerson, E. H.	Thomas Hooker and the reformed theology. The relationship of Hooker's conversion preaching to its background. (Louisiana State University); Ph.D, 1955.

2467	Esler, A. J.	The aspiring mind of the Elizabethan younger generation.(Duke University); Ph.D, 1961.
2468	Fines, J.	Heresy in the fifteenth and sixteenth centuries in the north of England. (University of Sheffield); Ph.D, 1964.
2469	Forbes, A. A.	'Faith and true allegiance' — The law and the internal security of England 1559-1714. A study of the evolution of the Parliamentary Legislation and the problem of its local administration and enforcement. (University of California) [Los Angeles]; Ph.D, 1960.
2470	Fulap, R. E.	John Frith and his relation to the origin of the reformation in England. (University of Edinburgh); Ph.D, 1956.
2471	Goheen, R. B.	The function of the Peers in early Tudor governance. (Yale University); Ph.D, 1968.
2472	Gransby, D. M.	Tithe disputes in the diocese of York 1540-1640. (University of York); M.Phil., 1968.
2473	Grun, R. E.	A study in seventeenth century English recusancy; The life and death of William Howard, Lord Stafford. (Bryn Mawr University); Ph.D, 1956.
2474	Greer, Y. C.	The place of Edmund Grindal in the Elizabethan church. (University of Cambridge); M.Litt., 1963.
2475	Haigh, C. A.	The reformation in Lancashire to 1558. (University of Manchester); Ph.D, 1969.
2476	Hamilton, C. L.	The covenanters and parliament 1640-1646; A study of Scottish relations with England during the British Civil War. (Cornell University); Ph.D, 1959.
2477	Hanlon, Sister Joseph D.	The effects of the Counter Reformation upon the English Catholics, 1603-1630. (Columbia

2478 Harper, K. J. — University); Ph.D, 1959. An introduction to the life and works of Francis Rous, puritan divine and parliamentarian 1581-1659. (University of Wales); M.A., 1960.

2479 Hawkins, E. M. — Theological and political aspects in the development of religious heterogeneity in England. A study of sixteenth and seventeenth century England. (University of Nebraska); Ph.D, 1957.

2480 Hays, R. W. — A history of the Abbey of Aberconway 1186-1537. (Columbia University); Ph.D, 1960.

2481 Head, M. C. — Pope Pius II and his relations with England. (Duke University); Ph.D, 1968.

2481 Heath, P. — The parish clergy in England 1450-1530.(University of London); M.A., 1961.

2483 Heinze, R. W. — Tudor Royal Proclamations, 1485-1533. (State University of Iowa); Ph.D, 1965.

2484 Hembry, P. M. — The bishops of Bath and Well 1535-1647; a social and economic study. (University of London); Ph.D, 1956.

2485 Hilton, J. A. — Recusancy in the diocese of Durham 1577-1625. (University of Leeds); M.Phil., 1968.

2486 Hitchcock, J. F. — Popular religion in Elizabethan England,(Princeton University); Ph.D, 1965.

2487 Hogg, I. W. — A survey of the diocese of York during the archbishoprics of Samuel Harsnett and Richard Neile, 1628-40. (University of Nottingham); M.A., 1961.

2488 Houlbrooke, R. A. — Church courts and people in the diocese of Norwich 1519-1570. (University of Oxford); D.Phil., 1970.

2489 Hudson, E. K. — Matthew Parker's contributions to

		the development of Anglican church government.(Indiana University); Ph.D, 1961.
2490	Huelin, G.	Peter Martyr and the English Reformation. (University of London); [External]; Ph.D, 1955.
2491	Hume, A. M. A.	A study of the writings of the English protestant exiles 1525-35, excluding their biblical translations. (University of London); Ph.D, 1961.
2492	Jack, S. M.	The monastic lands in Leicestershire after the dissolution of the monasteries.(University of Oxford); B.Litt., 1961.
2493	Johnston, P. F.	The life of John Bradford, the Manchester martyr c. 1510-1555. (University of Oxford); B.Litt., 1964.
2494	Jones, E. B.	The Anglican definition of the church as expounded by Bishop John Jewel. (University of St. Andrews); Ph.D, 1963.
2495	Jones, W.	The Elizabethan Church settlement in Wales. (General Theological Seminary, New York); S.T.B., 1956.
2496	Jones, W. R.	Conflict and co-operation of the royal and ecclesiastical courts in England during the later middle ages. (Harvard University); Ph.D, 1958.
2497	Kaplan, E.	Robert Recorde (c. 1510-1558). Studies in the life and work of a Tudor Scientist. (New York University); Ph.D, 1960.
2498	Keep, D. J.	Henry Bullinger and the Elizabethan Church.(University of Sheffield); Ph.D, 1970.
2499	Kelly, M. J.	Canterbury jurisdiction and influence during the episcopate of William Warham, 1503-32. (University of Cambridge); Ph.D, 1963.
2500	King, J. Jnr.	Official propaganda during the reign

2501 King, P. — Matthew Wren, bishop of Hereford, Norwich and Ely (1585-1667). (University of Bristol); M.A., 1969.

2502 Kirby, D. A. — The parish of St. Stephens, Coleman Street, London; a study in radicalism c. 1624-64. (University of Oxford); B.Litt., 1968.

2503 Kitching, C. J. — Studies in the re-distribution of collegiate and chantry property in the diocese and county of York at the dissolution. (University of Durham); Ph.D, 1970.

2504 Knox, R. B. — The ecclesiastical policy of James Ussher, archbishop of Armagh. (University of London) [External]; Ph.D, 1956.

2505 Lambert, D. — The lower clergy in Lancashire 1558-1662. (University of Liverpool); M.A., 1964.

2506 Leavy, A. P. — The theology of Herbert Thorndike 1598-1672. (University of Oxford); D.Phil., 1958.

2507 Loewen, A. L. — A survey of the correspondence of the early Tudor nobility 1492-1537. (Mississippi State University); Ph.D, 1967.

2508 Lomas, R. A. — Studies in the finance of Durham Priory in the early 16th century. (University of Durham); M.A., 1964.

2509 Lonsdale, E. L. — The episcopal administration of the diocese of Hereford 1400-1535. (University of Liverpool); M.A., 1957.

2510 Loomie, A. J. — Spain and the English catholic exiles 1580-1604. (University of London); Ph.D, 1957.

2511 Lunn, D. C. J. — The origins and early development of the revived English Benedictine congregation 1588-1647. (University of Cambridge); Ph.D, 1970.

2512 MaCauley, J. S. — Richard Montague, Caroline bishop 1575-1641. (University of Cambridge); Ph.D, 1964.

[preceding entry continued:] of Henry VIII. (Cornell University); Ph.D, 1955.

England and Wales

2513 McConica, J. K. — The continuity of humanist ideas during the English reformation to 1555. (University of Oxford); D.Phil., 1962.

2514 McDonald, E. H. — The piety of Englishmen under Henry VII, 1485-1509. (Washington University); Ph.D, 1957.

2515 MacDonald, W. W. — The early parliamentary career of John Pym. (New York University); Ph.D, 1965.

2516 McGuffie, D. S. — Archbishop Laud and the 'Via Media'. (University of Manchester); M.A., 1969.

2517 MacKaskey, R. A. — The life and thought of Balthasar Hübmaier 1485-1528. (University of Edinburgh); Ph.D, 1956.

2518 Maltby, W. S. — The Black legend in England 1558-1660. (Duke University); Ph.D, 1967.

2519 Marchant, R. A. — Puritanism and the church courts in the diocese of York 1560-1642. (University of Cambridge); Ph.D, 1956.

2520 Masek, R. — The English episcopate in the reign of Henry VII. (University of Illinois); Ph.D, 1965.

2521 Mason, R. J. — The income, administration and disposal of the monastic lands in Lancashire from the dissolution to c. 1558. (University of London); M.A., 1962.

2522 Miller, F. H. H. — The distribution of religious groups in England and Wales 1350-1550; a study in social geography. (University of London); M.Sc., 1965.

2523 Morgan, G. — Pregethau Cymraeg William Griffith (?1566-1612) ai Evan Morgan (c. 1574-1642) [The Welsh sermons of William Griffith and Evan Morgan] (University of Wales); M.A., 1969.

2524 Morgans, J. I. — The life and work of William Erbery (1604-54). (University of Oxford); B.Litt., 1968.

2525	Mott, A. D.	The Phenomenon of Ranterism in the Puritan Revolution: A study in the religion of the spirit 1640-1660. (University of California); Ph.D, 1956.
2526	Newton, J. A.	Puritanism in the diocese of York, excluding Nottinghamshire 1603-1640. (University of London) [External]; Ph.D, 1956.
2527	Niehaus, C. R.	The issue of law reform in the puritan revolution.(Harvard University); Ph.D, 1958.
2528	O'Connell, M. R.	Thomas Stapleton's critique of nascent protestantism.(Notre Dame University); Ph.D, 1959.
2529	O'Dwyer, M.	Catholic recusants in Essex c. 1580-c. 1600. (University of London); M.A., 1960.
2530	Olsen, V. H.	The concept of the church in the writings of John Foxe. (University of London); Ph.D, 1966.
2531	Orr, R. R.	Truth and authority; the development of William Chillingworth's ideas of religious toleration. (University of London); Ph.D, 1958.
2532	Owen, H. G.	The London parish clergy in the reign of Elizabeth I.(University of London); Ph.D, 1957.
2533	Paul, J. E.	Hampshire recusants in the reign of Elizabeth I. (University of Southampton); Ph.D, 1958.
2534	Peck, W. G.	The military and political career of John Dudley, Duke of Northumberland. (University of Alabama); Ph.D, 1964.
2535	Pfaff, R. W.	New liturgical observances in later medieval England. (University of Oxford); D.Phil., 1965.
2536	Pill, D. H.	The diocese of Exeter under Bishop Veysey. (University of Exeter); M.A., 1964.
2537	Platt, D. O.	The doctrine of the church in the church of England from the

		accession of Elizabeth I to the outbreak of the Civil War. (University of Cambridge); Ph.D, 1955.
2538	Poe, L. H.	The levellers and origin of the theory of natural rights.(University of Oxford); D.Phil., 1957.
2539	Porter, H. C.	Religious conflicts in Elizabethan Cambridge. (University of Cambridge); Ph.D, 1956.
2540	Prall, S. E.	Legal reform and the puritan revolution 1640-1660. (Columbia University); Ph.D, 1960.
2540	Pritchard, W. H.	Thomas Edwards (1599-1647) and theories against religious toleration. (University of Oxford); B.Litt., 1964.
2542	Pulman, M. B.	The Elizabethan Privy Council, 1568-1582. (University of California) [Berkeley]; Ph.D, 1964.
2543	Renold, P.	The Wisbech stirs 1595-1598; a critical edition of documents illustrating the conflicts among English catholics in the years preceding the appointment of George Blackwell, first archpriest. (University of London) [External]; Ph.D, 1959.
2544	Richardson, R. C.	Puritanism in the diocese of Chester to 1642. (University of Manchester); Ph.D, 1969.
2545	Roberts, J. D.	The rational theology of Benjamin Whichcote; father of the Cambridge Platonists. (University of Edinburgh); Ph.D, 1957.
2546	Roper, M.	The secular clergy in the diocese of Lincoln 1514-21. (University of Oxford); B.Litt., 1962.
2547	Rosenfield, M. C.	The disposal of the property of London monastic houses, with a special study of Holy Trinity, Aldgate. (University of London); Ph.D, 1961.
2548	Roszak, T. M.	Thomas Cromwell and the Henrician

	Reformation. (Princeton); Ph.D, 1959.
2549 Ryan, P. J.	The ecclesiology of William Laud. (University of S. Thomae de Urbe. Pars dissert. theolog.); 1964.
2550 Scarisbrick, J. J.	The Conservative Episcopate in England 1529-35. (University of Cambridge); Ph.D, 1955.
2551 Senning, C. F.	The Gondomar embassy, 1613-14; religious aspects. (University of Alabama); Ph.D, 1968.
2552 Shield, I. T.	The reformation in the diocese of Salisbury 1547-62. (University of Oxford); B.Litt., 1960.
2553 Shriver, F. H.	The ecclesiastical policy of James I; two aspects; the puritans (1603-5); the Arminians (1611-25). (University of Cambridge); Ph.D, 1967.
2554 Smith, K. L.	An archaeological analysis of MS Bodley 283. 'The Mirror of the World' produced by a publishing house of vernacular literature in mid-fifteenth century England. (University of California) [Berkeley] Ph.D, 1966.
2555 Snapp, H. F.	The interregnum bishops of the Anglican church, and the ideas of church and state in Caroline England. (Tulane University); Ph.D, 1963.
2556 Snell, L. S.	The suppression of the religious foundations of Devon and Cornwall. (University of Leicester); M.A., 1965.
2557 Solt, L. F.	Army of Saints: The religious and political ideas of the chaplains of the New Model Army 1645-1648. (Columbia University); Ph.D, 1955.
2558 Stockdale, W. H.	Richard Neile: A brief inquiry into his historical significance, 1562-1640. (New York University); Ph.D, 1958.
2559 Swan, C. M. J. F.	The introduction of the Elizabethan settlement into the universities of Oxford and Cambridge, with particular reference to the Roman Catholics

	1558-1603. (University of Cambridge); Ph.D, 1955.
2560 Thirlby, P. L.	The rise to power of William Laud 1624-1629. (University of Cambridge); M.Litt., 1960.
2561 Thomson, J. A. F.	Clergy and laity in London 1376-1531. (University of Oxford); D.Phil., 1960.
2561 Tjernagel, M. S.	Dr. Robert Barnes and Anglo-Lutheran relations, 1521-1540. (State University of Iowa); Ph.D, 1955.
2563 Tucker, A. W.	Matthew Parker and Cecil. (Ohio State University); Ph.D, 1964.
2564 Tyacke, H. R. N.	Arminianism in England, in religion and politics from 1604-1640. (University of Oxford); D.Phil., 1969.
2565 Tyler, P.	The court of High Commission in the province of York, 1561-1603. (University of Oxford); B.Litt., 1961.
2566 Tyler, P.	The ecclesiastical commission within the province of York 1562-1642. (University of Oxford); D.Phil., 1965.
2567 Walker, F. X.	The implementation of the Elizabethan statutes against recusants 1581-1603. (University of London); Ph.D, 1961.
2567 Walker, R. B.	A history of the Reformation in the archdeaconries of Lincoln and Stow 1534-94. (University of Liverpool); Ph.D, 1959.
2569 Walker, R. E.	The English General Baptists 1640-1660. (University of Manchester); Ph.D, 1969.
2570 Wark, K. R.	Elizabethan Recusancy in Cheshire. (University of Manchester); M.A., 1966.
2571 Warlick, R. K.	John Colet and Renaissance humanism. (Boston University Graduate School); Ph.D, 1965.
2572 Watts, S. J.	The county of Northumberland 1590-1635. (University of Maryland); Ph.D, 1965.

2573 Weinstein, M. F.	Jerusalem embattled. Theories of executive power in the early puritan revolution. (University of Maryland); Ph.D, 1965.
2573 Welsby, P. A.	The life and work of Bishop Lancelot Andrews 1555-1626. (University of Sheffield); Ph.D, 1958.
2575 White, B. R.	The development of the doctrine of the church among the English separatists, with special reference to Robert Browne and John Smyth. (University of Oxford); D.Phil., 1961.
2576 Williams, J. G.	The life and thought of Benjamin Whichcote. (Columbia University); Ph.D, 1964.
2577 Windsor, G.	The controversy between Roman Catholics and Anglicans from Elizabeth to the revolution. (University of Cambridge); Ph.D, 1967.
2578 Woodhouse, C. R.	Religious vitality in fifteenth century England. (University of California) [Berkeley]; Ph.D, 1963.
2579 Yost, J. K.	The Christian Humanism of the English Reformers, 1525-1555. A study in English Renaissance humanism. (Duke University); Ph.D, 1965.

SCOTLAND

compiled by

J. K. CAMERON

JOURNALS AND SOCIETY PUBLICATIONS CONSULTED

AUR	*Aberdeen University Review*	Aberdeen
	Abertay Historical Society Publications	Dundee
	Alumnus Chronicle of the University of St Andrews	St Andrews
	Ayrshire Archeological and Natural History Collections	Kilmarnock
	Bibliotheck	Glasgow
	Church Service Society Annual	Edinburgh
	College Courant	Glasgow
	Dumfriesshire and Galloway Natural History and Antiquarian Society	Dumfries
	Edinburgh University Journal	Edinburgh
	Forum for Modern Language Studies	St Andrews
	Historical Association	London
	History Today	London
IR	*Innes Review*	Glasgow
	Juridical Review	Edinburgh
	Old Edinburgh Club	Edinburgh
	Proceedings of the Society of Antiquaries of Scotland	Edinburgh
	St Andrews University Publications	Edinburgh
	Scottish Church History Society	Glasgow
	Scottish History Society	Edinburgh
ScHR	*Scottish Historical Review*	Edinburgh
	Scottish Law Times	Edinburgh
	Scottish Record Society	Edinburgh
ScS	*Scottish Studies*	Edinburgh
	Scottish Texts Society	Edinburgh
ScJTh	*Scottish Journal of Theology*	Edinburgh
	Society of the Friends of Brechin Cathedral	Arbroath
	Society of the Friends of Dunblane Cathedral	Edinburgh
	Spalding Club	Aberdeen
	Stair Society	Edinburgh
	The Stewarts	Edinburgh
	Transactions of the East Lothian Antiquarian and Field Naturalists Society	Haddington
	Transactions of the Gaelic Society of Inverness	Stirling
	Transactions of the Glasgow Archeological Society	Glasgow
	Transactions of the Scottish Ecclesiological Society	Aberdeen

SECTION 1. BOOKS AND PARTS OF BOOKS

S1	Anson, P. F.	*A Monastery in Moray: The Story of Pluscarden Priory, 1230-1948* (London 1959).
S2	Apted, M. R.	*The Painted Ceilings of Scotland 1550-1650* (Edinburgh 1966).
S3	Barclay, R. S. (ed)	*The Court Books of Orkney and Shetland 1612-13* (Edinburgh 1963).
S4	————	*The Court Books of Orkney and Shetland 1614-15* (Edinburgh 1967).
S5	Bell, H. E. and Ollard, R. L.	*Historical Essays 1600-1750: presented to David Ogg* (London 1963).
S6	Bennett, J. A. W.	*Devotional Pieces in Verse and Prose* (Edinburgh 1955).
S7	Berg, J. and Lagercrantz, B.	*Scots in Sweden* (Stockholm 1962).
S8	Beveridge, J. and Donaldson, G.	*The Register of the Privy Seal of Scotland,* 5, 1556-6, 2 parts (Edinburgh 1957).
S9	Bindoff, S. T. Hurstfield, J. and Williams, C. H.	*Elizabethan Government and Society: Essays presented to Sir John Neale* (London 1961).
S10	Bingham, C.	*The Making of a King, The Early Years of James VI and I* (London 1968).
S11	Boyd, W.	*Education in Ayshire through Seven Centuries* (London 1961).
S12	Burleigh, J. H. S.	*A Church History of Scotland* (Oxford 1960).
S13	Burnet, G.	*Holy Communion in the Reformed Church of Scotland* (Edinburgh 1960).
S14	Burns, J. H.	*Scottish Churchmen and the Council of Basle* (Glasgow 1962).
S15	Calderwood, A. B.	*The Buik of the Kirk of the Canagait 1564-1567* (Edinburgh 1961).
S16	Cameron, J. K. (ed)	*Letters of John Johnston and Robert Howie* (Edinburgh 1963).
S17	Cockburn, J. H.	*The Medieval Bishops of Dunblane and their Church* (Edinburgh/London 1959).

S18	Collinson, P.	*The Elizabethan Puritan Movement* (London 1967).
S19	Cowan, I. B.	*The Parishes of Medieval Scotland* (Edinburgh 1967).
S20	Cruden, S.	*Scottish Abbeys* (Edinburgh 1960).
S21	Dellavida, G. L.	*George Strachan: Memorials of a Wandering Scottish Scholar of the Seventeenth Century* (Aberdeen 1956).
S22	Dickinson, W. C.	*The Scottish Reformation and its Influence upon Scottish Life and Character* (Edinburgh 1960).
S23	———	*Scotland from Earliest Times to 1603: A New History of Scotland*, 1 (Edinburgh 1961, 2 ed 1965).
S23a	———	'John Knox', *Fathers of the Kirk*, pp 1-17. See S99.
S24	Donaldson, G. (ed)	*The Register of the Privy Seal of Scotland*, 6, 1567-74 (Edinburgh 1963).
S25	——— (ed)	*The Register of the Privy Seal of Scotland*, 7, 1575-80 (Edinburgh 1966).
S26	——— (ed)	*Registrum Secreti Sigilli Regum Scotorum*, 7, AD 1575-80 (Edinburgh 1965).
S27	———	*Scotland: James V – James VII: Edinburgh History of Scotland*, 3 (Edinburgh 1965).
S28	———	*The Making of the Scottish Prayer Book of 1637* (Edinburgh 1954).
S29	———	*Scotland, Church and Nation through Sixteen Centuries* (London 1960).
S30	———	*The Scottish Reformation* (Cambridge 1960).
S31	———	*Scottish Kings* (London 1967).
S31a	———	'David Lindsay', *c* 1531-1613', *Fathers of the Kirk*, pp 27-37. See S99.
S32	Dow, J.	*Ruthven's Army in Sweden and Esthonia* (Stockholm 1965).
S33	Drummond, A. L.	*The Kirk and the Continent* (Edinburgh 1956).

S33a Dunlop, A. Ian — John Spottiswoode 1565-1639, *Fathers of the Kirk*, pp 48-61. See S99.

S34 Dunlop, Annie I (ed) — *Acta Facultatis Artium Universitatis Sanctiandree 1413-1588* (Edinburgh 1964).

S35 Easson, D. E. — *Medieval Religious Houses: Scotland* (London 1957).

S36 ———— 'The Men of Faith', in *Veterum Laudes, being a tribute to the achievement of the members of St. Salvator's College during five hundred years* (Edinburgh 1950).

S37 Eeles, F. C. — *King's College Chapel, Aberdeen: Its Fittings, Ornaments and Ceremonial in the Sixteenth Century* (Edinburgh 1956).

S38 Elliott, K. (ed) — *Music of Scotland 1500-1700*, Song-texts ed H. M. Shire, *Musica Britannica*, 15 (London 1957).

S39 Fraser, A. — *Mary Queen of Scots* (London 1969).

S40 Gatherer, W. A. — *The Tyrannous Reign of Mary Stewart: George Buchanan's Account* (Edinburgh 1958).

S41 Giblin, C. (ed) — *The Irish Franciscan Mission to Scotland 1619-1646: Documents from the Roman Archives* (Dublin 1964).

S42 Gilbert, M. — *British History Atlas* (London 1968).

S42a Gullans, C. B. — See S250.

S43 Hammermayer, L. — *Deutsche Schottenklöster: Schottische Reformation, Katholische Reform und Gegenreformation in West- und Mittel-Europa 1560-1580* (Munich 1963).

S44 Hay, G. — *The Architecture of Scottish Post-Reformation Churches* (Oxford 1957).

S45 Henderson, G. A. — *The Kirk of St. Ternan, Arbuthnott: A Scottish Heritage* (Edinburgh 1962).

S46 Henderson, G. D. — *The Burning Bush: Studies in Scottish Church History* (Edinburgh 1957) pp 1-94.

S47	Horn, D. B.	*A short History of the University of Edinburgh 1556-1889* (Edinburgh 1967).
S48	Hurstfield, J.	See S9.
S49	Jacob, E. F.	*The Fifteenth Century, 1399-1485* (Oxford 1961).
S50	Jordan, W. K.	*Edward VI: The Young King* (London 1968).
S51	Ker, N. R.	*Medieval Libraries of Great Britain* (London 1964).
S52	Kingsley, J. (ed)	*William Dunbar: Poems* (Oxford 1958).
S53	Lagercrantz, B.	See S7.
S53a	Lamb, J. A.	'Samuel Rutherford 1600-61', *Fathers of the Kirk*, pp 73-84. See S99.
S54	Lamont, W. D.	*The Early History of Islay (500-1726)* (Glasgow 1967).
S55	Lee, M.	*John Maitland of Thirlestane and the Foundation of the Stewart Despotism in Scotland* (Oxford 1959).
S56	Lindsay, I. G.	*The Scottish Parish Kirk* (Edinburgh 1961).
S57	Lythe, S. G. E.	*The Economy of Scotland: 1550-1625, in its European Setting* (Edinburgh 1960).
S58	McElwee, W.	*The Wisest Fool in Christendom* (London 1958).
S58a	McEwen, J. S.	'John Erskine of Dun 1508-91', *Fathers of the Kirk*, pp 17-27. See S99.
S59	MacKenzie, A. M.	*Rival Establishments in Scotland 1560-1690* (London 1952).
S60	Mackie, J. D.	*The University of Glasgow, 1451-1951* (Glasgow 1954).
S61	———	*A History of the Scottish Reformation* (Edinburgh 1960).
S62	———	*John Knox* (London 1951).
S63	Mackie, R. L.	*King James IV of Scotland: A Brief Survey of His Life and Times* (Edinburgh 1958).
S64	———	*A Short History of Scotland*, rev G. Donaldson (Edinburgh 1962).
S65	MacNeill, D. H. (trans)	*The Art and Science of Government among the Scots: being George Buchanan's 'De Jure Regni apud Scotos'* (Glasgow 1964).

S66	McRoberts, D. (ed)	*Essays on the Scottish Reformation* (Glasgow 1962).
S67	Mathew, D.	*Scotland under Charles I* (London 1955).
S68	———	*James I* (London 1967).
S69	Mechie, S.	*The office of Lord High Commissioner* (Edinburgh 1957).
S69a	———	'Andrew Melville 1545-1622', *Fathers of the Kirk*, pp 37-48. See S99.
S70	Miller, A. C.	*Sir Henry Killigrew, Elizabethan Soldier and Diplomat* (Leicester 1963).
S71	Mitchell, W. S.	*A History of Scottish Bookbinding, 1432-1650* (Aberdeen 1955).
S72	Naiden, J. R.	*The Sphera of George Buchanan* (Philadelphia 1952).
S72a	Niven, W. D.	'Robert Leighton, 1611-84', *Fathers of the Kirk*, pp 84-94. See S99.
S73	Ollard, R. L.	See S5.
S74	Paton, H. M.	*Accounts of the Masters of Works, 1, 1529-1615* (Edinburgh 1957).
S75	Phillips, J. E.	*Images of a Queen: Mary Stuart in Sixteenth-Century Literature* (Los Angeles 1964).
S76	Pryde, G. S.	*Scotland from 1603 to the Present Day: A New History of Scotland*, 2 (Edinburgh 1962).
S77	Quinn, F.	*The Meroure of Wyssdome, by Johannes de Irlandia*, bks 3-4, vol 2 (Edinburgh 1965).
S78	Rae, T. I.	*The Administration of the Scottish Frontier, 1513-1603* (Edinburgh 1966).
S79	Rankin, W. E. K.	*The Parish Church of the Holy Trinity, St Andrews: Pre-Reformation* (Edinburgh 1955).
S80	Reid, R. C. (ed)	*Protocol Book of Mark Carruthers 1531-1561* (Edinburgh 1956).
S81	——— (ed)	*Wigtownshire Charters* (Edinburgh 1960).
S82	Ridley, J.	*John Knox* (Oxford 1968).
S83	Scarisbrick, J. J.	*Henry VIII* (London 1968).

S84	Shaw, D.	*The General Assemblies of the Church of Scotland, 1500-1600: Their Origins and Development* (Edinburgh 1964).
S85	———	*Reformation and Revolution: Essays presented to Hugh Watt* (Edinburgh 1967).
S86	Simon, J. R.	*Le Livre du Roi (The Kingis Quair) attribué à Jacques Ier d'Ecosse* (Paris 1967).
S87	Skelton, J.	*A Ballade of the Scottish Kynge* (Detroit 1969).
S88	Slavin, A. J.	*Politics and Profit. A Study of Sir Ralph Sadler* (Cambridge 1966).
S89	Smout, T. C.	*A History of the Scottish People, 1560-1830* (London 1969).
S90	Thomson, J. A. F.	*The Later Lollards, 1414-1520* (Oxford 1965).
S91	Thomson, R. L.	*The Gaelic Version of John Calvin's Catechismus Ecclesiae Genevensis* (Edinburgh 1962)
S92	Trevor-Roper, H. R.	*George Buchanan and the Ancient Scottish Constitution, EHR* suppl 3 (London 1966).
S93	Wightman, W. P. D.	*Science and the Renaissance* (Edinburgh 1962)
S94	Williams, C. H.	See S9.
S95	Willson, D. H.	*James VI and I* (London 1956).
S96	Wood, M. (ed)	*Book of Records of the Ancient Privileges of the Canongate* (Edinburgh 1956).
S97	Wood-Legh, K. L.	*Perpetual Chantries in Britain* (Cambridge 1965).
S98	Wright, R. S.	*The Kirk in the Canongate* (Edinburgh 1956).
S99	——— (ed)	*Fathers of the Kirk* (Oxford 1960).

SECTION 2. JOURNALS, PERIODICALS AND OCCASIONAL PUBLICATIONS

S100 Adamson, M. R., Burns, J. H., Anderson, W. J., McLaren, R., The Ordination of John Knox: A Symposium, *Innes Review*, 6, 1955, pp 99-106.

S101 Anderson, W. J. William Thomson of Dundee, Friar Minor Conventual, *Innes Review*, 18, 1967, pp 99-111.

S102 ——— John Knox as Registrar, *Innes Review*, 7, 1956, p 63.

S103 ——— The Protestant's Trial, *Innes Review*, 7, 1956, p 63.

S104 ——— Narratives of the Scottish Reformation, I: Report of Father Robert Abercrombie, S. J., in the year 1580, *Innes Review*, volume 7, 1956, pp 27-59.

S105 ——— Narratives of the Scottish Reformation, II: Thomas Innes on Catholicism in Scotland, *Innes Review*, 13, pp 1962, pp 112-21.

S106 ——— Narratives of the Scottish Reformation, III: Prefect Ballentine's Report, circa 1660, Part I, *Innes Review*, 8, 1957, pp 39-66.

S107 ——— Narratives of the Scottish Reformation, IV: Prefect Ballentine's Report, circa 1660, Part II, *Innes Review*, 8, 1957, pp 99-129.

S108 ——— Presbyteries Triall, *Innes Review*, 8, 1957, pp 86-90.

S109 ——— William Ballentine, Prefect of the Scottish Mission, 1653-1661, *Innes Review*, 8, 1957, pp 19-20.

S110 ——— George Buchanan's Paschal Lamb, *Innes Review*, 9, 1958, pp 139-44.

S111 ——— Nidaros and Aberdeen, *Innes Review*, 9, 1958, pp 130-4.

S112 ——— A Jesuit that calls himself Ogilvy, *Innes Review*, 15, 1964, pp 56-65, 182-5.

S113 ——— Three Sixteenth-Century Scottish Missals, *Innes Review*, 9, 1958, pp 204-9.

S114	———	Two Documents of the Scottish Reformation, 1. The "Twopenny Faith". 2. The Excommunication of Edinburgh Town Council, 1558, *Innes Review*, 10, 1959, pp 287-94.
S115	———	Rome and Scotland, 1513-1625, *Innes Review*, 10, 1959, pp 173-93.
S116	——— (ed)	Abbé Paul MacPherson's History of The Scots College, Rome, *Innes Review*, 12, 1961, pp 3-161.
S117	———	Andrew Lundy's Primer, *Innes Review*, 11, 1960 pp 39-51.
S118	———	John Knox at Dieppe, *Innes Review*, 13, 1962, p 104.
S119	———	On the early career of James Beaton II, Archbishop of Glasgow, *Innes Review*, 16, 1965, pp 221-4.
S120	———	Frater Jacobus Maxwell, Scotus, *Innes Review*, 18, 1967, pp 142-4.
S121	———	William Thomson of Dundee, Friar Minor Conventual, *Innes Review*, 18, 1967, pp 99-111.
S122	———	See S100.
S123	Anton, A. E.	Medieval Scottish Executors and the Courts Spiritual, *Juridical Review*, 67, 1955, pp 129-54.
S124	———	Handfasting in Scotland, *Scottish Historical Review*, 37, 1958, pp 89-102.
S125	Apted, M. R. and Robertson, W. N.	Late Fifteenth Century Church Paintings from Guthrie and Foulis Easter, *Proceedings of the Society of Antiquaries of Scotland*, 95, 1961-2, pp 262-79.
S126	Arbuckle, W. F.	The Gowrie Conspiracy, *Scottish Historical Review*, 36, 1957, pp 1-24, 89-110.
S127	Barkley, J. M.	'Episcopate' and 'Presbyterate' in the Anglican 'Ordinal', *Scottish Journal of Theology*, 11, 1958, pp 134-49.
S128	Batho, G. R.	The Execution of Mary, Queen of Scots, *Scottish Historical Review*, 39, 1960, pp 35-42.

S129 Baxter, J. H. — Dr. Richard Hildyard in St. Andrews 1540-1543, *The Alumnus Chronicle of the University of St. Andrews*, no 44, 1955, pp 2-10.

S130 ——— Dundee and the Reformation, *Abertay Historical Society Publications*, no 7, 1960, p 26.

S131 Black, H. M. — Archbishop Law's books in Glasgow University Library, *Bibliotheck*, 3, 1962 pp 107-21.

S132 Bonaventure, Brother — The Popular Theology of John Ireland, *Innes Review*, 13, 1962, pp 130-46.

S133 Brown, A. L. and Duncan A. A. M. — The Cathedral of Lismore, *Transactions of the Scottish Ecclesiological Society*, 15, part I, 1957, pp 41-50.

S134 Brown, A. L. — The Cistercian Abbey of Saddell, Kintyre, *Innes Review*, 20, 1969, pp 130-7.

S135 Bulloch, J. — Conformists and Nonconformists, *Transactions of East Lothian Antiquarian and Field Naturalists' Society*, 8, 1960, pp 70-84.

S136 ——— Bothans Kirk, *Transactions of East Lothian Antiquarian and Field Naturalists' Society*, 9, 1963, pp 24-40.

S137 ——— Stobo Kirk, *Church Service Society Annual*, 38, 1968, pp 27-32.

S138 Burleigh, J. H. S. — The Scottish Reforming Councils, 1549 to 1559, *Records of the Scottish Church History Society*, 11, 1955, pp 189-211.

S139 ——— The Scottish Reformation as seen in 1660 and 1760, *Records of the Scottish Church History Society*, 13, 1959, pp 241-56.

S140 Burns, C. — Curious Altar Dedication in Dunkeld, *Innes Review*, 9, 1958, pp 215-16.

S141 ——— Scottish Bishops at the General Councils of the late middle ages, *Innes Review*, 16, 1965, pp 135-9.

S142 ——— Papal Gifts to Scottish Monarchs:

		The Golden Rose and the Blessed Sword, *Innes Review*, 20, 1969, pp 150-94.
S143	Burns, J. H.	John Ireland and "The Meroure of Wyssdome", *Innes Review*, 6, 1955, pp 77-98.
S144	———	Knox and Bullinger, *Scottish Historical Review*, 34, 1955, pp 90-1.
S145	———	The Political Ideas of the Scottish Reformation, *Aberdeen University Review*, 36, 1956, pp 251-68.
S146	———	The Political Background of the Reformation, 1513-1625, *Innes Review*, 10, 1959, pp 199-236.
S147	———	Scottish Churchmen and the Council of Basle, *Innes Review*, 13, 1962, pp 3-53, 157-89.
S148	———	The Conciliarist Tradition in Scotland, *Scottish Historical Review*, 42, 1963, pp 89-104.
S149		See S100.
S150	Burrell, S. A.	The Apocalyptic Vision of the Early Covenanters, *Scottish Historical Review*, 43, 1964, pp 1-24.
S151	Cameron, J. K.	The Uproar of Religion, *Alumnus Chronicle of the University of St. Andrews*, no 50, 1959, pp 20-3.
S152	———	A St. Andrews Manuscript of Poems by John Johnston (*c.* 1565-1611), *The Aberdeen University Review*, 39, 1961, pp 230-2.
S153	———	Further information on the Life and Likeness of George Buchanan, *Scottish Historical Review*, 42, 1963, pp 135-42.
S154	Campbell, W. M.	Robert Boyd of Trochrigg, *Records of the Scottish Church History Society*, 12, 1958, pp 220-34.
S155	Cant, R. G.	The Scottish Universities in the Seventeenth Century, *Aberdeen University Review*, 43, 3, 1970, pp 223-33.
S156	Chadwick, H.	An Important Letter on Blessed

		John Ogilvie, *Innes Review*, 15, 1964, pp 182-3.
S157	Christensen, T. L.	Scoto-Danish relations in the sixteenth century: the historiography and some questions, *Scottish Historical Review*, 48, 1969, pp 80-97.
S158	———	Scots in Denmark in the sixteenth century, *Scottish Historical Review*, 49, 1970, pp 125-45.
S158a	Clouston, R. W. M.	See S241.
S159	Cockburn, J. H.	The Scottish Reformation in outline, *Society of Friends of Dunblane Cathedral*, 8, 1960, pp 51-68.
S160	———	Parochial Clergy of the Medieval diocese of Dunblane (part III), *Society of Friends of Dunblane Cathedral*, 9, 1963, pp 20-4.
S161	———	Parochial Clergy of the Medieval Diocese of Dunblane (part IV), *Society of Friends of Dunblane Cathedral*, 9(2), 1964, pp 70-5.
S162	———	Post-Reformation years of peril and uncertainty, 1560-1573, *Society of Friends of Dunblane Cathedral*, 9 (2), 1964, pp 51-64.
S163	———	Post-Reformation Clergy of Dunblane, (cont.), *Society of Friends of Dunblane Cathedral*, 9, 1965, pp 92-100.
S164	———	Post-Reformation Clergy of Dunblane, *Society of Friends of Dunblane Cathedral*, 9, 1966, pp 129-36.
S165	———	Dr. Alexander Leighton, c. 1568-1649, *Society of the Friends of Dunblane Cathedral*, 10, 1968, pp 41-3.
S166	Coutts, A.	Ninian Winzet: Abbot of Ratisbon, 1577-1592, *Records of the Scottish Church History Society*, 11, 1955, pp 240-53.
S167	Cowan, I. B.	Some Aspects of the Appropriation of Parish Churches in Medieval Scotland, *Records of the Scottish Church History Society*, 13, 1959, pp 203-22.

S168 ———	The Pre-Reformation Parish Churches of East Lothian, *Transactions of East Lothian Antiquarian and Field Naturalists' Society*, 8, 1960. pp 61-9.
S169 ———	The development of the parochial system in medieval Scotland, *Scottish Historical Review*, 40, 1961, pp 43-55.
S170 ———	The organization of Scottish secular cathedral chapters, *Records of the Scottish Church History Society*, 14, 1962, pp 19-47.
S171 ———	The Religious and the cure of souls in medieval Scotland, *Records of the Scottish Church History Society*, 14, 1963, pp 215-30.
S172 ———	The Covenanters: a revision article, *Scottish Historical Review*, 47, 1968, pp 35-53.
S173 ———	Vicarages and the cure of souls in medieval Scotland, *Records of the Scottish Church History Society*, 16, 1969, pp 111-27.
S174 ———	The Vatican Archives: a report on pre-reformation Scottish Material, *Scottish Historical Review*, 48, 1969, pp 227-42.
S175 Cruden, S.	Seton Collegiate Church, *Proceedings of the Society of Antiquaries of Scotland*, 89, 1958, pp 417-37.
S176 Dell, R. F.	The Glasgow City Archives Office, *Scottish Historical Review*, 47, 1968, pp 211-13.
S177 ———	Some Fragments of Medieval manuscripts in Glasgow City Archives, *Innes Review*, 18, 1967, pp 112-17.
S178 Dellavida, G. L.	George Strachan: Memorials of a wandering Scottish Scholar of the seventeenth century, *The Third Spalding Club*, 1956, pp 1-110.
S179 Dickinson, G. (ed)	Report by de la Brosse and D'Oysel on conditions in Scotland, 1559-1560.

S180 Dillon, W. J.   *Scottish History Society*, 3 series, 50, *Miscellany*, 9, 1958, pp 85-125.
The spittals of Ayrshire. The hospitals of Celtic and mediaeval times, *Ayrshire Archaeological and Natural History Collections*, 6, 1958-60, pp 12-42.

S181 Dilworth, M.   Two Necrologies of Scottish Benedictine Abbeys in Germany, *Innes Review*, 9, 1958, pp 173-203.

S182 ——— Prayer Book of Mary Queen of Scots, *Innes Review*, 15, 1964, pp 96-7.

S183 ——— The first Scottish monks at Ratisbon, *Innes Review*, 16, 1965, pp 180-98.

S184 ——— New light on Alexander Montgomerie, *Bibliotheck*, 4, 1966, pp 230-5.

S185 ——— Benedictine Monks of Ratisbon and Würzburg in the 17th and 18th Centuries: Emigrés from the Highlands of Scotland, *Transactions of the Gaelic Society of Inverness*, 44, (1964-6) 1967, pp 94-110.

S186 ——— Two Scottish pilgrims in Germany, *Innes Review*, 18, 1967, pp 19-24.

S187 ——— *Germania Christiana*. A Seventeenth-Century Trilogy, *Innes Review*, 18, 1967, pp 118-40.

S188 ——— Scottish Students at the Collegium Germanicum, *Innes Review*, 19, 1968, pp 15-22.

S189 ——— Book of Hours of Mary of Guise, *Innes Review*, 19, 1968, pp 77-80.

S190 Dobson, R. B.   The last English monks on Scottish soil: Coldingham priory 1461-78, *Scottish Historical Review*, 46, 1967, pp 1-25.

S191 Donaldson, G.   The Polity of the Scottish Church, 1560-1600, *Records of the Scottish Church History Society*, 11, 1955, pp 212-26.

S192 ——— Inter-Diocesan and Inter-Provincial Communication Before and After the Reformation, *Records of the Scottish Church History Society*, 12, 1958, pp 73-81.

S193	———	The Church Courts, *The Stair Society*, 20, 1958, pp 363-73.
S194	———	The Parish Clergy and the Scottish Reformation, *Innes Review*, 10, 1959, pp 5-20.
S195	———	Bishop Adam Bothwell and the Reformation in Orkney, *Records of the Scottish Church History Society*, 13, 1959, pp 85-100.
S196	———	'Flitting Friday' the Beggars' Summons and Knox's Sermon at Perth, *Scottish Historical Review*, 39, 1960, pp 175-6.
S197	———	Scottish Presbyterian exiles in England 1584-8, *Records of the Scottish Church History Society*, 14, 1962, pp 67-80.
S198	——— (ed)	A Scottish Liturgy of the reign of James VI, *Scottish History Society*, 4 series, 2, *Miscellany*, 10, 1965, pp 87-117.
S199	———	Map of the Siege of Leith, 1560, *The Book of the Old Edinburgh Club*, 32, 1966, pp 1-7.
S200	———	The rights of the Scottish Crown in episcopal vacancies, *Scottish Historical Review*, 45, 1966, pp 27-35.
S201	Donaldson, R.	Henry Danskin's *De Remoris*: a Bio-Bibliographical note, *Bibliotheck*, 1, 1957, pp 15-25.
S202	Donn, T. M.	The Scots Gaelic Bible and its Historical Background, *Transactions of the Gaelic Society of Inverness*, 43, 1966, pp 335-56.
S203	Doughty, D. W.	Notes on the provenance of books belonging to Lord James Stewart, afterwards the Regent Moray, *Bibliotheck*, 3, 1961, pp 75-88.
S204	Dow, J.	Scottish Trade with Sweden, 1512-80, 1580-1622, *Scottish Historical Review*, 48, 1969, pp 64-79, 124-50.
S204a	Duncan, A. A. M.	See S133.
S205	Dunlop, A. Ian	The Polity of the Scottish Church 1600-1637, *Records of the Scottish*

S206 Dunlop, Annie I.   *Church History Society,* 12, 1958, pp 161-84.
Remissions and indulgences in fifteenth-century Scotland, *Records of the Scottish Church History Society,* 15, 1966, pp 153-67.

S207 ——— Note on the Grey Friars at Kirkcudbright, *Transactions of the Dumfriesshire and Galloway Natural History and Antiquarian Society,* 35, 1958, pp 127-9.

S208 Durkan, J. Relic of Blessed John Ogilvie, *Innes Review,* 6, 1955, pp 148-9.

S209 ——— Hospital Scholars in the Middle Ages, *Innes Review,* 13, 1956, pp 125-7.

S210 ——— The Dominicans at the Reformation, *Innes Review,* 9, 1958, pp 216-17.

S211 ——— and Ross A. Early Scottish Libraries, *Innes Review,* 9, 1958, pp 5-167.

S212 ——— St. Salvator's College, Castle Inventory, *Innes Review,* 16, 1965, pp 128-30.

S213 ——— Buchanan's Judaising Practices, *Innes Review,* 15, 1964, pp 185-7.

S214 ——— Some local Heretics, *Transactions of the Dumfries and Galloway Natural History and Antiquarian Society,* 36, 1959, pp 67-77.

S215 ——— Education in the Century of the Reformation, *Innes Review,* 10, 1959, pp 67-90.

S216 ——— Care of the Poor: Pre-Reformation Hospitals, *Innes Review,* 10, 1959, pp 268-80.

S217 ——— The Cultural Background in Sixteenth-Century Scotland, *Innes Review,* 10, 1959, pp 382-439.

S218 ——— Henry Scrimgeour, Fugger Librarian: A biographical Note, *Bibliotheck,* 3, 1960, pp 68-70.

S219 ——— The Library of St. Salvator's College, St. Andrews, *Bibliotheck,* 3, 1961, pp 97-100.

S220 ———	An Arbroath Book Inventory of 1473, *Bibliotheck,* 3, 1961, pp 144-6.
S221 ———	Paisley Abbey and Glasgow Archives: Some New Directions, *Innes Review,* 13, 1962, pp 46-53.
S222 ———	Alexander Dickson and S. T. C. 6823, *Bibliotheck,* 3, 1962, pp 183-90.
S223 ———	Cardinal Farnese and a Possible Scots Livy Original, *Innes Review,* 13, 1962, p 74.
S224 ———	The Sanctuary and College of Tain, *Innes Review,* 13, 1962, pp 147-56.
S225 ———	Foundation of the Collegiate Church of Seton, *Innes Review,* 13, 1962, pp 71-6.
S226 ———	Scots at the Franciscan General Chapter in Lisbon, *Innes Review,* 13, 1962, pp 218-19.
S227 ———	A Note on Scottish Medieval Hospitals, *Innes Review,* 13, 1962, pp 217-18.
S228 ———	St. Andrews University Medieval Theological Statutes: Revised Dating Suggested, *Innes Review,* 13, 1962, pp 104-8.
S229 ———	David Lowis or Lauxius of Edinburgh, *Bibliotheck,* 4, 1965, pp 200-1, [A Scottish schoolmaster in France, 1496-1539].
S230 ———	Three Manuscripts with Fife Associations: and David Colville of Fife, *Innes Review,* 20, 1969, pp 47-58.
S231 ———	David Colville: An Appendix, *Innes Review,* 20, 1969, pp 138-49.
S232 ———	George Buchanan: some French connections, in *Bibliotheck,* 4, 1965, pp 66-72.
S233 ———	Two Jesuits: Patrick Anderson and John Ogilvie, *Innes Review,* 21, 1970, pp 157-61.
S234 ———	John Ogilvie's Glasgow Associates,

	Innes Review, 21, 1970, pp 153-6.
S235 ———	The Career of John Brown, Minim, *Innes Review*, 21, 1970, pp 164-70.
S236 ———	A Minim's Obituary, *Innes Review*, 21, 1970, pp 161-3.
S237 ———	John Francis Maitland, Minim, *Innes Review*, 21, 1970, pp 163-4.
S238 Easson, D. E. (ed)	Map of Monastic Britain — North Sheet, (Ordnance Survey) 1950, and second edition 1954.
S239 ———	The Reformation and the Monasteries in Scotland and England: Some Comparisons, *Transactions of the Scottish Ecclesiological Society*, 15, part I, 1957, pp 7-22.
S240 ———	The Medieval Hospital of Haddington, *Transactions of the East Lothian Antiquarian and Field Naturalists' Society*, 6, 1955, pp 9-18; 7, 1958, pp 37-43.
S241 Eeles, F. C. and Clouston, R. W. M.	The Church and Other Bells of Aberdeenshire, *Proceedings of the Society of Antiquaries of Scotland*, volume 94, 1963, pp 272-300.
S242 Elliott, K.	Scottish Music of the Early Reformed Church, *Transactions of the Scottish Ecclesiological Society*, 15, 1961, part 2, pp 18-41.
S243 Finlayson, C. P.	A volume associated with John Knox, *Scottish Historical Review*, 38, 1959, pp 170-2.
S244 Foster, W. R.	The operation of Presbyteries in Scotland, 1600-1638, *Records of the Scottish Church History Society*, 15, 1964, pp 21-33.
S245 Fowler, J. J.	The Presbytery of Ayr: its schools and schoolmasters 1642-1746, *Ayrshire Archeological and Natural History Collections*, 6, 1958-60, pp 81-174.
S246 Fraser, A.	The murder of David Riccio, *History Today*, 16, 1966, pp 243-50.
S247 Gerrish, B. A.	Biblical Authority and the

	Continental Reformation, *Scottish Journal of Theology,* 10, 1957, pp 337-60.
S248 Giblin, C.	John Brown and John Francis Maitland, Scottish Minims, *Innes Review,* 6, 1955, pp 145-8.
S249 Gualdo, G.	The Earliest Correspondence of Pope Paul II and King James III, *Innes Review,* 15, 1964, pp 117-21.
S250 Gullans, C. B.	The English and Latin Poems of Sir Robert Ayton, *Scottish Text Society,* 4 series, 1, 1963.
S251 Haden-Guest, E.	A Pseudo-Scot in sixteenth century Glasgow, *The College Courant,* 16, 1964, pp 94-107.
S252 Hargreaves, H.	The Mirror of our Lady, *Aberdeen University Review,* 42, 1968, pp 267-80.
S253 Haws, C. H.	Scottish Religious Orders at the Reformation, *Records of the Scottish Church History Society,* 16, 1969, pp 203-24.
S254 Hay, G.	A Scottish Altarpiece in Copenhagen, *Innes Review,* 7, 1956, pp 5-10.
S255 ———	Scottish Post-Reformation Church Furniture, *Proceedings of the Society of Antiquaries of Scotland,* 88, 1956, pp 47-56.
S255a	See S312.
S255b	See S370.
S256 ——— and McRoberts, D.	Rossdhu Church and its Book of Hours, *Innes Review,* 16, 1965, pp 3-17.
S257 Hill, G.	The Sermons of John Watson, Canon of Aberdeen: with a note on John Royaerts, O.F.M., *Innes Review,* 15, 1964, pp 3-34.
S258 Hogg, A.	Sidelights on the Perth Charterhouse, *Innes Review,* 19, 1968, pp 168-9.
S259 Horn, B. L. H.	List of references to the pre-Reformation altarages in the parish church of Haddington, *Transactions of the East Lothian Antiquarian and Field Naturalists' Society,* 10, 1966, pp 55-91.

S260 Horn, D. B.	The origins of the University of Edinburgh, *Edinburgh University Journal*, 22, 1966, pp 213-25, 297-312.
S261 Hunter, D. M.	Kinneil Church, *Transactions of the Glasgow Archeological Society*, 15, 1965, pp 189-99.
S262 Innes, G. P.	Ecclesiastical Patronage in Scotland in the Later Middle Ages, *Records of the Scottish Church History Society*, 13, 1959, pp 73-84.
S263 Innes, T.	The Grange-Fortress of the Abbey of Kinloss at Strathisla in Banffshire, *Transactions of the Scottish Ecclesiological Society*, volume 15, 1961, part II, pp 9-13.
S264 Jack, R. D. S.	Sir William Mure and the Covenant, *Records of the Scottish Church History Society*, 17, 1969, part I, pp 1-14.
S265 Jexlev, T.	Scottish History in the light of records in the Danish National Archives, *Scottish Historical Review*, 48, 1969, pp 98-106.
S266 Johnson, I.	The Benedictines of Aberdeen: A Ghost Laid, *Innes Review*, 9, 1958, pp 220-1.
S267 Kenneth, Brother	The Popular Literature of the Scottish Reformation, *Innes Review*, 10, 1959, pp 295-310.
S268 Kerr, T. A.	The Early Ministry of John Craig at St. Giles 1562-1566, *Records of the Scottish Church History Society*, 14, 1962, pp 1-17.
S269 ———	John Craig in St. Giles 1567-1572, *Records of the Scottish Church History Society*, 14, 1962, pp 81-99.
S270 ———	The Early Life of John Craig, Scottish Reformer 1512-1560, *Records of the Scottish Church History Society*, 17, 1969, part I, pp 65-79.
S271 Kilpatrick, J.	The Rev. Robert Douglas, A. M.,

		1594-1674, *Records of the Scottish Church History Society*, 12, 1958, pp 29-46.
S272	Lamb, J. A.	Archbishop Alexander Burnet, 1614-1684, *Records of the Scottish Church History Society*, 11, 1955, pp 133-48.
S273	———	The Kalendar of the Book of Common Order, 1564-1644, *Records of the Scottish Church History Society*, 12, 1958, pp 15-28.
S274	Lee, M.	The Scottish Reformation after 400 Years (Revision Article), *Scottish Historical Review*, 44, 1965, pp 135-47.
S275	———	John Knox and his History, *Scottish Historical Review*, 45, 1966, pp 79-88.
S276	Louden, R. S.	Robert Leighton: the bishop, *Scottish Journal of Theology*, 20, 1967, pp 198-205.
S277	Lythe, S. G. E.	Life and Labour in Dundee from the Reformation to the Civil War, *Abertay Historical Society Publications*, no 5, 1958, p 30.
S278	MacDonell, A. and McRoberts, D.	The Mass Stones of Lochaber, *Innes Review*, 17, 1966, pp 71-81.
S279	McFarland, H. S. N.	The Book of Discipline, *Aberdeen University Review*, 38, 1960, pp 246-8.
S280	———	The Education of James Melvill (1556-1614), *Aberdeen University Review*, 36, 1956, pp 362-70.
S281	MacFarlane, L.	Some Recent Research on the Founder of the University, *Aberdeen University Review*, 36, 1956, pp 225-41.
S282	———	William Elphinstone's Library, *Aberdeen University Review*, 37, 1958, pp 253-71.
S283	———	The Book of Hours of James IV and Margaret Tudor, *Innes Review*, 11, 1960, pp 3-21.
S284	———	William Elphinstone, Founder of

		the University of Aberdeen, *Aberdeen University Review*, 39, 1961, pp 1-18.
S285	———	The Primacy of the Scottish Church, 1472-1521, *Innes Review*, 20, 1969, pp 111-29.
S286	McHardy, J.	The Priesthood of Knox, *Innes Review*, 13, 1956, p 62.
S287	MacIan, D. J.	George Strachan of the Mearns, *Innes Review*, 8, 1957, pp 131-2.
S288	MacInnes, J.	Baptism in the Highlands, *Records of the Scottish Church History Society*, 13, 1959, pp 1-24.
S289	———	The historical background of the Westminster Confession, *Records of the Scottish Church History Society*, 15, 1964, pp 57-75.
S290	MacIvor, I.	The King's Chapel at Restalrig and St. Triduana's Aisle: A Hexagonal Two-Storied Chapel of the Fifteenth Century, *Proceedings of the Society of Antiquaries of Scotland*, 96, 1962-3, pp 247-63.
S291	McKay, D.	Parish Clerks called Clark, *Innes Review*, 15, 1958, pp 95-6.
S292	———	Parish Life in Scotland, 1500-1560, *Innes Review*, 10, 1959, pp 237-67.
S293	———	Ayrshire Parish clerks, *Collections of the Ayshire Archeological and Natural History Society*, 7, 1966, pp 39-46.
S294	———	The Election of Parish Clerks in Medieval Scotland, *Innes Review*, 18, 1967, pp 25-35.
S295	———	The Duties of the Medieval Parish Clerk, *Innes Review*, 19, 1968, pp 32-8.
S296	———	The Four Heid Pilgrimages of Scotland, *Innes Review*, 19, 1968, pp 76-7.
S297	———	The Induction of the Parish Clerk in Medieval Scotland, *Innes Review*, 20, 1969, pp 59-64.
S298	MacKenzie, A.	Extracts from Kirk Session Book of John Welch, 1604-1605, *Collections*

		of the Ayshire Archeological and Natural History Society, 7, 1966, pp 47-52.
S298a	McLaren, R.	See S100.
S299	McMahon, G. I. R.	The Scottish courts of high commision, 1610-38, *Records of the Scottish Church History Society*, 15, 1966, pp 193-209.
S300	McNeill, P. G. B.	Sir James Balfour of Pittendreich, *Juridical Review*, new series, 5, 1960, pp 1-28.
S301	———	The legal aspect of the Scottish Reformation, *Scottish Law Times*, 1962, p 84.
S302	———	The Conquests of Scotland, *Scottish Law Times*, 1963, p 49.
S303	———	The Scottish Regency, *Juridical Review*, 12, 1967, pp 127-48.
S304	McNeill, W. A.	Documents Illustrative of the History of the Scots College, Paris, *Innes Review*, 15, 1964, pp 66-85.
S305	———	Scottish Entries in the Acta Rectoria Universitatis Parisiensis 1519-c. 1633, *Scottish Historical Review*, 43, 1964, pp 66-87.
S306	MacQueen, J.	Some aspects of the early renaissance in Scotland, *Forum for Modern Language Studies*, 3, 1967, pp 201-22.
S307	———	Two Versions of Henryson's Fabillis, *Innes Review*, 13, 1962, pp 3-9.
S308	McRoberts, D.	The Medieval Scottish Liturgy illustrated by surviving documents, *Transactions of the Scottish Ecclesiological Society*, 15, part I, 1957, pp 24-40.
S309	———	Was Blessed John Ogilvie a Highlander? *Innes Review*, 15, 1964, pp 183-5.
S310	———	Scottish Medieval Chalice Veils, *Innes Review*, 15, 1964, pp 103-16.
S311	———	The Priesthood of John Knox, *Innes Review*, 16, 1965, pp 134-5.
S312	——— and Hay, G.	Rossdhu Church and Its Book of Hours, *Innes Review*, volume 16, pp 3-17, 1965.

S313 ——— Hermits in Medieval Scotland, *Innes Review*, 16, 1965, pp 199-216.
S314 ——— Catholic Ayrshire, *Innes Review*, 9, 1958, pp 221.
S315 ——— A Sixteenth-Century Picture of St. Bartholomew from Perth, *Innes Review*, 10, 1959, pp 281-6.
S316 ——— Material Destruction Caused by the Scottish Reformation, *Innes Review*, 10, 1959, pp 126-72.
S317 ——— Notes on Scoto-Flemish Artistic Contacts, *Innes Review*, volume 10, 1959, pp 91-6.
S318 ——— Scottish Sacrament Houses, *Transactions of the Scottish Ecclesiological Society*, 15, part III, 1965, pp 33-56.
S319 ——— Notes on Glasgow Cathedral, *Innes Review*, 17, 1966, pp 40-9.
S320 ——— Some Post-Reformation Chalices, *Innes Review*, 18, 1967, pp 144-6.
S321 ——— The Painted Ceilings of Scotland, 1550-1650, *Innes Review*, volume 18, 1967, pp 66-7.
S322 ——— The Scottish Church and Nationalism in the fifteenth century, *Innes Review*, 19, 1968, pp 3-14.
S323 ——— Dean Brown's Book of Hours, *Innes Review*, 19, 1968, pp 144-67.
S324 ——— Two Hebridean Liturgical Items, *Innes Review*, 19, 1968, pp 170-5.
S325 ——— The Boy Bishop in Scotland, *Innes Review*, 19, 1968, pp 80-2.
S326 ——— Scottish Pilgrims to the Holy Land, *Innes Review*, 20, 1969, pp 80-106.
S326a ——— See S256.
S327 Mahoney, M. The Scottish Hierarchy, 1513-1565, *Innes Review*, 10, 1959, pp 21-66.
S328 Makey, W. H. The Elders of Stow, Liberton, Cannongate and St. Cuthberts in the Mid-Seventeenth Century, *Records of the Scottish Church History Society*, 17, part II, 1970, pp 155-67.

S329 Marshall, P. (ed)	The Diary of Sir James Hope, 24th January – 1st October, 1646, *Scottish History Society*, 3 series, 50, *Miscellany* 9, 1958, pp 129-94.
S330 Matheson, A.	Bishop Carswell, *Transactions of the Gaelic Society of Inverness*, 42 (1953-59) 1965, pp 182-205.
S331 Mechie, S.	Episcopacy in Post-Reformation Scotland, *Scottish Journal of Theology*, 8, 1955, pp 20-35.
S332 ——	Education for the Ministry in Scotland since the Reformation: 1. *Records of the Scottish Church History Society*, 14, 1963, pp 115-33.
S333 Meier, H. H.	A Pre-Reformation Biblical Paraphrase, *Innes Review*, 17, 1966, pp 11-23.
S334 Merriman, M. H.	The assured Scots: Scottish Collaborators with England during the Rough Wooing, *Scottish Historical Review*, 47, 1968, pp 10-34.
S335 Mill, A. J.	The Perth Hammerman's play, A Scottish Garden of Eden, *Scottish Historical Review*, 49, 1970, pp 146-53.
S336 Miner, B.	John Ireland and the Immaculate Conception, *Innes Review*, 17, 1966, pp 24-39.
S337 Mitchell, G. A. G.	The Medical History of Aberdeen and its Universities, *Aberdeen University Review*, 37, 1958, pp 225-38.
S338 Montgomerie, A.	The Death-Bed Dispositions of Elizabeth, Prioress of the Abbey of Haddington, 1563, *Transactions of the East Lothian Antiquarian and Field Naturalists' Society*, 6, 1955, pp 1-5.
S339 Morgan, P.	Some bibliographical aspects of the Scottish Prayer Book of 1637, *Bibliothek*, 5:1 (1967) pp 1-23.
S340 Muirhead, I. A.	A Quignonez Breviary, *Innes Review*, 13, 1962, p 74.
S341 Murray, A.	Exchequer and Council in the

		Reign of James V, *Juridical Review*, new series, 5, 1960, pp 209-25.
S342	Murray, A. L.	The revenues of the bishopric of Moray in 1538, *Innes Review*, 19, 1968, pp 40-56.
S343	Murray, J. E. L.	The Agriculture of Crail, 1550-1600, *Scottish Studies*, 8, 1964, pp 85-95.
S344	O'Dea, J.	Inventory of the Holy Cross Altar, Dumbarton, in the Year 1449, *Innes Review*, 17, 1966, p 60.
S345	Oldham, A.	Scottish Polyphonic Music, *Innes Review*, 13, 1962, pp 54-61.
S346	Park, W. (ed)	Letter of Thomas Randolph to the Earl of Leicester, 14th February 1566, *Scottish Historical Review*, 34, 1955, pp 135-9.
S347	Paton, H. M.	Haddington Records: Books of the Common Good, *Transactions of the East Lothian Antiquarian and Field Naturalists' Society*, 7, 1958, pp 46-80.
S348	Reid, R. C.	Papists and Non-Communicants in Dumfries, *Transactions of the Dumfriesshire and Galloway Natural History and Antiquarian Society*, 32, 1955, pp 186-90.
S349	———	The Archdeacons of Galloway, *Transactions of the Dumfriesshire and Galloway Natural History and Antiquarian Society*, 33, 1956, pp 66-72.
S350	———	The Election of Parish Clerks, *Transactions of the Dumfriesshire and Galloway Natural History and Antiquarian Society*, 34, 1957, pp 22-8.
S351	———	The Priory of St. Mary's Isle, *Transactions of the Dumfriesshire and Galloway Natural History and Antiquarian Society*, 36, 1959, pp 9-26.
S352	Robertson, W. N.	Fragments of Sculptured Stone-work from the Tomb of Henry Wardlaw, Bishop of St. Andrews, *Proceedings*

S352a ——— See S125.
S353 Ross, A. More about the archbishop of Athens [Alexander Gordon of Galloway], *Innes Review*, 13, 1962, pp 30-7.
S354 ——— Reformation and Repression, *Innes Review*, 10, 1959, pp 338-81.
S355 ——— The Scottish Conventual Franciscan Province, *Innes Review*, 13, 1962, pp 220-1.
S356 ——— Libraries of the Scottish Blackfriars, 1481-1560, *Innes Review*, 20, 1969, pp 3-36.
S357 Rupp, G. Luther and the Doctrine of the Church, *Scottish Journal of Theology*, 9, 1956, pp 384-92.
S358 Sanderson, M. H. B. Some Aspects of the Church in Scottish Society in the Era of the Reformation: Illustrated from the Sheriffdom of Ayr, *Records of the Scottish Church History Society*, 17, part II, 1970, pp 81-98.
S359 ——— Catholic Recusancy in Scotland in the Sixteenth Century, *Innes Review*, 21, 1970, pp 87-107.
S360 Scanlan, J. D. Husband and Wife: Pre-Reformation Canon Law of Marriage in the Officials' Courts, *The Stair Society*, 20, 1958, pp 69-81.
S361 Shaw, D. The Inauguration of Ministers in Scotland: 1560-1620, *Records of the Scottish Church History Society*, 16, 1969, pp 35-62.
S362 Shearman, Father Alexander McQuhirrie, S. J. *Innes Review*, 6, 1955, pp 22-45.
S363 Shirley, G. W. A Dumfries Rental (1548), *Transactions of the Dumfriesshire and Galloway Natural History and Antiquarian Society*, 39, 1962, pp 50-79.
S364 Simpson, G. C. and Webster B. The Archives of the Medieval Church of Glasgow: An Introductory survey, *Bibliotheck*, 3, 1962, pp 195-201.

S365	———	Letters of Father Thomas Innes about the Archives of the Church of Glasgow, *Innes Review,* 13, 1962, pp 62-70.
S366	Smith, D. B.	Florence Wilson: two early works, *Bibliotheck,* 4, 1966, pp 228-9.
S367	Smith, J. I.	The Transition to the Modern Law 1532-1600 *in* An Introduction to Scottish Legal History, *The Stair Society,* 20, 1958, pp 25-43.
S368	Stewart, C.	James V and the Reformation in England, *The Stewarts,* 11, 1963, pp 240-72.
S369	Stewart, A. M.	Regensburg and Scotland, *Aberdeen University Review,* 43, 1970, pp 48-52.
S370	Stones, E. L. G. and Hay, G.	Notes on Glasgow Cathedral, *Innes Review,* 18, 1967, pp 88-98.
S371	Taylor, M.	The Conflicting Doctrines of the Scottish Reformation, *Innes Review,* 10, 1959, pp 97-125.
S372	Thoms, D. B.	Church and School in Brechin, 1560-1872, *Book of the Society of Friends of Brechin Cathedral,* no 9, 1956, pp 10-36.
S373	———	Communion at Brechin during the Seventeenth Century, *Book of the Society of Friends of Brechin Cathedral,* no 10, 1957, pp 20-5.
S374	———	The Cathedral Kirk of Brechin, *Book of the Society of Friends of Brechin Cathedral,* no 11, 1958, pp 13-27.
S375	———	The Kirk Fabric in the Seventeenth Century, *Book of the Society of Friends of Brechin Cathedral,* no 13, 1960, pp 7-26.
S376	Thomson, D. S.	Gaelic Learned Orders and Literati in Medieval Scotland, *Scottish Studies,* 12, 1968, pp 57-78.
S377	Thomson, J. A. F.	Some new light on the elevation of Patrick Graham, *Scottish Historical Review,* 40, 1961, pp 83-8.
S378	———	Innocent VIII and the Scottish

	Church, *Innes Review*, 19, 1968, pp 23-31.
S379 Walker, G. S. M.	Scottish Ministerial Orders, *Scottish Journal of Theology*, 8, 1955, pp 238-54.
S380 Watt, D. E. R.	Scottish Masters and Students at Paris in the Fourteenth Century, *Aberdeen University Review*, 36, 1955, pp 169-80.
S381 Whitaker, I.	The Reports on the Parishes of Scotland, 1627, *Scottish Studies*, 3, 1959, pp 229-33.
S382 Winning, T.	Church Councils in Sixteenth-Century Scotland, *Innes Review*, 10, 1959, pp 311-37.
S383 Withrington, D. J.	Schools in the Presbytery of Haddington in the 17th Century, *Transactions of the East Lothian Antiquarian and Field Naturalists' Society*, 9, 1963, pp 90-111.

SECTION 3. REVIEW ARTICLES (listed under authors reviewed)

S384	Anson, P. F.	S1	*ScHR* 39, 1960, pp 145-6; *IR* 11, 1960, pp 69-70.
S385	Apted, M. R.	S2	*ScHR* 48, 1969, pp 183-4; *ScS* 11, 1967, pp 119-20.
S386	Barclay, R. S. (ed)	S3	*ScS* 7, 1963, pp 245-7.
S387	————	S4	*ScS* 12, 1968, pp 201 *et seq.*
S388	Bell, H. E. and Ollard, R. L.	S5	*ScHR* 44, 1965, pp 161-4.
S389	Bennett, J. A. W.	S6	*ScHR* 36, 1957, pp 147-50.
S390	Berg, J. and Lagercrantz, B.	S7	*ScS* 7, 1963, pp 126-8.
S391	Beveridge, J. and Donaldson, G.	S8	*ScHR* 37, 1958, pp 54-61.
S392	Bindoff, S. T.; Hurstfield, J. and Williams, C. H.	S9	*ScHR* 42, 1963, pp 66-8.
S393	Bingham, C.	S10	*ScHR* 48, 1969, pp 193-4.
S394	Boyd, W.	S11	*ScHR* 42, 1963, pp 54-7.
S395	Burleigh, J. H. S.	S12	*ScHR* 42, 1963, pp 141-3.
S396	Burnet, G.	S13	*ScHR* 42, 1963, pp 66-8.
S397	Burns, J. H.	S14	*ScHR* 43, 1964, pp 52-3. *AUR* 40, 1963, pp 37-8.
S398	Calderwood, A. B.	S15	*ScHR* 42, 1963, pp 63-4.
S399	Cameron, J. K.	S16	*ScHR* 44, 1965, pp 159-60.
S400	Cockburn, J. H.	S17	*ScHR* 39, 1960, pp 53-5.
S401	Collinson, P.	S18	*ScHR* 47, 1968, pp 89-90.
S402	Cowan, I. B.	S19	*ScHR* 47, 1968, pp 87-8; *IR* 18, 1967, p 141.
S403	Cruden, S.	S20	*ScHR* 42, 1963, pp 70-1.
S404	Dellavida, G. L.	S21	*AUR* 37, 1958, pp 383-4.
S405	Dickinson, W. C.	S23	*ScHR* 42, 1963, pp 41-6; *ScS* 7, 1963, pp 117-20.
S406	Donaldson, G.	S24	*ScHR* 43, 1964, pp 148-9.
S407	————	S25	*ScHR* 46, 1967, pp 161-3.
S408	————	S27	*ScHR* 45, 1966, pp 207-10.
S409	————	S28	*ScHR* 34, 1955, pp 161-3.
S410	————	S29	*ScHR* 40, 1961, pp 68-70.
S411	————	S30	*ScHR* 40, 1961, pp 161-4.
S412	————	S31	*ScHR* 47, 1968, pp 168-9.
S413	Dow, J.	S32	*ScHR* 45, 1966, pp 210-11.
S414	Dunlop, Annie I.	S34	*ScHR* 44, 1965, pp 152-3.
S415	Easson, D. E.	S35	*ScHR* 37, 1958, pp 146-52; *IR* 8, 1957, pp 132-4.

S415a ———
S416 Eeles, F. C.
S417 Elliott, K.
S418 Fraser, A.
S419 Gatherer, W. A.
S420 Giblin, C.
S421 Gilbert, M.
S422 Hammermayer, L.
S423 Hay, G.
S424 Horn, D. R.
S425 Jacob, E. F.
S426 Jordan, W. K.
S427 Ker, N. R.
S428 Kingsley, J.
S429 Lee, M.

S430 Lindsay, I. G.
S431 Lythe, S. G. E.
S432 McElwee, W.
S433 MacKenzie, A. M.
S434 Mackie, J. D.
S435 ———
S436 Mackie, R. L.

S437 ———
S438 MacNeill, D. H.
S439 McRoberts, D.
S440 Mathew, D.
S441 Matthew, D.
S442 Miller, A. C.
S443 Mitchell, W. S.
S444 Naiden, J. R.
S445 Phillips, J. E.
S446 Quinn, F.
S447 Rae, T. I.
S448 Rankin, W. E. K.
S449 Ridley, J.
S450 Scarisbrick, J. J.
S451 Shaw, D.
S452 ———
S453 Simon, J. R.
S454 Skelton, J.
S455 Slavin, A. J.

S238 *ScHR* 31, 1952, pp 84-6;
ScHR 35, 1956, pp 163-5.
S37 *ScHR* 37, 1958, pp 163-5.
S38 *AUR* 37, 1958, pp 287-90.
S39 *ScHR* 49, 1970, pp 203-4.
S40 *ScHR* 39, 1960, pp 57-9.
S41 *ScHR* 44, 1965, pp 160-1.
S42 *ScHR* 48, 1969, pp 209-10.
S43 *ScHR* 44. 1965, pp 157-8.
S44 *ScHR* 37, 1958, pp 158-60.
S47 *ScHR* 48, 1969, pp 191-2.
S49 *ScHR* 42, 1963, pp 61-3.
S50 *ScHR* 49, 1970, pp 110-11.
S51 *ScHR* 44, 1965, pp 150-1.
S52 *AUR* 37, 1958, pp 387-9.
S55 *ScHR* 42, 1963, pp 71-4;
ScS 4, 1960, pp 108-13.
S56 *ScHR* 42, 1963, pp 69-70.
S57 *ScHR* 40, 1961, pp 72-3.
S58 *ScHR* 38, 1959, pp 82-3.
S59 *ScJTh* 8, 1955, pp 104-5.
S60 *ScHR* 34, 1955, pp 144-7.
S62 *ScHR* 41, 1962, pp 165-7.
S63 *ScHR* 38, 1959, pp 133-6;
AUR 37, 1958, pp 379-81.
S64 *ScHR* 42, 1963, pp 160-1.
S65 *ScHR* 48, 1969, pp 190-1.
S66 *ScHR* 43, 1964, pp 145-7.
S67 *ScHR* 35, 1956, pp 153-7.
S68 *ScHR* 48, 1969, pp 193-4.
S70 *ScHR* 43, 1964, pp 53-4.
S71 *AUR* 36, 1956, pp 405-7.
S72 *ScHR* 34, 1955, pp 62-4.
S75 *ScHR* 44, 1965, pp 153-5.
S77 *ScHR* 48, 1969, pp 179-80.
S78 *ScHR* 47, 1968, pp 171-3.
S79 *ScHR* 35, 1956, pp 172-4.
S82 *ScHR* 48, 1969, pp 184-6.
S83 *ScHR* 48, 1969, pp 181-3.
S84 *ScHR* 44, 1965, pp 155-6.
S85 *ScHR* 48, 1969, pp 186-8.
S86 *ScHR* 49, 1970, pp 115-17.
S87 *ScHR* 49, 1970, pp 199-200.
S88 *ScHR* 48, 1969, pp 181-3.

S456 Smout, T. C.
S457 Thomson, J. A. F.
S458 Thomson, R. L.
S459 Trevor-Roper, H. R.
S460 Wightman, W. P. D.
S461 Willson, D. H.
S462 Wood-Legh, K. L.
S463 Wright, R. S.
S464 ———

S89 *ScHR* 49 1970, pp 200-2.
S90 *ScHR* 46, 1967, pp 63-4.
S91 *ScHR* 43, 1964, pp 158-9.
S92 *ScHR* 48, 1969, pp 188-90.
S93 *AUR* 40, 1963, pp 29-31.
S95 *ScHR* 36, 1957, pp 52-8.
S97 *ScHR* 47, 1968, pp 88-9.
S98 *ScHR* 37, 1958, pp 171-2.
S99 *ScHR* 40, 1961, pp 74-6.

SECTION 4. COMPLETED THESES

S465 Anderson, M. W.	Biblical humanism and Catholic reform, 1444-1562: a study of Renaissance philology in the revival of New Testament criticism. (Aberdeen University) Ph.D., 1964.
S466 Apted, M. R.	Painting in Scotland from the fourteenth to the seventeenth centuries, with particular reference to painted domestic decoration, 1550-1650. (Edinburgh University), Ph.D., 1964.
S467 Bohn, R. P.	The controversy between Puritans and Quakers, to 1660. (Edinburgh University) Ph.D., 1956.
S468 Bullough, F.	Supernaturalism in the thought of James VI and his circle. (Aberdeen University) Ph.D., 1967.
S469 Carter, J. K.	Sunday observance in Scotland, 1560-1606. (Edinburgh University) Ph.D., 1957.
S470 Christie, W.	The episcopal church in the diocese of Brechin. (Dundee University) Ph.D., 1967.
S471 Cowan, I. B.	Appropriation of parish churches in medieval Scotland. (Edinburgh University) Ph.D., 1961.
S472 Crawford, J. R.	History of the doctrine of the Priesthood of Believers. (Aberdeen University) Ph.D., 1958.
S473 Dilworth, G. M.	The Scottish abbey in Würzburg, 1595-1696. (Edinburgh University) Ph.D., 1968.
S474 Donaldson, G.	The organisation and worship of the Scottish Church in the sixteenth and early seventeenth centuries. (Edinburgh University) D.Litt., 1955.
S475 Donaldson, R.	Patronage and the church: a study in the social structure of the secular clergy in the diocese of Durham, (1311-1540). (Edinburgh University) Ph.D., 1956.

S476 Durkan, J.	The medieval universities of Scotland (1410-1560). (Edinburgh University) Ph.D., 1959.
S477 Foster, W. R.	Ecclesiastical administration in Scotland, 1600-38. (Edinburgh University) Ph.D., 1963.
S478 Fredericks, R. S.	Death practices and burial rites in Scotland from the later medieval period to 1780, with particular reference to the influence of theology. (Edinburgh University) Ph.D., 1967.
S479 Fulop, R. E.	John Firth and his relation to the origin of the Reformation in England. (Edinburgh University) Ph.D., 1957.
S480 Galbraith, J. D.	The sources of the Aberdeen Breviary. (Aberdeen University) M.Litt., 1970.
S481 Gatherer, W. A.	An annotated edition of George Buchanan's account of the personal reign of Mary Stuart, with a critical introduction. (Edinburgh University) Ph.D., 1956.
S482 Jones, E. B.	An Examination of the Anglican Definition of the Church as expounded by Bishop John Jewel. (St. Andrews University) Ph.D., 1964.
S483 Kerr, T. A.	John Craig (1512-1600), with special reference to his contribution to the upbuilding of the reformed church in Scotland. (Edinburgh University) Ph.D., 1955.
S484 Kitshoff, M. C.	Aspects of Arminianism in Scotland. (St. Andrews University) Ph.D., 1968.
S485 Larner, C. J.	Scottish demonology in the sixteenth and seventeenth centuries and its theological background. (Edinburgh University) Ph.D., 1962.
S486 Mackie, R. L.	King James IV of Scotland. (St. Andrews University) D.Litt., 1959.
S487 Main, A.	The origins of John Knox's doctrine of Just Rebellion. (Aberdeen University) Ph.D., 1963.
S488 Matheson, P. C.	Cardinal Contarini at Regensburg: a

	study in Ecumenism, Catholicism and Curialism. (Edinburgh University) Ph.D., 1968.
S489 Moore, E. B.	The Political Theories of Martin Luther and Ulrich Zwingli: A Study in Contrasts. (St. Andrews University) Ph.D., 1965.
S490 Murray, A. L.	The exchequer and Crown revenue of Scotland, 1437-1542. (Edinburgh University) Ph.D., 1961.
S491 MacDonald, E. G.	Scottish-Polish relations, 1550-1800. (Strathclyde University) M.Litt., 1970.
S492 Mackoskey, R. A.	The life and thought of Balthasar Hübmaier, 1485-1528. (Edinburgh University) Ph.D., 1957.
S493 McNally, F. W.	The Westminster Directory: its origin and significance. (Edinburgh University) Ph.D., 1958.
S494 McNeill, P. G. B.	The jurisdiction of the Scottish privy council, 1532-1708. (Glasgow University) Ph.D., 1961.
S495 Percival, S. M.	Some sixteenth-century French artists having connections with Scotland: the Quesnel family and Jehan Decourt. (Edinburgh University) Ph.D., 1962.
S496 Prugh, J. W.	The theory and practice of discipline in the Scottish Reformation. (Edinburgh University) Ph.D., 1959.
S497 Shaw, D.	The origin and development of the General Assembly of the Church of Scotland, 1560-1600. (Edinburgh University) Ph.D., 1962.
S498 Stevenson, D.	The Covenanters and the government of Scotland, 1637-51. (Glasgow University) Ph.D., 1970.

IRELAND

compiled by

DEREK BAKER

JOURNALS AND SOCIETY PUBLICATIONS CONSULTED

An H	Analecta Hibernica	Dublin
	Apollo	London
AR	Archiv für Reformationsgeschichte	Gütersloh
Ar H	Archivum Hibernicum	Maynooth
	Augustiniana	Louvain
	Breifne	Cavan
BICHS	Bulletin of the Irish Commission of Historical Sciences	Dublin
	Carmelus	Rome
CHR	Catholic Historical Review	Washington
CH	Church History	Chicago
CQR	Church Quarterly Review	London
	Cîteaux	Westmalle
CR	Clogher Record	Monaghan
	Collectanea Franciscana	Rome
Coll H	Collectanea Hibernica	Dublin
COCR	Collectanea Ordinis Cisterciensium Reformatorum	Rome/Westmalle
DA	Donegal Annual	Londonderry
DHR	Dublin Historical Record	Dublin
	Eigse	Dublin
	Franciscan College Annual	Rome
	Galvia	Galway
Herm	Hermathena	Dublin
HS	Historical Studies	Dublin/Belfast
	Iris Hibernia	Fribourg
IER	Irish Ecclesiastical Record	Dublin
IG	Irish Genealogist	London
IHS	Irish Historical Studies	Dublin
IJ	Irish Jurist	Dublin
	Irish Rosary	Dublin
IS	Irish Sword	Dublin
	Irish Text Society	London
ITQ	Irish Theological Quarterly	Maynooth
JClHAS	Journal of the Clonmel Historical and Archeological Society	Clonmel
JCoHAS	Journal of the Cork Historical and Archeological Society	Cork
JDHS	Journal of the Donegal Historical Society (Donegal Annual from 1951)	Donegal
JEH	Journal of Ecclesiastical History	London

JGAHS	Journal of the Galway Archeological and Historical Society	Galway
JFHS	Journal of the Friends' Historical Society	London/Philadelphia
JIMA	Journal of the Irish Medical Association	Dublin
JKAS	Journal of the County Kildare Archeological Society	Dublin
JLAS	Journal of the County Louth Archeological Society	Dundalk
JRSAI	Journal of the Royal Society of Antiquaries of Ireland	Dublin
NMAJ	North Munster Antiquarian Journal	Limerick
OKR	Old Kilkenny Review	Kilkenny
PICHC	Proceedings of Irish Catholic Historical Committee	Dublin
PRIA	Proceedings of the Royal Irish Academy	Dublin
RH	Recusant History	Bognor Regis
RHA	Revue d'Histoire Ardennaise	Charleville-Mèzieres
RN	Reportorium Novum	Dublin
Ríocht	Ríocht Na Midhe	Drogheda
SA	Seanchas Ardmhacha	Armagh
SH	Studia Hibernica	Dublin
	Studies	Dublin
	Terminus	
	Topic 13, A Journal of the Liberal Arts	Washington
UJA	Ulster Journal of Archaeology	Belfast

Ireland

SECTION 1. BOOKS AND PARTS OF BOOKS

I 1	Ainsworth, J. (ed)	*The Inchiquin Manuscripts* (Dublin 1961).
I 1a	Aylmer, G. E.	*The King's Servants: The civil service of Charles I 1625-42* (London 1961).
I 1b	Bagwell, R.	*Ireland under the Tudors*, 3 vols (repr London 1963).
I 1c	———	*Ireland under the Stuarts*, 3 vols (repr London 1963).
I 2	Balic, C. M.	Wadding the Scotist, *Father Luke Wadding* pp 463-507.
I 3	Beckett, J. C.	*A Short History of Ireland* (rev 1958, 3 ed London 1966).
I 4	———	*The Making of Modern Ireland 1603-1923* (London 1966).
I 5	Beckinsdale, B. W.	*Elizabeth I* (London 1963).
I 6	Bindoff, S. T. (ed)	*Elizabethan Government and Society: essays presented to Sir John Neale* (London 1961).
I 7	Bolton, F. R.	*The Caroline tradition of the Church of Ireland with particular reference to Bishop Jeremy Taylor* (London 1958).
I 8	Brady, J.	Keeping the faith at Gormanston 1569-1629, *Father Luke Wadding* pp 405-13.
I 9	Byrne, P. F.	*Witchcraft in Ireland* (Cork 1967).
I 10	Castro, M. de	Wadding and the Iberian peninsular, *Father Luke Wadding* pp 119-70.
I 11	Ceyssens, L.	*La première bulle contre Jansénius: sources relatives à son histoire (1644-53)*, 2 vols (Brussels 1961-2).
I 12	———	*Sources relatives au débuts du Jansénisme et de l'Antijansénisme 1640-3* (Louvain 1957).
I 13	———	Florence Conry, Hugh de Burgo, Luke Wadding and Jansenism, *Father Luke Wadding* pp 295-404.
I 14	Clarke, A.	*The 'Old English' in Ireland 1625-42* (London 1966).
I 15	Coonan, T. L.	*The Irish Catholic Confederacy and the Puritan Revolution* (Dublin/London/New York 1954).

I 16	Corish, P. J. (ed)	*History of Irish Catholicism* (Dublin).
I 17	———	The beginnings of the Irish College at Rome, *Father Luke Wadding*, pp 284-94.
I 18	Dewar, M.	*Sir Thomas Smith, a Tudor intellectual in office* (London 1964).
I 19	Edwards, R. D.	The Irish catholics and the puritan revolution, *Father Luke Wadding* pp 93-118.
I 20	———	Ireland, Elizabeth I and the Counter-Reformation, *Elizabethan Government and Society* pp 315-39.
I 21	———	The kings of England and papal provisions in the fifteenth century, *Studies presented to Aubrey Gwynn* pp 265-80.
I 22	Egan, P. K.	*The parish of Ballinasloe: its history from the earliest times to the present day* (Dublin 1960).
I 23	Flanagan, U.	*Luke Wadding* (Cork 1961).
I 24	Franciscan Fathers (ed) (Dún Mhuire, Killiney)	*Father Luke Wadding: Commemorative volume* (Dublin 1957).
I 25	Giblin, C. (ed)	*Liber Lovaniensis: a collection of Irish Franciscan documents 1629-1717* (Dublin 1956).
I 26	——— (ed)	*The Irish Franciscan Mission to Scotland, 1619-46* (Dublin 1964).
I 27	———	The Processus Datariae and the appointment of Irish bishops in the seventeenth century, *Father Luke Wadding*, pp 508-616.
I 28	———	See I 36.
I 28a	Gleeson, D. F.	*A History of the diocese of Killaloe*, 1, parts 2-4 (Dublin 1962).
I 29	Gwynn, A.	*Anglo-Irish Church Life: fourteenth and fifteenth centuries*, in *History of Irish Catholicism* 2, fasc 4 (Dublin/Sydney 1968).
I 30	———	Archbishop Ussher and Father Brendan O'Conor, *Father Luke Wadding*, pp 263-83.
I 31	Hammermayer, L.	*Herrschaftlich-staatliche Gewalt, Gesellschaft und Katholizismus in Irland vom 16-18 Jahrhundert* (Munich 1970).

I 32	Hand, G. J.	The medieval chapter of St Mary's Cathedral, Limerick, *Studies presented to Aubrey Gwynn*, pp 74-89.
I 33	Hogan, J. and O'Farrell, N. M. (ed)	*The Walsingham letter book or register of Ireland, May 1578 – December 1579* (Dublin 1959).
I 34	Jackson, D.	*Intermarriage in Ireland 1550-1650* (Montreal 1970).
I 35	Jennings, S. B. (ed)	*Wadding Papers 1614-38* (Dublin 1955).
I 36	———— and Giblin, C.	*Louvain Papers 1606-1827* (Dublin 1968).
I 37	Jones, F. M.	The Counter-Reformation, in *History of Irish Catholicism* 3, fasc 3 (Dublin/Melbourne 1967).
I 38	Kearney, H. F.	*Strafford in Ireland 1637-41: a study in absolutism* (Manchester 1959).
I 39	Knox, R. B.	*James Ussher, Archbishop of Armagh* (Cardiff 1967).
I 39a	Knox, S. J.	*Walter Travers: paragon of Elizabethan puritanism* (London 1962).
I 40	Larramendi, M. L.	See I 69.
I 40a	Leask, H. G.	*Irish Church and Monastic Buildings* III [1400 - Reformation] (London 1960).
I 41	Longfield, A. K. (ed)	*Fitzwilliam accounts 1560-65* (Dublin 1960).
I 42	Love, H. W.	*The records of the archbishops of Armagh* (Dundalk 1965).
I 43	MacDonagh, O.	*Ireland* (Englewood Cliffs 1968).
I 44	McGrath, C.	Toirdhealbhach Ó Conchubhair (floruit circa 1645), *Father Luke Wadding*, pp 414-37.
I 45	MacLysaght, E.	*Irish Families, their names, arms and origins* (Dublin 1957).
I 46	————	*More Irish Families* (Dublin 1960).
I 47	————	*Supplement to Irish Families* (Dublin 1964).
I 48	————	*Guide to Irish Families* (Dublin 1964).
I 49	MacLysaght, P. J.	*Irish Life in the seventeenth-century* (3 ed Shannon 1969).
I 50	McNeill, C. and Otway-Ruthven, A. J. (ed)	*Dowdall Deeds* (Dublin 1960).

I 51	Magee, J.	*Ferment and change: a survey of British and Irish History,* bk 1: 1485-1660 (London/Belfast 1964).
I 52	Martin, F. X.	*Friar Nugent: a study of Francis Lavalin Nugent (1569-1635) agent of the counter-reformation* (London/Rome 1962).
I 53	———	The Irish Augustinian reform movement in the fifteenth century, *Studies presented to Aubrey Gwynn* pp 230-64.
I 54	——— (ed)	See I 57.
I 55	——— (ed)	See I 80.
I 56	Millett, B.	Guide to material for a biography of Father Luke Wadding, *Father Luke Wadding* pp 229-62.
I 57	Moody, T. W. and Martin, F. X. (ed)	*The course of Irish history* (Cork 1967).
I 58	Mooney, C.	Was Wadding a patriotic Irishman?, *Father Luke Wadding* pp 15-92.
I 59	———	The first impact of the reformation, in *History of Irish Catholicism* 3, fasc 2 (Dublin 1967).
I 60	———	The church in gaelic Ireland: thirteenth to fifteenth centuries, in *History of Irish Catholicism* 2, fasc 5 (Dublin 1969).
I 61	Morrall, J. B.	See I 80.
I 62	Mould, D. D. C. P.	*The Irish Dominicans: the friars preacher in the history of catholic Ireland* (Dublin 1957).
I 63	Ó Cuiv, B. (ed)	*Seven centuries of Irish learning 1000-1700* (Dublin 1961).
I 64	O'Donnell, T. (ed)	*Father John Colgan: essays in commemoration of the third centenary of his death* (Dublin 1959).
I 65	O'Farrell, N. M.	See I 33.
I 66	O Murchu, M. (ed)	*Kilcrea Friary: 500th anniversary of foundation, 1465-1965* (Kilcrea 1966).
I 67	Otway-Ruthven, A. J.	The medieval church lands of county Dublin, *Studies presented to*

		Aubrey Gwynn pp 54-73.
I 67a	———	*A History of Medieval Ireland* (London 1968).
I 68	———	See I 50.
I 69	Olarra Garmandia, J. de and Larramendi, M. L. (ed)	*Correspondencia entre la Nunciatura en España y la Santa Sede, reinado de Felipe III* (1598-1621) vols 5-6 (Rome 1965-6).
I 70	Powell, J. R. and Timings, E. K. (ed)	*Documents relating to the Civil War 1642-48* (London 1963).
I 71	Quinn, D. B.	*The Elizabethans and the Irish* (Ithaca 1966).
I 71a	Renwick, W. L. (ed)	E. Spenser, *A View of the present state of Ireland* (rev ed Oxford 1970).
I 72	Silke, J. J.	*Ireland and Europe 1559-1607* (Dundalk 1966) Dublin Historical Association, *Irish History Series* 7.
I 73	———	*Kinsale: The Spanish intervention in Ireland at the end of the Elizabethan wars* (Liverpool 1970).
I 74	Seymour, St J. D.	*The Puritans in Ireland, 1647-61* (repr Oxford 1969).
I 75	Talbot, C. H. (ed)	*Letters of the English abbots to the chapter at Cîteaux 1442-1521*, Camden 4 series, 4 (London 1967).
I 76	Timings, E. K.	See I 70.
I 76a	Trevor-Roper, H. R.	Religion, the Reformation and Social Change, *Historical Studies* 4 (London 1963).
I 77	Twemlow, J. A. (ed)	See I 95.
I 78	Wall, T.	Bars and Bruodins, *Father Luke Wadding* pp 438-62.
I 79	Watt, J. A.	*The church and the two nations in medieval Ireland* (Cambridge 1970).
I 80	——— and Morrall, J. B. Martin, F. X. (ed)	*Medieval Studies presented to Aubrey Gwynn, S. J.* (Dublin 1961).
I 81	Wernham, R. B. (ed)	*List and analysis of State Papers, foreign series, Elizabeth, I, I, August 1589-June 1590* (London 1964).
I 82	White, N. B. (ed)	*Registrum dioicesis Dublinensis: a sixteenth-century Dublin precedent book* (Dublin 1959).

SECTION 2. DICTIONARIES, BIBLIOGRAPHIES ETC

I 83	Backova, A. N.	*Istoriya Anglii i Irlandii: bibliograficheskii ukazateli literaturi izdannoi v USSR za 1918-1962* (Moscow 1963).
I 84	Conyers Read	See I 92.
I 84a	Cross, F. L.	*Oxford Dictionary of the Christian Church* (London 1957).
I 85	Eager, A. R.	*A guide to Irish bibliographical material: being a bibliography of Irish bibliographies and some sources of information* (London 1964).
I 86	Edwards, R. D. and Quinn, D. B.	Sixteenth-century Ireland 1485-1603, *IHS* 16 (1968) pp 15-32.
I 86a	Fryde, E. B. (ed)	See I 90a.
I 87	Gwynn, A.	*Bibliographie de la Réforme (1450-1648) 1940-55,* fasc 2 (Leyden 1960) pp 51-61.
I 87a	———	*Medieval Religious Houses: Ireland* (London 1970).
I 87b	Hayes, R. J. (ed)	*Manuscript sources for the history of Irish civilization,* 11 vols (Boston 1966).
I 88	Hayes-McCoy, G. A.	*Ulster and other maps c* 1600 (Dublin 1964).
I 89	Johnston, E. M.	*Irish history: a select bibliography* (London 1968). Historical Association *Helps for Students of History* 73.
I 90	Otway-Ruthven, J.	Medieval Ireland 1169-1485, *IHS* 15 (1967) pp 359-65.
I 90a	Powicke, F. M. and Fryde, E. B. (ed)	*Handbook of British Chronology* (2 rev ed London 1961).
I 91	Quinn, D. B.	See I 86.
I 92	Read, Conyers (ed)	*Bibliography of British History, Tudor Period 1485-1603* (2 ed Oxford 1959).
I 92a	Simms, J. G.	Seventeenth-century Ireland, *IHS* 15 (1967) pp 366-75.
I 93		*Acts of the Privy Council, England, May 1629-May 1630* (London 1960).
I 94		Alphabetical list of articles contri-

	buted to the Journal from vol 1, 1904 to vol 13, 1957, *JLAS* 14 (1961) pp 232-60.
I 95	*Calendar of entries in the papal registers relating to Great Britain and Ireland.* 13, *Papal Letters 1471-84* (London 1955); 14, *Papal Letters 1484-92* (London 1960).
I 96	*Calendar of the patent rolls preserved in the Public Record Office, Elizabeth I, 5, 1569-72* (London 1966).
I 97	Handlist of Irish Diocesan Histories, *PICHC* (1957) pp 31-7.
I 98	*Sources for the study of local history in Northern Ireland: a catalogue* for an exhibition January-July 1968 (Belfast n.d.).
I 99	The September numbers of *IHS* list the annual writings on Irish history, and, though not always complete, supply a useful bibliographical introduction to Irish history.

SECTION 3. ARTICLES IN ACADEMIC JOURNALS AND SOCIETY PUBLICATIONS

I 100 Barron, T. J.   Rev Alexander McWhidd: a seventeenth-century minister in Knockbride, Co Cavan, *Breifne* 1 (1959) pp 154-8.

I 100a Becket, J. C.   The Confederation of Kilkenny reviewed, *HS* 2 (1959).

I 101 Bradshaw, B.   George Browne, first reformation archbishop of Dublin, 1536-54, *JEH* 21 (1970) pp 301-26.

I 102 Brady, J.   Some Kilmore clergy of the seventeenth and eighteenth centuries, *Breifne* 1 (1960) pp 215-24.

I 103 ———   The Irish colleges in Europe and the counter-reformation, *PICHC* (1957) pp 1-8.

I 104 ———   The medieval diocese of Meath, *Ríocht* 1, 3 (1957) pp 34-40.

I 105 ——— (ed)   Some inquisitions relating to Louth clergy during the reign of Henry VIII, *SA* 3 (1959) pp 333-6.

I 106 Brooke-Tyrell, A.   Michael Jones, governor of Dublin, *DHR* 24 (1970) pp 159-72.

I 106a Browne, P.   The 'Brevis relatio' of the Irish Discalced Carmelites, 1625-70 (ed Glynn, M. and Martin, F. X.) *Ar H* 25 (1962) pp 136-63.

I 107 Buckley, D.   The Church in Ireland in the fifteenth century: III, Diocesan organisation, Cloyne, *PICHC* (1956) pp 8-11.

I 108 Clarke, A.   The policies of the 'Old English' in parliament 1640-41, *HS* 5 (1965) pp 85-102.

I 109 Clohosey, T. J. (ed)   Obligationes pro annatis dioicesis Ossoriensis 1413-1531, *Ar H* 20 (1957) pp 1-37.

I 110 Coen, M.   The post-reformation catholic bishops of Kilfenora, *NMAJ* 12 (1969) pp 53-62.

I 111 Collins, J. T.   Church government in the south of

I 112 Conway, C.
[see also nos I 201-2a]
Ireland 1471-1484, *JCoHAS* 62 (1957) pp 14-21.

I 113 ——— The cistercian abbey of Inislounaght, *JClHAS* 1, 4 (1956) pp 3-52.

I 114 ——— The Irish Cistercian documents in Octavian's Register, Armagh, *SA* 2 (1957) pp 269-94.

I 114a ——— The decline and attempted reform of the Irish cistercians (1445-1531), *COCR* 18 (1956) pp 290-305; 19 (1957) pp 146-62.

I 114b ——— The abbatial succession of Mellifont 1142-1539, *JLAS* 15 (1961) pp 23-38.

I 114c Conway, D. (ed)
The Lands of St. Mary's Abbey, Dublin, at the dissolution of the abbey, *RN* 3 (1962) pp 94-107.

I 115 Coombes, J.
Guide to documents of Irish and British Interest in Fondo Borghese, series 1, *Ar H* 23 (1960) pp 1-147; series 2-4, *Ar H* 24 (1961) pp 31-102.

I 116 Corish, P. J.
The life and times of Archbishop Denis O'Driscoll (1600-1650), *JCoHAS* 70 (1965) pp 108-19.

I 117 ——— Irish ecclesiastical history and the papal archives: introduction, *PICHC* (1956) pp 17-20.

I 118 ——— The Church in Ireland in the fifteenth century: V, summing up, *PICHC* (1956) pp 14-16.

I 119 ——— An Irish counter-reformation bishop: John Roche, *ITQ* 25 (1958) pp 14-32, 101-23; 26 (1959) pp 101-16, 313-30.

I 120 ——— Father Luke Wadding and the Irish Nation, *IER* 5 series 88 (1957) pp 377-95.

I 121 ——— (ed)
The reorganisation of the Irish Church 1603-41, *PICHC* (1957) pp 9-14.

Two reports on the catholic church in Ireland in the early seventeenth century, *Ar H* 22 (1959) 140-62.

I 122 Cregan, D. F.   Irish recusant lawyers in politics in the reign of James I, *IJ* 5 (1970) pp 306-20.

I 123 Dodd, R. (ed)   Vatican archives: instrumenta, miscellanea. Documents of Irish interest, *Ar H* 19 (1956) pp 135-40.

I 124 Douglas, J. M.   Early Quakerism in Ireland, *JFHS* 48 (1956) pp 5-32.

I 125 Dowling, P. J.   The continuity of education in Ossory, *IER* 5 series 85 (1956) pp 243-51, 416-26.

I 126 Doyle, S.   The Confederation of Kilkenny and Catholic Europe, *BICHS* 79 (1957) pp 4-5.

I 127 Edwards, R. D.   The Irish reformation parliament of Henry VIII, 1556-7, *HS* 6 (1968) pp 59-84.

I 128 ———   Conflict of papal and royal jurisdictions in fifteenth-century Ireland, *PICHC* (1961) pp 3-9.

I 129 Egan, P. K.   The Church in Ireland in the fifteenth century: II, Diocesan organisation. Clonfert, *PICHC* (1956) pp 4-8.

I 130 Faulkner, A.   Father O'Finachty's miracles, *IER* 5 series 104 (1965) pp 349-62.

I 131 Fenning, H.   The Dominicans of Trim: 1263-1682, *Ríocht* 3, 1 (1963) pp 15-23.

I 132 ———   The Dominicans of Mullingar: 1237-1610, *Ríocht* 3, 2 (1964) pp 105-13.

I 133 ———   The Dominicans of Mullingar: 1622-1654, *Ríocht* 3, 4 (1966) pp 299-314.

I 134 Gallagher, P.   Sources for the history of the clergy of a diocese: seventeenth-century Clogher, *PICHC* (1957) pp 25-30.

I 135 Galligan, L.   Luke Wadding — Franciscan student and scholar, *Franciscan College Annual* (1957) pp 68-71.

I 136 Gibling, C.   Aegidius Chaissey, O.F.M., and James Ussher, protestant archbishop of

I 137 —— Armagh, *IER* 5 series 85 (1956) pp 383-405.

I 138 —— The *Processus Datarie* for Denis O'Driscoll 1640, *Coll H* 8 (1965) pp 38-42.

I 139 —— The Franciscan ministry in the diocese of Clogher, *CR* 7 (1970) pp 149-203.

I 140 —— (ed) The Irish Franciscan mission to Scotland 1619-1647, *PICHC* (1957) pp 15-24.

Catalogue of material of Irish interest in the collection *Nunziatura di Fiandra,* Vatican archives, *Coll H* 1, 3, 4, 5, 9, 10, 11, 12, 13 (1958-70) 9 parts.

I 141 Goodbody, O. C. Anthony Sharp, wool merchant 1643-1707, and the Quaker community in Dublin, *JFHS* 48 (1956) pp 38-50.

I 142 —— Ireland in the sixteen-fifties. A background to the coming of Quakerism, *JFHS* 48 (1956) pp 33-7.

I 143 —— Seventeenth-century Quaker marriages in Ireland, *JFHS* 4 (1964) pp 248-9.

I 144 Gwynn, A. Irish society in the fifteenth century, *Iris Hibernia* 3, 5 (1957) pp 33-42.

I 145 Hand, G. The Church in Ireland in the fifteenth century: IV, medieval cathedral chapters, *PICHC* (1956) pp 11-14.

I 146 —— The rivalry of the cathedral chapters in medieval Dublin, *JRSAI* 92 (1962) pp 193-206.

I 147 Harrison, P. A sixteenth-century Spanish wooden statue from Co. Clare, *NMAJ* 12 (1969) pp 35-40.

I 148 Hayes-McCoy, G. A. Sir John Davies in Cavan in 1606 and 1610, *Breifne* 1 (1960) pp 177-91.

I 149 —— Gaelic Society in Ireland in the late sixteenth century, *HS* 4 (1963) pp 45-61.

I 150 ———— The renaissance and the Irish wars, *Iris Hibernia* 3, 5 (1957) pp 43-51.

I 151 Hawkes, W. The liturgy in Dublin 1200-1500: manuscript sources, *RN* 2 (1958) pp 33-67.

I 152 Henning, J. Irish saints in the Martirloge in englyssche (1526), *IER* 5 series 90 (1958) pp 173-82.

I 153 Henry, F. Irish cistercian monasteries and their carved decoration, *Apollo* (Oct 1966) pp 260-7.

I 154 Jennings, B. Ecclesiastical appointments in Ireland August 1643-December 1649, *Coll H* 2 (1959) pp 16-65.

I 155 ———— Theses defended in St Isidore's College, Rome, 1631-49, *Coll H* 2 (1959) pp 95-104.

I 156 ———— (ed) Acta sacrae congregationis de propaganda fide 1622-50, *Ar H* 22 (1959) pp 28-139.

I 157 ———— (ed) The indictment of F. John Preston, Franciscan, *Ar H* 26 (1963) pp 50-5.

I 158 ———— (ed) The Irish Franciscans in Poland, *Ar H* 20 (1957) pp 38-56.

I 159 ———— (ed) Irish preachers and confessors in the archdiocese of Malines, 1607-1794, *Ar H* 23 (1960) pp 148-66.

I 160 Kearney, H. F. Ecclesiastical politics and the counter-reformation in Ireland 1618-48, *JEH* 11 (1960) pp 202-12.

I 161 Kelly, J. P. Rectors of Trim — fourteenth and fifteenth centuries, *Ríocht* 3 (1966) pp 388-9.

I 162 Kingston, J. Catholic Families of the Pale, *RN* 1 (1956) pp 323-50; 2 (1960) pp 236-56.

I 163 ———— The Carmelite nuns in Dublin 1644-1829, *RN* 3 (1963/4) pp 331-60.

I 164 Knox, R. B. A Caroline trio: Ussher, Laud and Williams, *CQR* (1963) pp 442-57.

I 165 Leader, M. Irish Parish Registers, *IG* 3 (1957) pp 60-3.

Ireland

I 166 Logan, P.	The medical history of Father Luke Wadding, *JIMA* 40 (1957) pp 175-8.
I 167 Lowe, J.	Some aspects of the wars in Ireland 1641-9, *IS* 4 (1959) pp 81-7.
I 168 Mac Airt, S.	The seventeenth-century Franciscan house 'at Drowes', *DA* 4 (1958) pp 12-15.
I 169 Mac An Ghallóglaigh, D.	The 1641 rebellion in Leitrim, *Breifne* 2 (1965) pp 441-54.
I 170 McBride, P. P. (ed)	Some unpublished letters of Mateo de Oviedo, archbishop of Dublin, *RN* 1 (1955) pp 91-117; (1956) pp 351-68.
I 171 MacCurtain, B.	An Irish agent of the counter-reformation, Dominic O'Daly, *IHS* 15 (1967) pp 39-406.
I 171a Mac Fhinn, C. E.	Dhá athchuinge as Achaidh Chonaire, *Galvia* 8 (1961) pp 27-30.
I 172 McGovern, P.	Father Edmund Deane 1647-1717, *Breifne* 1 (1959) p 162.
I 173 MacNiocaill and Mallon, P. (ed)	Cairt ó Mhaolmhordha Ó Raighilligh 1558, *Breifne* 1 (1959) pp 134-6.
I 174 Martin, F. X.	An Irish Capuchin missionary in politics: Francis Nugent negotiates with James I, 1623-4, *BICHS* 90 (1960) pp 1-3.
I 175 ———	A thwarted project: the Capuchin mission to England and Scotland in the seventeenth century, 1608-60, *Miscellanea Melchor de Pobladura* 2 (Rome 1964) pp 211-41.
I 176 ———	Ireland, the renaissance and the counter-reformation, *Topic* 13 (1967) pp 23-33.
I 177 ———	La mission capuchine irlandaise à Sedan, 1639-1654, *Revue d'Histoire Ardennaise* 1 (1969) pp 27-37.
I 178 ———	The Augustinian friaries in pre-reformation Ireland, *Augustiniana* 6 (1956) pp 346-84.
I 179 ———	Sources for the history of the Irish Capuchins, *Collectanea Franciscana* 26 (1956) pp 67-79.
I 180 ———	The Irish friars and the observant

I 181 ———— and Meijer, A.
I 182 Meagher, J.
I 183 Meijer, A.
I 184 Millett, B.
I 185 ————
I 186 ————
I 187 ————
I 188 ————
I 189 Mooney, C.
I 190 ————
I 191 ————
I 192 ————
I 193 ————
I 194 ————
I 195 ————

movement in the fifteenth century, *PICHC* (1961) pp 10-16.
Irish material in the Augustinian general archives Rome, 1354-1624, *Ar H* 19 (1956) pp 61-134.
Presentments of recusants in Dublin 1617-18, *RN* 2 (1960) pp 269-73.
See I 181.
Irish ecclesiastical history and the papal archives: II. The archives of the Sacra Congregatio de Propaganda Fide, *PICHC* (1956) pp 20-7.
Catalogue of Irish material in the *Scritture originali riferite nelle congregazioni generali* in the Propaganda archives, *Coll H* 8-13 (1965-70) *passim*.
Calendar of vol 1 (1625-68) of the *Scritture riferite nei Congressi, Irlanda, Coll H* 6 (1964) pp 18-211.
The pastoral zeal of Robert Wauchope, *SA* 2, 1 (1956) pp 32-60.
Irish Scotists at St Isidore's College, Rome, in the seventeenth century, in *De Doctrina Iohannis Duns Scoti* 4 (Rome 1968) pp 399-419.
The Franciscans in Ireland: The Third Order, *Terminus* 12 (1956) pp 14-17, 41-4, 58-62, 88-92, 105.
Father John Colgan and the Louvain School, *DA* 4 (1958) pp 1-5.
A French bishop of Annaghdown, *JGAHS* 30 (1962) p 2.
The Irish Church in the sixteenth century, *IER* 5 series 99 (1963) pp 102-13.
Franciscan Architecture in pre-reformation Ireland, III, *JRSAI* 77 (1957) pp 1-38, 103-24.
Francis Magruairk, *SA* 2 (1957) pp 229-52.
A day in the life of Father Luke Wadding, *Franciscan College Annual* (1957) pp 19-22.

I 196 ———	The Franciscan Friary at Drowse, *DA* 3, 1 (1957) pp 1-7.
I 197 ———	The letters of Luke Wadding, *IER* 5 series 88 (1957) pp 396-409.
I 198 Morrissey, T.	The strange letters of Mathew O'Hartegan, S. J., 1644-45, *ITQ* 37 (1970) pp 159-72.
I 199 Mould, D. C. D. P.	The Dominican Third Order: its history in Ireland, *Irish Rosary* 60 (1956) pp 225-30.
I 200 Nicholls, K. W.	Visitation of the dioceses of Clonfert, Tuam and Kilmacduagh c 1565-7 *An H* 26 (1970) pp 144-57.
I 201 Ó Conbhuidhe, C. [= Conway, C. See nos I 112-114b]	Studies in Irish cistercian history: I. The Irish Cistercians under the Tudors, 1539-1603, *Cîteaux* 16 (1965) pp 5-25.
I 202 ———	Studies in Irish Cistercian history: II. The Irish Cistercians under the Stuarts, *Cîteaux* 16 (1965) pp 177-87.
I 202a ———	The lands of St Mary's Abbey Dublin, *PRIA* 62, sect c (1962) pp 21-84.
I 203 O'Connell, M. R.	The church in Ireland in the fifteenth century: 1, Diocesan organisation, Kerry, *PICHC* (1956) pp 1-4.
I 204 Ó Cuiv, B.	James Cotter, a seventeenth-century agent of the crown, *JRSAI* 89 (1959) pp 135-59.
I 205 Ó Doibhlin, E.	Domhnach Mór: the insurrection of 1641 and its background, *SA* 3 (1959) pp 401-29.
I 206 O'Dwyer, P.	The Carmelite order in pre-reformation Ireland, *IER* 5 series 110 (1968) pp 350-63.
I 207 ———	The Carmelite order in pre-reformation Ireland, *Carmelus* 16 (1969) pp 264-78.
I 208 Ó Gallachair, P.	Clogherici: a dictionary of the catholic clergy of the diocese of Clogher 1535-85, *CR* 1-7 (1956-1969) *passim*.

I 209 ——— (ed)	A Fermanagh survey, 1622, *CR* 2 (1958) pp 293-310.
I 209a ———	The 1641 War in Clogher, *CR* 4 (1962) pp 135-47.
I 210 Ó Maidin, P.	A true historical relation of the conversion of Sir Tobie Matthew, *JCoHAS* 70 (1965) p 71.
I 211 Ó Mearáin, L.	Complaint against Miler McGrath, 1591, *CR* 2 (1957) pp 204-6.
I 211a ———	Miler McGrath, archbishop of Cashel 1571-1622, *CR* 2 (1959) pp 432-44.
I 212 Ó Mordha, P. B.	The MacMahons of Monaghan 1600-40, *CR* 2 (1958) pp 311-27.
I 212a ———	The battle of Clones, 1643, *CR* 4 (1962) pp 148-54.
I 213 Ó Mordha, S. P.	Hugh O'Reilly (1581?-1653): a reforming primate, *Breifne* 4 (1970) pp 1-42.
I 214 Ó Riordan, W. M.	A list of seventeenth-century Dublin diocesan priests, *RN* 2 (1958) pp 109-19; 2 (1960) pp 257-68; 3 (1962) pp 137-52.
I 214a O'Sullivan, A. (ed)	Poem in praise of John Cantwell, archbishop of Cashel, 1452-82, *Éigse* 10 (1962) pp 103-19.
I 215 O'Sullivan, H.	The Franciscans in Dundalk, *SA* 4 (1961) pp 33-71.
I 216 O'Sullivan, W.	Ussher as a collector of manuscripts, *Herm* 88 (1956) pp 34-58.
I 217 Olden, M. (ed)	Episcopal comments on the 'Decreta pro recto regimine ecclesiarum Hiberniae', 1635-6, *Ar H* 27 (1964) pp 1-12.
I 218 ———	Counter-reformation problems: Munster, *IER* 5 series 104 (1965) pp 42-54.
I 219 ———	Counter-reformation problems: Munster, *PICHC* (1967) pp 21-32.
I 220 Oulton, J. E. L.	Ussher's work as a patristic scholar and church historian, *Herm* 88 (1956) pp 3-11.
I 221 Paterson, T. G. F. (ed)	County Armagh in 1622: a plantation survey, *SA* 4 (1961) pp 103-40.

Ireland

I 222 Purcell, M. St Vincent de Paul and Ireland 1640-60, *IER* 5 series 102 (1964) pp 1-16.

I 223 Quane, M. The diocesan schools 1570-1870, *JCoHAS* 66 (1961) pp 26-50.

I 224 Quinn, D. B. (ed) Calendar of Irish Council Books, 1 March 1581-1 July 1586, *An H* 24 (1967) pp 91-180.

I 225 ——— Henry VIII and Ireland 1509-34, *IHS* 12 (1961) pp 318-44.

I 226 ——— Additional Sidney State Papers 1566-70, *An H* 26 (1970) pp 91-102.

I 227 Ryan, M. The Franciscan houses of Thomond in 1616, *NMAJ* 10 (1967) pp 112-15.

I 228 Sheehy, M. P. (ed) The parish of Athenry in 1434, *JGAHS* 21 (1964/5) pp 8-10.

I 229 Silke, J. J. The Irish appeal of 1593 to Spain: some light on the genesis of the 'Nine years' war, *IER* 5 series 92 (1959) pp 279-90, 362-71.

I 229a ——— (ed) The Irish College, Seville, *Ar H* 24 (1961) pp 103-47.

I 230 ——— Spanish intervention in Ireland 1601-2: Spanish bibliography, *SH* 3 (1963) pp 179-90.

I 231 ——— Hugh O'Neill, the Catholic question and the papacy, *IER* 5 series 104 (1965) pp 65-79.

I 232 ——— Spain and the invasion of Ireland 1601-2, *IHS* 14 (1965) pp 295-312.

I 233 Somerville, B. The Spanish expedition to Ireland, 1601, *IS* 7 (1965) pp 37-57.

I 234 Styles, P. James Ussher and his times, *Herm* 88 (1956) pp 12-33.

I 235 Sykes, N. Ussher as a churchman, *Herm* 88 (1956) pp 59-80.

I 236 Treadwell, V. The Survey of Armagh and Tyrone, 1622, *UJA* 3 series 23 (1960) pp 126-37.

I 237 Valkenburg, A. Walter Wellesley, bishop of Kildare 147?-1539, *JKAS* 14 (1970) pp 518-43.

1238 Walsh, D. The Dominicans of Arklow 1264-1793, *RN* 3 (1963-4) pp 307-23.

I 239 White, D. G.   Henry VIII's Irish kerne in France and Scotland 1544-45, *IS* 3 (1958) pp 213-25.

I 240 ——— The reign of Edward VI in Ireland: some political, social and economic aspects, *BICHS* 89 (1960) pp 3-4.

I 241 ——— The reign of Edward VI in Ireland: some political, social and economic aspects, *IHS* 14 (1965) pp 197-211.

I 242 Williams, P.   The council in Munster in the late sixteenth century, *BICHS* 94 (1961) pp 2-3.

SECTION 4. REVIEWS (listed by authors reviewed)

Reviews of titles in this bibliography may generally be found in the volumes of *Irish Historical Studies*. Only major reviews are noted here. The numbers given in column 3 identify the work under review.

I 243 Ainsworth, J.	I 1	*IHS* 13 (1962) pp 188-9.
I 244 Coonan, T. L.	I 15	*IHS* 11 (1958) pp 52-5.
I 244a Giblin, C.	I 25	*IHS* 10 (1957) pp 333-4.
I 245 Jennings, B.	I 35	*IHS* 10 (1956) pp 228-36.
I 246 Knox, R. B.	I 39	*IHS* 16 (1968) pp 215-19.
I 247 MacLysaght, E.	I 45	*IHS* 11 (1958) pp 173-8.
I 248 Martin, F. X.	I 52	*IHS* 14 (1964) pp 71-2.
I 249 ———	I 78	*IHS* 11 (1959) pp 233-5.
I 249a Twemlow, J. A.	I 95	*IHS* 10 (1957) pp 328-33.

SECTION 5. COMPLETED THESES

I 250 Bradshaw, B. I. — George Browne, archbishop of Dublin 1536-1554 (University College, Dublin) M.A. 1966.

I 251 Carville, G. — The Cistercians in Ireland and their economy 1142-1541 (Belfast) M.A. 1969.

I 252 Clarke, A. — The Old English in Ireland 1625-42 (Trinity College, Dublin) Ph.D. 1959.

I 253 Curtin, M. B. — Dominic O'Daly, 1595-1662: a study of Irish-European relationships in the seventeenth century (University College, Dublin) M.A. 1958.

I 253a Doyle, S. — The register of letters of the confederation of Kilkenny to 1645 (University College, Dublin) M.A. 1956.

I 253b Elkin, R. E. — The interactions between the Irish rebellion and the English Civil Wars (University of Illinois) Ph.D, 1961.

I 254 Jones, F. M. — Clement VIII and the counter-reformation in Ireland, 1592-1605 (Galway) Ph.D. 1957.

I 255 Knox, R. B. — The ecclesiastical policy of James Ussher, archbishop of Armagh (London) ext Ph.D. 1956.

I 256 Millerick, M. D. — The role of the Dublin parliament 1640-1 (University College, Dublin) M.A. 1966.

I 257 Morrissey, T. — James Archer and the Jesuit mission to Ireland 1597-1602 (University College, Dublin) M.A. 1970.

I 258 O'Neill, W. — John Bale 1495-1563 (Trinity College, Dublin) Ph.D. 1970.

I 259 Ranger, T. O. — The career of Richard Boyle, first earl of Cork, in Ireland, 1588-1643 (Oxford) Ph.D. 1959.

I 260 Silke, J. J. — The Spanish Expedition to Munster, 1601-2 (University College, Dublin) Ph.D. 1963.